About t

Call-up for National Service in 1953 offered the Navy. Initially training at sea on aircraft-carrier then frigate where an police ex-cadet on board inspired me to join.

Soon I was at large in Soho and the West End, Plaistow, Wanstead, Holloway, City Road, Leman Street and secondment to the LSE, reading Economics.

After Holborn I met my second wife, marrying in 1980 and starting again with two daughters and a lively criminal practice in wig and gown.

My last client felt reminded of her grandfather. Enough! We decided it was time to cut stress and write about my lives.

Three Lives

Barry Forward

Three Lives

Olympia Publishers

London

www.olympiapublishers.com

OLYMPIA PAPERBACK EDITION

A CIP catalogue record for this title is
available from the British Library.

ISBN: 978-1-84897-978-9

First Published in 2018

Olympia Publishers
60 Cannon Street
London
EC4N 6NP
Printed in Great Britain

Dedication

To both my families.

THREE LIVES

Contents

Photographs of particular Interest

Chapter 1
A Brush With the Law

"Oi!" a voice bellowed. "You there, stop!" Looking round, I saw a large, corpulent figure emerge from a deep dark doorway, a line of silver buttons running down his jacket and a shiny badge on his helmet glinting from the street lights. He beckoned me over, so I got off the bicycle and went over to him.

The police officer was quite old, possibly in his 60s, and since the cycle had no lights on, and it was after midnight, his attitude revealed that I was in trouble. He told me I was committing an offence and reached for his notebook. Being dressed in naval uniform, I explained I was on leave from my ship, had been to a local dance, and had borrowed the bike, as the bus services ended at about 8p.m.

Licking the tip of his stubby pencil, and starting to write in his notebook, he took my name and address, and proceeded to report me for the offence with full solemnity and obvious satisfaction. My excuse and uniform did nothing to help my situation, and I was sent on my way and told to walk home. It was some six miles away, and since he could never have caught up with me -- his was a more ancient bicycle, and had to carry some twenty stone -- I rode home.

As I did so I realised that if I had not stopped for him I would never have been reported. I also thought that a simple matter of this kind – a young serviceman in uniform, doing his National Service, who had been frank, honest and respectful with the policeman, having no lights on a pedal cycle, in the middle of the night, in a tiny village -- would not have led to my being reported with a view to prosecution.

However, with minimal effort on his part, he had caught a young offender (hence the satisfaction), and had got another notch on his belt. Some months later, I was fined, and had a conviction recorded against me. The year was 1955, and I carried that record with me for many years. It was not to be the end of this matter.

Chapter 2
Starting National Service in the Navy

I had reached the age for National Service in 1953, and at that time had joined the Civil Service. I was keen to sign up. At first I was interviewed for the Army, but I fancied the Royal Navy. I pressed the recruiting officer to reconsider, stressing my long service as a sea cadet. (This was not entirely true. I had hoped to get the uniform quickly, but as it did not materialise after a few weeks I opted out.)

It was virtually impossible to get into the Navy, but after I pushed, and told of my educational successes and two uncles in the Navy, the recruiting officer said that I could take a series of exams and he would see.

I took five exams, academic, current affairs and technical (woodwork and metalwork). (My wife will howl with laughter at the thought that I once knew about tools, carpentry or any skill that would assist around the house!) Having obtained 98%, I was then offered the Royal Navy, as a seaman or stoker; the Royal Marines; or the Fleet Air Arm and the opportunity of becoming a 'coder.' This position involved going to university and learning Russian for eighteen months. Afterwards, I would spend the remaining six months on decoder duties. I guessed that spying would have been involved, and reasoned that I would be a completely willing victim of any inducement offered by a foreign female operative under the age of forty-five.

My concern as to which to choose was largely dismissed, but he gave me one minute to decide. I tried to remonstrate that this choice this would determine the next two years of my life. He told me I now had half a minute, and so I plumped for becoming a seaman. Having been nothing but a schoolboy, and then a civil servant in an office full of women, I wanted to do a man's job and see the world.

This turned out to be only partly successful, as the furthest abroad I ever got was Calais, and then only once, as I was denied shore leave due to some minor peccadilloes, one involving throwing waste ("gash") overboard just as all the ships' officers came up from the wardroom and stepped out on deck behind me.

I did try. During the first few weeks of the training course, a rumour circulated that the ship was to sail to the Caribbean for a three-month cruise. This is why I had been so determined to join the Navy.

Accordingly, I let my marks slip, until I was border-line to pass. Though I would have to re-sit the exams, this was a price well worth paying.

The latest rumour provided the devastating detail that the cruise was to be for Iceland, so I was able to make an effort to get through and passed the course. Shortly afterwards, of course, the carrier sailed to the Caribbean for three months!

After my seamanship training, we were sent back to HMS Victory, the barracks at Portsmouth, ready for polishing off before posting. It was not long before I realised that the best job there was in the Guard. It required spit and polish by the bucketful, Blanco on belt and gaiters, and immaculately creased and well-presented uniform.

The duties were mainly ceremonial, but included maintaining a twenty-four-hour armed guard on the Admiral's residence, and one tour in the naval detention centre – the equivalent of its prison –which terrified me, as I did the night shift. Sailors who were detained in punishment cells were the hardest cases, and being in charge while looking like a schoolboy in uniform was one of my worst experiences ever.

The advantages of being in the Guard were having the best quarters; clean, luxurious beds; washing machines in the laundrette and excellent ironing facilities; superb food in the restaurant and as much of it as you wanted; every evening off; and being out in the centre of Portsmouth every night -- in civvies, as uniform was stowed in a massive locker in the NAAFI building just outside the gates. I would happily have stayed there for months, but was posted to my first ship within weeks.

Chapter 3
Life On Board and a Near Disaster

I joined HMS Redpole, a frigate with some ninety men on board, and thus started what I came to regard as my first life. The role of the ship was to train officers in navigation, which meant that we went to sea from 9am to 5pm, had weekends off, and a two to three week cruise usually around Scotland or Northern Ireland, in the autumn – a far cry from the West Indies.

However, our own navigational skills, coupled with mild eccentricity might well have alerted those in high Command about our suitability for the task, had they known. I cite some instances.

On one occasion coming back into Portsmouth through a fairly narrow channel, our coxswain put 30 degrees of starboard on the wheel rather than 30 of port. Standing beside him I pointed out his error with more urgency than tact, thus risking insubordination, and disaster was averted.

Again, on an exercise to the Channel Islands, we left the port without casting off some cables, which resulted in our towing out to sea half of Sark's jetty. This, together with drinking the island's pub dry, ensured this exercise was never repeated.

Our Scottish cruise took us once around the Hebrides, and our captain instructed me, as ship's DJ, to play Fingal's Cave, with full power, thus deafening the inhabitants–fortunately so we just missed the islands. The job of ship's DJ was for fun only, no pay.

Finally, still in Scotland, as we were steaming through a narrow mountainous area our Captain spotted a tiny figure, high above us, and at least half a mile away, walking along a cliff edge. He jovially greeted the man as loudly as possible with his loud-hailer. We could see the man jump in the air, twist and turn, clearly startled and in complete shock. Being on the edge of the path, he nearly fell off the cliff. Had he actually fallen, a negligence suit might have provoked amusement in the High Court. Fortunately, Health and Safety did not exist then – one reason why such times are now regarded quite fondly. 'Health and Efficiency' was more in vogue.

My job was in the wheelhouse with the radar but I also became ship's secretary, schoolmaster (my qualifications were higher than those of anyone else on board, and the ratings needed English and Maths tuition for promotion exams), as well as being the ship's painter.

The reason for these positions was purely financial. My pay for eighteen months was twenty shillings per week, after eight shillings had been deducted by the paymaster to send to National Service ratings' mothers. This touch of maternal concern on our part was mandatory.

Careful budgeting would fund very little in the way of socialising, but each job I undertook brought in an extra eight pence a day. The total allowed for more than one night out, a few glasses of rough cider, and the odd bag of chips. On this some social life could be managed, but room always had to be left for the dances, without which, in those days, opportunities for romance in a strange town hardly existed. In the sixth form of my grammar school we had all been sent helpfully to a dance studio in town to learn ballroom dancing - and told to keep our backs to the wall! For the first few lessons we were only trusted to dance with chairs.

Returning to our parlous finances, buying drinks for your dance partner when ashore called for swift financial reassessment, and it goes without saying that any girl had to be met **inside** a cinema.

As a National Serviceman's pay increased six hundred per cent in his last six months-to induce signing on permanently - this was to be the time for serious relationships and high living. Despite this, the temptation to sign on after the two years had no appeal to any of us.

Finally, on the subject of allowances, we were given, each week, a tin of about 100 cigarettes (called blue liners). Quite why this came about I still have no idea. Initially I sold mine to the smokers, despite them being pretty awful, as I found when boredom and the 'glamour' of smoking kicked in for me too.

Since everyone including myself ended up smoking, the cynic in me now considers that the free provision of poor quality cigarettes must have been in order for some cigarette manufacturer to increase the sale of proper cigarettes. This must surely be the case otherwise, why give them away?

Similarly, providing us with very rough and ill-fitting uniforms meant we had to buy smoother, tailored, comfortable uniforms from the private tailors who came on board. This applied to all ranks.

The ratings wore them so flatteringly tight that you had to get a friend to help pull them over your head after a night out. Both wearers and pullers usually being legless, this was a constant source of amusement for those of us who had remained soberly on board.

Our daily task much of the time, when not at sea, was to dangle overboard on cradles, chipping at the paintwork with tiny hammers. This was followed by re-painting the ship all over again. My role as ship's painter only allowed me some respite to dole out the paint and then go back over the side.

Interestingly, our day uniform was what was called number eights- a light blue denim shirt and trousers. They seemed to be the forerunners of the jeans and denim tops that were to follow years later. They were probably derived from the US, where the term 'blue collar workers' was used, and cowboys in the films seemed to wear them.

Being so young, the relief of the daily allowance of a tot of rum was denied us: we were allowed lemonade for another year. The pageantry of the time-honoured ceremony of its allocation, together with the exchange and barter of halves, or other fractions, of the tot, to settle debts, scores, and cigarette exchanges, was another delight to watch. This would be enhanced at sea when the helmsmen, at the appointed time, would rock the ship from side to side -- to howls up to the wheelhouse from the queuing recipients.

Nevertheless, much of daily life was a mindless routine, only punctuated by nights out, or a weekend spent at home after hitchhiking back to Aylesbury. As I believe happens to other servicemen spending time at home alone, the routine becomes dull, even with their parents. Restlessness seems to set in after a day or two.

I had grown up fast in the Navy. As an only child I could do virtually nothing for myself, but studied incessantly, since I loved school and homework. On a small ship living in a tiny mess with ten others, everything had to be ship-shape, and we had to be fully organised and self-reliant. No more having a bedroom in such a state that my mother, having frequently threatened to throw all my things out into the garden, actually did so. Coming home from school that day, I found that my room had been transported on to our lawn: clothes, furniture, everything. It did not achieve the desired effect, but it ended up with my mother and I laughing helpless together at the spectacle.

Just one instance typifying the daily routine (recounted on a recent trip to Turkey, where I visited an identical class of frigate for the first time since leaving the Redpole) was that every morning started with a bucket on the floor, and all ten of us squatting round peeling a sack of potatoes for lunch. The Turkish sailors who encouraged my reminiscences were in utter disbelief that this happened every day, and in the twentieth century.

Since my father was a prison officer at an open prison, I would compare the prisoners' lives to mine. Apart from some restrictions, they could walk to the pub for a drink, go out on work parties, and enjoy all the sport on offer. They enjoyed watching tennis, especially when I brought girlfriend home for a game, some of whom would wonder why a hundred men would all stand around their end, and none behind mine. I think the prisoners appreciated the spectacle, cheering loudly for every shot made by my opponent, wherever the ball ended up.

During my time on the Redpole, life was not always mundane for within a few months I was told to attend a Board for an interview for promotion to the rank of Lieutenant. My mother had always visualized me in the smart uniform of a naval officer, and was excited at the prospect. She need not have been, for the interview took about two minutes and I was asked one question.

As I faced the Board the chairing senior officer asked me if I had private means. I replied I did not. He explained courteously that in that case it would be impossible for me to attain officer rank. I would have to buy several full uniforms, and the costs of the gold rings on the sleeves and on the bridge of the caps, of the high quality of the uniforms and formal mess dress, of the mess bills that had to be paid for the pink gins that were the order of the day for officers, and of the general expense, would have left me destitute. Life would have been desperate, with very little income for me, especially at a National Serviceman's rate, and a very miserable existence.

This did not come as much of a surprise, as the midshipmen I had seen – trainee officers -- were a pretty dismal sight: uniforms grubby, collars and cuffs grey, and everything creased. One of my duties had been to clean the officers' cabins, where their difficulties were more than obvious. They were ill at ease socially in the officers' mess and struggled to survive and keep up the standards expected of an officer.

The technical officers, engineers, etc., seemed slightly out of place in the social ladder without the public school accents and confidence of the other officers. Their technical abilities and approachability made them very different. The officers' mess, known as the wardroom, provided a clear picture of the social structure and the significance of private means.

The non-commissioned officers, petty officers, were untroubled by any distinctions, and were the best paid onboard. I was their cook and mess-man for a while. They had the highest standard of living, which is why I took on that job, but I had to learn to cook, never having peeled a potato before joining the Navy.

After twelve months, I was again summoned to go before another promotion board. It lasted for about as long, and followed exactly the same pattern. This time, I was able to welcome the Board's frankness and concern for my welfare. To be considered twice had made me feel respected, having been at the lowest rank in the Navy, not just as a seaman, but a National Service seaman to boot, and so the bottom of the pile.

Later our captain's concern saved me from what could have been a life-changing situation. I was awoken in the middle of the night, dragged out of my hammock and marched to the quarterdeck. There, sat behind a desk, were the captain and several other officers. The atmosphere was cold, the language formal, and everyone, including the Master-of-Arms responsible for discipline, looked frighteningly serious.

They told me that the informal leader of my mess – a reprobate with all the vices and faults of a seasoned matelot (what we usually called our experienced seamen) – had gone ashore when forbidden to do so, due to his being on watch. This was a most serious and flagrant misdemeanour on his part, and may have been regarded as his last straw. I was still not wide awake enough, or capable of appreciating how that affected me, but was told that he had given me as his alibi, saying that we had been together on board all evening, and that I would readily confirm that to them. "Is that right?" I was asked. I seem to remember that the prisoner, as he clearly was, sat looking at me, nodding at me confidently, although plainly terrified.

I stumbled to answer, trying to help him under extreme pressure. Because of the formality of the procedure, there were certain to be drastic consequences. I knew of his life and family, and had liked him enormously. Yet what he had said was a lie.

I was pressed to be clearer in my evidence and the word perjury was muttered quietly by the Master of Arms to the captain. The Master of Arms was in charge of the procedure, and as it went on, it was obvious that things would get dreadfully serious for me if I fully supported him. From all the faces, nobody believed me in my increasingly half-hearted and utterly unlikely support for him.

The silence was deafening, as the Captain stared hard at my face for minutes. He then told me that he didn't believe a word I had said, but that I had been put in an awful position, and he could understand that I was trying to help a shipmate who was from my own mess, but who was also a persuasive and complete rogue, with an appalling record.

I was fortunate, in that our Captain was a follower of Billy Graham – the evangelist – and was a powerful believer in Christianity and morality. He gave me informal words of advice, and I was dismissed from the hearing, much to the disgust of the Master of Arms. The seriousness of such a major criminal charge being proved would have put paid to all that I was to accomplish later in my later 'lives'.

My time in the 'Andrew', as it was called, took me quickly to maturity, and I was no longer the smallest boy in the class, nor so unworldly. Yes, I was more tolerant, fitter, and could even cope with the female sex. I could cook quite well, could wash and iron my clothes, could manage money, could deal with my senior officers, and was regarded in my final report as being fairly competent as a seaman. My washing skills were such that, very soon after being assigned to the ship, my navy blue collar was almost white, indicating that I was an old sweat. Such things mattered.

The diet in our mess was dreary, too, since although our leader (mentioned above as the rogue who had tried to use me as his alibi) was the ship's butcher and caterer, we had the same joint roasted every day, and tinned carrots were the only vegetable he bought for me as caterer. His philosophy was to buy and eat cheap, so that, when we got our mess allowance, what was left over could be spent in one massive night out.

After semi-starvation, I acted as mess-man for the Petty officers, who were the best-paid on board and were happy to spend freely: and this was at a time when rationing and shortages for the general population still persisted. When nearly all the Petty officers got their bikes out and went home for the weekend, the few who were left feasted on what I could conjure up, with no expense spared. We lived like kings at the weekend.

Much of the work I found tedious, but I loved going to sea, and going ashore in different places: the Firths and mountains in Scotland during the autumn; the pretty Scottish coastal resorts such as Tobermory Bay, which at that time was being searched for treasure by divers, as well as Kirkcaldy, Oban and Greenock.

Elsewhere, we enjoyed our visits to Torbay and Londonderry, and nights ashore there. My favourite spot in Torbay was the small fishing village of Brixham, where I went on leave for a few days to meet a girl I had met there. Having been injudiciously explicit in a letter to her, her parents had barred me from seeing her, with good reason. I ended up being mothered by the landlady of a small hotel, eating with the staff in the kitchen, and having a most enjoyable time – but a far cry from what had been intended.

Approaching such popular resorts from the sea, with the lights twinkling along the front, promised adventure, and, in our naval uniform, we were usually quite popular and well-behaved. The shore patrols did not need to keep an eye on us, for any transgressions would have had serious repercussions.

Entering the estuary of the Dart on our way past Dartmouth and the Naval College was truly spectacular, and we were allowed to visit the College, in which most of our officers (except the technical or electrical grades) had been trained.

We did, however, on one such voyage, so misjudge our negotiations around the ferry that crossed the river that we ended up perilously close to it. Fortunately, the passengers failed to notice our panic, as we ran frantically along the deck placing fenders overboard so as not to damage the ferry or ourselves. The passengers smiled and waved happily at us, while we missed them literally by an inch in places.

What I had always enjoyed, whilst in training, was our early morning PE on the flight deck of the carrier, with the Royal Marine band practicing at full blast, and usually keeping in time. Again, strutting through the streets of Portsmouth in nineteenth-century naval uniform to mark the Coronation was huge fun, and the Band was as usual in top form.

Of all those institutions which the Navy prided itself on retaining, the one which I found loathsome was the kit inspection. Generally, it was ordered on set occasions; but in my case they were more frequent, and designed to teach me my place (as I was regarded as a bit uppity) or to punish me for some minor indiscretion or lack of respect.

For instance, a humorous article about our trip to Sark, which I had written and published on board, was leaked to the local paper. As a lesson a kit inspection would have followed, rather than a formal response.

To prepare for such an inspection all the clothing and kit that had been supplied, down to the shoe brushes stamped with your number, had to be laid out on the floor in a set order. Hours of spit and polish brought footwear up to a shine which you could literally see your face in, and even laces had to be ironed flat, so as not to appear twisted.

The inspecting officer, with his baton under his arm, would ensure the right order of the items was maintained, and then he would examine article after article, lifting some disdainfully with his baton. This was in front of one's mess-mates. This would be accompanied by comment on the cleanliness of some of the clothing and its need to be washed again, as well as by remarks on other items, but always with the closest scrutiny of footwear.

A constant concern was whether the legs of bell-bottoms bore the necessary seven creases (to represent the Seven Seas). Further, that the creases should be sharp and distinct, but also alternately external or inverted; and, of course, each type had to be parallel on each leg.

No ingenuity was required to find some fault, and the experience was utterly humiliating. Having one's issued underwear lifted on the end of a baton, for all to see, was excruciating. Given every inducement, e.g. to have as much money as I would want, to travel all over the world, and to have the best job available, with a delectable personal assistant, signing on without the abolition of kit inspections would have been unthinkable.

Now the time was approaching when I needed to consider my future. At school or afterwards, I had never known what I wanted to do, and only joined the Civil Service at my parents' insistence, as the job was safe, clean, and came with a good pension; it also had sufficient different departments for at least one of them to appeal to me.

With a few months to go, a new National Serviceman joined the ship. He turned out to be a Metropolitan Police cadet. He was the most impressive, decent and caring individual I had ever met, and his sense of morality and public duty very much appealed to me during the frequent chats we had. The more I admired him, the longer and deeper were our conversations.

That a policeman worked outdoors and in London, was provided with a smart uniform, and was clearly accorded both status and respect, were strong selling points. Importantly, this really was a man's job.

When I left the ship, needless to say, my application was sent immediately to the Metropolitan police. What was remarkable, supporting the impression this young man had made, was that I later found that two more such applications had been sent from two of the other National Servicemen on board. He should have been on commission!

I had been to London only once before, and that was for an interview for the post of Executive officer or for one in the Diplomatic service. This interview arose from my achieving a high mark in an open national competition, and took place just off Regent Street.

Despite my marks in the written examination – I had been in the top few – the interview was utterly intimidating, as all the candidates seemed to be from public school, judging by their accents, and had the complete confidence that came with such an education. The Board's first question was about my tie. I told them, with a trace of the 'Brummie'accent I had proudly acquired, in the two years we had lived there, that it was from my grammar school in Birmingham.

Though it was a decent grammar school, it was apparent from the faces of large number of the interviewers that I was well out of place. Next, since it was noticed that I had lived in Germany after the war, and spoke good German, I was asked what the German was for bed. I had a total mental block, and after a deafening silence , they announced that the correct word was Bett - I fell apart. So ended, *thankfully*, the chance of a career to which I would have been completely unsuited.

Some months later, I presented myself at Beak Street, just off Regent Street, for a physical examination and interview.

My previous experience did not encourage any optimism, as I sat in front of two senior police officers dazzling me with silver braid, medals and epaulettes bristling with pips and crowns. They were immaculately attired, and quite forbidding. At the end of the table was an older man in a dark suit, with a notebook in front of him. In no time, my criminal conviction was brought up. There was nothing I could say as an excuse or in mitigation – these officers would not be impressed by any such story and would see through any attempt to lessen its seriousness. I was surprised that we carried on. I was on safer ground as the interview continued with, "What makes you want to be a policeman?" I was able to make my best point: that I had been so impressed with the cadet that I wanted to join an organisation that could boast such officers. I also touched on other elements which attracted me.I felt that my conviction might have completely prejudiced my case, but I kept going, telling them that I wanted to do a man's job. They half-smiled, and I continued to explain that I had joined the Civil Service, working almost entirely with women, in an atmosphere of pettiness: the boredom of tallying telephone rental accounts and modifying changes of rates; forever correcting figures; the staff's paramount concern as to the warmth and strength of the cups of tea drunk all day; never-ending gossip; and ...

The police officers turned to the figure in civvies, pointing at him, and roaring with laughter, teasing him unmercifully about being a civil servant, and how true of his job my description was. He had the grace, or misfortune, not having the choice of arguing with the officers, to accept the teasing with good grace. They would not let him off the hook for several minutes.

Still laughing, they told me that I had passed, and, as I left, I could hear them still ribbing their colleague. Unwittingly I had made their day, and so was to commence my second life.

Chapter 4
Another Brush with the Law and not the last

To consider my service in the Navy as a 'life' may at first seem bizarre. The truth is that it was a totally different way of life, separated even from other services by its own language.

For the previous nineteen years I had basically been a grammar schoolboy in a single sex school, progressing through the various educational stages. The routine was home, school and a little work at the end, before being called up for National Service.

Since many of these years were spent during the war, to dismiss it as routine would be to ignore events which are worthy of mention. My education will follow, since it is probably of central relevance to my lives. That my children will be able to read the whole story once I have the time and leisure to tell it has been my motivation, and I have been told that some of the incidents that have occurred are worthy of repetition, especially since they are unvarnished and are utterly factual. They very much present images of different moments, but I have decided that the harrowing times that family life has presented are better left undiscussed.

Moving around the country, due to my father having been, first, in the Royal Ulster Rifles, and, then, the Catering Corps, we arrived from Dover in Leigh-on-Sea towards the end of the war. Dover had been under bombardment, and we spent much of the time under the table, or under the stairs; we were reluctant to venture out into the garden to stay in our Anderson shelter, though such shelters were furnished with lighting and bedding. Things came to a head when the house in the street opposite was utterly demolished by a bomb, and became a huge crater.

I am sure this prompted my being given my small brown attaché case, and despatched to Grantham as an evacuee. Whilst the lady caring for me was very kind, she had her own children to bring up, and I began to feel a bit left out. Realising this, my mother arrived after a few weeks, and we returned to Dover.

The next move was to Leigh, as my father took up his army catering job and left for Germany. Just before the war ended, my mother and I were returning home when, above us, we could see the German rocket we called the doodle bug, and noticed its flaming exhaust suddenly switched off. Panicking, I thought that we should take cover but my mother was not going to have to go out of her way 'for any bloody German.' The war soon ended, and it was in the same street that we enjoyed our VE Day street party (see below).

Due to the bombing and fatalities, there were many bombed-out or abandoned properties at Leigh. There was nobody to stop us exploring them, and one property I remember had a huge conservatory, with a grape vine from which dangled dozens of bunches of juicy, black grapes. Discovering such grapes was a real find in rationing Britain at the time, and the memory of picking them off the vine has never faded.

Several years later, we joined my father in Germany, in our very comfortable married quarters. He had declined officer rank, since he very much enjoyed being a Quarter Master Sergeant Instructor, with a better income and quality of life.

It was during the war that we lost one of my uncles who had been serving in the Navy, and another to tuberculosis, after his discharge from one of the Stalag prisoner-of-war camps. Fortunately, my other uncle survived. He was a submariner, and was renowned for his exploits in resisting the capture of his submarine in China: he reappears in my second life.

We were in Germany for some two years, ending up in Berlin, before returning to Dover and the same grammar school.

After that, my father joined the Prison service, as a cook and baker, and this time we moved to Birmingham. Education was still a priority, and a short summary is appropriate to grasp much of what is to follow.

At Dover, we were told that Matriculation was required for university: five subjects, with Maths and English, as well as Latin. Moving again, as ever, it was at Birmingham (Handsworth Grammar School) that the educational penny seemed to drop. I obtained Distinctions in Geography and English Literature at A level, and the same in French Literature and Geography at Scholarship level.

Though my teachers were disappointed, because of my results, that I did not sit the Oxford University entrance exam, my father thought the grant insufficient. The other factor was that I could not satisfy my parents of my intentions to pursue a career which might justify the expense.

The only possibility that had appealed was to be a barrister but having seen and admired Robert Donat as a QC in the film *The Winslow Boy*, I was no Robert Donat, and the demands for such a position were impossible.

It was also obvious that I was too immature and unworldly to go to any University, and I think it fortunate that I did not make the attempt which would, I am sure, have been disastrous.

After this digression, I return to life on board ship. We were National Service, Ordinary Seamen -- not even Able Seamen -- schoolboys from sixth forms in uniform. Not being traditional seamen, we were subjected all round to criticism and ridicule until we conformed. Howls of derision would greet us if we talked about going up or down stairs, for instance. Rapidly we learnt that we went 'down below' or 'up top', 'aft' or 'forrard' (as it was pronounced), 'port' and 'starboard'.

We began each day by rolling up and stowing our hammocks to clear our mess, visit the heads (toilets), prepare our food in the galley, and return to the mess to eat it whilst peeling potatoes for dinner. If at sea, for me it was the wheelhouse with the coxswain; or, if in port, removing paintwork, re-applying it to the whole ship, bright work polishing, some duties in the ship's office or teaching in the classroom, or cleaning an officer's quarters.

The start of the process of socialisation and fitting in was language. Though my father was in the Army and in the Prison service for many years, I never picked up any jargon from him. Yet from the time my first family started at primary school until my second followed, and in all over fifty years after my naval service, I have continued to hear in their conversation at home naval slang, jargon and amusing quirks that originated on the Redpole.

I started by listing a number that were peculiar to the service, and having reached more than two pages decided that it was becoming tedious. Suffice it to say that my university-educated families are still open to naval language.

On board a ship, boat or ferry, they will use the proper terms which I had to learn; or, at play, they enjoy being 'Number One' to my skippering.

The ship provided our entertainment, film shows, music (I played much of it over the ship's tannoy), food, clothing, cigarettes, drink, work, friendship, social order and normative behaviour, pay - collected by queuing up and presenting one's cap to be filled - writing and reading facilities; in short, everything, as I remember, even down to a barber.

It is a tribute to the concept of National Service that I had gone from being a spoilt sixth-form student, with a few weeks in work behind a desk, to being someone who was largely self-sufficient, self-protective, and a responsible and effective member of a team in the Armed Forces.

Despite a tendency to end up, generally, behind a desk and in an office, even on board a ship, this was not going to happen in my new adventure. I could not wait to get started and then go on to the streets of London. We were going to change the world and put much to rights, and have the power to do so.

My training took place at the police training school at Hendon, which was a huge complex for training all ranks up to Inspector, and for other relevant organisations(detective school and the cadet school). The course lasted for some months, with frequent examinations to weed out those who could not make it or realised it was not for them. It was so prestigious that the sons of foreign dignitaries, and ruling sovereigns were allowed to attend the course, and we had one such person. After some time, he learned to stop waiting at doors for them to be opened for him; so we at least taught him how to open a door.

The officer in charge of the course not only frightened the life out of us, but when he came into our class to observe or to put a few questions to our lecturers, themselves seasoned inspectors, they would become completely intimidated. Their hands would tremble visibly, so we knew this was not play-acting.

He would usually reduce the women officers to tears; we were not far behind. He teased, ridiculed and plainly bullied whomever he wanted; he would make you stand to receive it before your classmates. His rudeness and language were legendary.

When we came to give the evidence for our arrests in the parade ground, in the mock Magistrates' court which had been setup, he would be the magistrate. Again, we were belittled, shouted at, treated sneeringly, asked where was our evidence, what was our power of arrest in the circumstances and reduced to such a bundle of nerves that we could hardly read our notes because our hands shook so much. This happened without exception to all; and it must be borne in mind that most of us had been in the armed orces.

We were to realise, though he would never have told us, that this was utterly deliberate. The phrase used to be, 'You'll get much worse on the street.' One could then see his treatment of the women officers in context, although then the women were as tough as we were, and quite forbidding in their uniform.

Marching and drilling was the order of the day (sorry). It was interminable, but was something we could all handle. The instructors loved the Army style of drill, with knees raised high, and feet, in huge boots, brought crashing to the ground. This was not the naval style. We had been allowed shoes, and slid our feet together somewhat elegantly when brought to attention. We could show our own tradition, even on the police training ground, grinning at each other as we did so. It goes without saying that the others stamped twice as hard and loudly to do the same, and it was a good game.

The school encouraged us in athletics, but particularly in road walking, which seemed a bit like 'coals to Newcastle.' Since mincing along public roads in proper road-walking style probably afforded the instructors considerable amusement, I cannot blame them for their encouragement.

Then there was self-defence. How we hated self-defence. Our torturer had the qualifications and looks of a professional wrestler, and, in our introduction to him, we were told he would carry his motorcycle up three flights of stairs to his flat every day. It is also a fact that, some years later, he was featured in the headlines of national newspapers for having entered a world-wide wrestling competition in Japan. He had lifted the Japanese champion up in his arms like a baby, and had thrown him out of the ring.

With us he was fair. He would only pick on the biggest and strongest recruit to throw around, whilst the rest of us practised being invisible and avoided any eye-contact, on pain of virtual death. If he had not been so professional with his holds and locks, we would have welcomed it, since we realised that we would at some time need to know how to handle ourselves out on the street.

Essentially, we had to learn our powers of arrest, some basic law, and rules of evidence. We were allocated a case, had to arrest our instructor, take him first to be charged, and then to our mock court. To maintain realism in some cases, they would not let themselves be arrested, or would not stay arrested, but would run away. The trainee would have to chase them, sometimes for up to a hundred yards -- or even around the football pitch, if the trainee looked unfit or overweight.

One of our class had won a medal as an athlete in a previous year's Olympics. Having broken nearly all the school's athletic records, he was a special case. After the arrest, we had the harrowing task of proving the case in the mock court, as described before.

Every month we had exams which had to be passed. If not,if you could not cope with the job or found it was not for you, dismissal was immediate. Learning whole sections of our instruction book by rote was essential, and I spent many hours going round and round the Circle line, which was oddly conducive to the task.

The time soon came for us to find out where we were to serve. those who lived in London would be posted closer to home, but not too close to their previous environment. For the others, it was random. My posting, I was delighted to see, was to West End Central, in Savile Row, in the very centre of London. It was the only part of London I had been to, at my interviews, and it seemed to be where most of the action would be.

Turning up for duty there was an exhilarating thought, and I could not wait to start, and to exercise my new powers. Fortunately, we had instruction classes for the next twelve months, learning report-writing, how to deal with and report traffic accidents and offences, and the myriad of matters that we would doubtless come across.

It became obvious that even though we were only constables, if one was the only officer at a scene or on the street, or was called in for an emergency, one had to take charge. Rarely could help be summoned. A police officer was required at times, to demonstrate leadership qualities, and he often had a huge responsibility placed on his shoulders.

It was encouraging to know that if we were challenged in court over the procedure or were mistaken about the law, the High Court, we were told, had expressed sympathy with an officer who had had to act immediately, and without the recourse to law books which a defence solicitor could have. Arguments from such solicitors over the rules of hearsay, over the Judge's rules – directions to be strictly adhered to in interrogations -- and over the lawfulness of arrest, were matters on which we had received little training, yet had to deal with in our conduct of prosecutions in the Magistrates courts. Not only did this require cross-examining defendants and their witnesses, but also making a closing speech prior to that of the defence, if permitted.

At first we were to 'learn beats' – accompanying for several weeks another officer who had been picked for his experience and competence. A beat would be a small area of perhaps four to five backstreets and a section of a main road. This was the case in Soho, but on the other side of Regent Street, in Mayfair, as far as Park Lane, there was less action, but a greater need to protect private property, exclusive shops, stores and embassies, and to monitor the very best hotels, where famous members of foreign governments or other influential guests might be staying.

Those with whom we patrolled were nothing less than most helpful, advising us constantly and recounting all manner of experiences in an effort to man us up, teaching us to protect ourselves and to cope with what would be thrown at us. Such help was in their interests, too, as they would need support, in the physical sense and as witnesses to arrests in court.

Needless to say, our continuing instruction in our classes was vital, and included practical advice, local knowledge, memos on how to deal with up-to-date changes to procedure, both local and general, and mnemonics for report writing, especially for including all the relevant items for traffic accidents. It was our good fortune that the Inspector who ran our classes was particularly brilliant.

Stepping out on my own for the first time onto the street involved a mixture of sensations. It was something I had looked forward to, but now the responsibility bore down on my shoulders. Did I know enough? Where should I go to get to my beat? What should I do? How should I manage traffic points directing traffic, especially buses, as well as crowds of pedestrians, crossing here, there, and everywhere? These were all questions which incessantly troubled me at first.

It was not long before my first arrest. This involved a drunk flat out in an alleyway. Back at the station, a search of his property revealed a photograph of him with a mayoral chain round his neck. Mild panic set in, but at court he pleaded guilty, and there were no repercussions or press interest.

The second drunk we found turned out to be the cousin of my girlfriend, up from Monmouth; but she had never liked him anyway, she said.

The third was a solicitor, and he pleaded not guilty so there was a trial. He called three other solicitors to say he had never had a drink in his life. I was perplexed as to what disease he might have been suffering from, and which could have made him thoroughly unsteady on his feet, his speech almost incomprehensible, and breath to reek of what I had thought was alcohol. He was found not guilty by the magistrate.

Day duty arrived, with its first challenge. As I patrolled Oxford Street, I was faced with a street trader, selling fruit from his barrow. What was more to the point it was a stationary barrow, and was supposed to move on the approach of the uniform. The trader carried on selling and ignored me. This was not to be permitted. I went up to him slowly and very deliberately. He ignored me, and I was clearly being defied.

Local arrangements had been made to deal with the regulations affecting the treatment of street traders and, if they were arrested and taken to the police station, the protection of their produce. I was not entirely sure of the current policy. I told him that he was committing an offence, and asked why was he not moving, as was the practice. His response was that he had been chased from pillar to post on the other side of the road, policed by another division and he had had enough. He wasn't going anywhere, so he said.

I told him there was nothing for it but...and produced my notebook. Excruciatingly slowly, I turned the pages, not letting him see that there was nothing yet in it. Staring hard at him, I searched for my pencil, taking as much time as was possible, and then asked him for his full name. With my stubby pencil, I made a meal of writing this down. By the time I had finished and looked up, he was scampering across Oxford Street with his barrow. Lesson learnt! This job might not be as difficult as I had thought.

Prostitution was endemic in the West End, and over the boundary into Hyde Park. My first police accommodation was at Paddington, in a section house where the room resembled a Salvation Army cubicle. This was on the north side of the park, and on the south side, in Kensington, in her room, lived the girl whom I had met on my first night out, and who was to become my first wife.

I used to cross the park, diagonally, to meet her, and on my first walk there in broad daylight, saw a couple on a bench. The girl was giving the man a helping hand, in a manner of speaking, and was oblivious to all the passers-by – since this was her livelihood.

Later the park turned into a modern Sodom and Gomorrah, with the prostitutes and clients performing on, under, and across benches and deckchairs, or up against most of the trees by the path. There was no sign of any police.

Couples disappeared into bushes, the men to emerge a few minutes later, embarrassingly adjusting their dress as they hurried away, to be followed by the next customer.

Moving closer to Kensington, there were queues of cars crawling past the line of girls who were tapping on their windows asking if the drivers wanted a good time. Again, there was no police presence.

At least in Soho, where much the same was occurring in the street and in doorways, arrests were being made, or the girls would run when the officers appeared. Once they had been seen to solicit, they became 'common prostitutes' in law, and could then be arrested if soliciting on the street or if caught in the act. At first I could not arrest them for soliciting, leaving it to the more experienced officers in the vice unit, but if caught in the act I could do so, as they were 'outraging public decency'. Sometimes, in Brewer Street, where I was regularly posted at night they would lift their skirts up, as if doing the Can-Can, to attract customers, or otherwise flashing their best points.

As all sorts frequented the area, especially coming from the theatres to restaurants, or to wherever they had parked, some control was necessary. Personally, I felt it right to protect the drunks with money in their pockets from a temptation which could have had serious repercussions. Drugs did not then seem a problem, as they later turned out to be, becoming a major factor inducing prostitution.

The most regular method of control, however, was by checking, from the bail notices which the girls carried, or from receipts showing that they had paid their fines, whether they had been arrested within the previous fortnight. Once arrested, they would usually be bailed, to allow them to earn the fine and to look after their children.

If they wanted to be arrested, and kept free for a few weeks, they would meet one of the vice squad in a taxi, and drive to the police station with him and, sometimes, another officer and his accompanying beat-learner (I speak from experience). Once at the station, they were then released on bail and back out in minutes. It was a system that provided control, but it was fair to all, and put no pressure on the detention rooms or other resources at the police station. They were only sentenced to a short term of custody if their fines went unpaid on their next arrest, and this could not be avoided. The system showed how ingenuity and flexibility, coupled with discretion, could achieve effective and equitable results.

My first arrest of a suspected criminal was about to present itself, though little detection was involved. I had just seen someone climb through the kitchen windows of the section house in the centre of Soho, aptly named Trenchard House, after Lord Trenchard, the Marshal of the Air force who had become the Commissioner of Police a decade or so before.

I searched the kitchen, and found the thief stuffing food and money into his pockets as fast as he could. He was charged, and pleaded guilty in court. Since he was obviously impoverished, I gave what mitigation I could as to what he had stolen, and he was treated leniently by one of the stipendiary magistrates who sat in the Magistrates courts at that time. The more experienced officers drily observed that he must have been desperate to have stolen food from our canteen.

Another day, on my usual beat around Brewer Street, I noticed a crowd at its junction with Lexington Street. Quickening my pace, I approached the junction, which also led to Piccadilly Circus, and saw more people gathering on the pavements, and starting to block the traffic, with their car horns beeping noisily. As I got closer, people were pouring into the junction from all directions, and crowds thickening on all four corners.

On the first corner was situated a large showroom or garage, the forecourt of which was congested, with more and more people packing onto it. As I strode to the centre, there were a number of photographers standing around, whilst the current Miss World posed quite happily for them. They wanted me to pose with her, and I replied gruffly that I was more concerned with their colleague, who was hanging out of the first floor window of the showroom waving and beckoning an ever-increasing crowd to come closer. The scene was chaotic, and the noise deafening. Mayhem would be a fair description -- and on my beat!

I ordered him to stop and come down, and, as he faced me, we were surrounded by five of his colleagues. I told him he was causing obstruction to the traffic and pedestrians, and proceeded to report the facts for his prosecution to be considered. I was booking him, in other words, for the offence.

This caused consternation to his colleagues, who started arguing and abusing me. Keeping cool, though thoroughly annoyed by his behaviour, I went through the procedure as fully as was possible. I had realised that the best way of dealing with complaints or arguments was to be both dispassionate and formal. Whilst doing so, the other reporters got out their notebooks and wrote down every word I said, whilst advising me to buy the next day's newspapers to see something which might interest me.

I finished reporting him, and the crowd dispersed and the traffic flowed again. As I returned to the Section House, the enormity of what I had just done dawned on me – reporting for prosecution a member of the press. I got straight on the phone and told my duty officer, the inspector of my relief. This was too important for my sergeant.

He listened quietly, and then stated that I had been quite right to have done what I had, right even to have reported him. Calmly, he ordered me to make a completely detailed report, and present it to him when I booked off.

I ordered the papers, and, sure enough, there were full reports of the whole matter, with my actual words being included. However, I heard no more of it, to my relief, but found out it was not being proceeded with: that came as no surprise, but then the result was not my concern.

For instance, on the other side of Bond Street, in Mayfair, were several prestigious hotels, where we would assist with their famous guests in fan control, for security, or just to help staff. A relationship developed between the hotel and police, to the extent that they would welcome the officer on the beat in for a very early breakfast.

The Dorchester provided silver service on a platter which was carried down to the kitchen, to be amply filled and eaten in a private room. I liked Claridge's hotel better. There we were supplied with a menu, and served as any other customer would have been. Two other things made that the best. Firstly, we could see how much the guests were paying for what we were eating for free on our wages, that felt good. Secondly, a copy of The Times was placed on the tray, and I, for one, felt that this acknowledgment that a mere 'copper' would want and could enjoy such a paper was something of a tribute.

The control of parking in the narrow streets of Soho was a never-ending problem. There was but one approach, to book the driver with as little conversation as possible. This also prevented being talked out of it, with all the charm that could be mustered by an alternative (and often female) response.

Anticipating a complaint from one encounter with the type who would say, 'Do you realise who you are talking to,' I gave him the full formal treatment, informing him his parking was causing serious obstruction to the whole area. I got to the station first, and was amused to hear him vociferously complaining to my sergeant. The main thrust of the complaint was the officer was so bloody polite, and kept calling me 'sir' all the damn time. He was infuriating.'

I have no doubt that to my sergeants, too, I could be a pain at times. One of the first times was when I assisted a very distressed and helpless young lady who started to become embarrassingly grateful once indoors. It was very well decorated for a 'seamstress.' Looking around I soon noticed the pornographic pictures, especially in the bedroom, and certain specialist equipment. This indicated that the damage incurred in gaining entry, and the time spent away from my beat in the company of a lady of ill repute, should be fully reported.

I made out my report, and handed it in to my sergeant. He said that he could not understand quite a lot of it, and I told him that that was probably because it was in French. As she spoke no English, I had to write her statements in French to convey her actual words, as advised in report-writing. My sergeant became nearly apoplectic. I pointed out that on the next page I had written a translation, so complying with instructions but ensuring comprehension.

I behaved similarly towards my other sergeant, to whom I handed the report of a stop in the street, on the Mayfair side. Stops in the street had to be justified by reasonable suspicion, and he asked what it was about. I told him that the guy had a case full of guns and revolvers, and turned to walk away. He grabbed me and screamed "And you let him go away?" Before I could answer he wanted to know exactly where this was so efforts could be made to find him.

I told him it was not necessary, as the man I had stopped was the producer of *The Goon Show*, and he was taking home all the props for the show. My sergeant failed to be amused, and I was marked down for a traffic point posting.

This came as no punishment, as we mostly liked this duty: the time passed swiftly and other officers would relieve you constantly. I think the attraction was to really work your point – the busier and trickier the better. Oxford Circus was the favourite, once the routes of the buses were mastered namely, which would turn left, which would turn right, and which would go straight on, once the hordes of pedestrians crossing were under control, and once emergency vehicles were speeded through.

That it was pure power that motivated us is perhaps best illustrated by the histrionics and styles used abroad, by the more extrovert traffic officers working there. You probably needed to audition to relieve a traffic officer on his point in Italy.

It was not long before I was in trouble with much higher ranks. My girlfriend and I wanted to live together in a flat, and sought permission to change my address to one in Notting Hill, from which bus services ran to both our workplaces, and where the rent was affordable.

I was also given an indication that I would be permitted to marry her, also essential, I suppose, after a criminal conviction check. My Chief Superintendent told me that he had received a message from his counterpart at Notting Hill to the effect that our choice of residence was most unsuitable. He would not say why, but there had been trouble with the landlady and it was inadvisable.

As we were committed, and thought we could handle it, we moved in. It was in an insalubrious part of Notting Hill, and had at least one brothel directly opposite, fully and openly functioning. The landlady very much liked us, and gave my wife a good alarm clock as a present.

Soon afterwards our neighbours, two legitimate models, were given eviction notices, which they very much disputed.

Nevertheless, they were evicted, and all their possessions 'confiscated.'

Not many weeks later we were served immediate eviction notices. This was clearly her practice and it was this that had resulted in civil court actions which had earned the premises' reputation. Ours was supported by an allegation of theft of an alarm clock. We obtained the services of a friend with a van, and lowered our belongings out of the window of the first floor and down to the ground below. Whilst one of us held her shut in the toilet, the other ran up and downstairs with smaller items. We did a moonlight flit, as it was called.

All sorts of letters, from solicitors as well as from her, were sent to the police station. I was called in over it several times, for our landlady was livid that she had been out-witted, with all her legal knowledge and experience in these activities. I received strong advice about her letters and official complaints, and for avoiding the good advice I had been given. Even though criminal allegations were made, nothing formal came of it. I would think most of these matters were written up in my personal record, but we kept the clock, as a sign of victory over a very cunning, sly and vicious adversary.

The next time I went even higher. As my now pregnant wife was getting off the bus in which we travelled home, I helped her off the step. I was in full uniform, but had my armlet off. This small band on the wrist of the uniform jacket was to indicate that I was off duty. I helped her down the step and off the bus. Thereupon an elderly and very smart gentleman shouted "What the hell do you think you are doing?" I turned to face him and we had the time-honoured question, "Do you know who I am?"

I replied in the negative, and he announced that he was an Assistant Commissioner, one of the top three in the Force. Having learnt in training school that the top echelon carried silver tokens, not warrant cards, I then stated that if that were the case, I would like to see his silver token. He started searching his clothing, and became thoroughly frustrated not to find it. He had to give up, and strode away, his face purple with rage, offering vague threats about my future in the Force.

Needless to say, I was soon summoned before my Superintendent. Words of advice followed, but the fact that I could not be faulted, and had been perfectly polite (with the impression that the very senior officer involved was not much liked, nor the most pleasant or reasonable of ranking officers) all saved me again.

On the following night duty, an event occurred which outweighed the significance of some of the criticisms on my record and reputation.

I was approached on my beat in Old Compton Street and informed by a member of the public that there was a sizeable group of young guys, armed with iron bars, roaming the streets. Although we were not permitted to stray off our beat, even across the road on to another, it was clearly important to find another PC on an adjacent beat.

Telling him what I had been told, we decided to team up and see if we could find them. Since the group was more than two of us could handle, we found another two officers and suggested that they should follow behind us in our quest as back up if necessary.

It was not long before we found the group and shepherded them against a wall, with the other PCs joining us. As we did so lengths of iron bar were dropped or fell from their sleeves. We stood facing a group of ten or so and earmarked those who clearly were the leaders for arrest, looking for further help or the arrival of some transport.

Two of them, who were on the fringe, slowly backed away further and further until they turned and ran off. Immediately the two colleagues who were our back-up turned and chased them. That left the two of us with some eight of them. An uneasy silence and a sort of truce ensued for a minute or so; then another backed away, getting ready to run, and then did so. We moved closer to the three whom we had thought were the ringleaders, ready to arrest them when it became feasible.

We had no choice but to let the next one run as well and the next and eventually the last two; there were three of them and two of us and these odds were now manageable.

Accordingly, we arrested them physically without much resistance on their part, and took them to the police station, where the CID were called and took over the case. We wrote up our notes and made statements for trial, and contributed to the recording of the details in the Crime Book. As I remember, arrests were written in red ink in the books, the Stop book and the Crime book. The CID and our uniformed senior officers were quite impressed with us: little was said about the ill-advised pursuit of two of them by our back-up pair, leaving us with the majority of the others. I believe it was discussed in a training class as a useful lesson.

Later, after they had pleaded guilty to possessing offensive weapons in what were clearly circumstance intimidating to someone or to a club, they were sentenced, almost certainly to custody.

I was then called up before an extremely senior officer and commended: I have no doubt that my first colleague was similarly commended, as we acted together.

A commendation looked good on my record. I did not complain, but thought it was more a victory for common sense rather than for Bravery, which is how it was listed, with other lessons to be learnt.

Other functions we could undertake were to police film premiers, and be paid overtime for it as well. My best time was in Charing Cross Road, at the premier of Doctor in the House. This featured Brigitte Bardot who dashed out of the cinema, running to her limousine in the bikini she wore in the film, with a flimsy cover. I was out front monitoring the traffic, so that the stars could be despatched home in the traffic that had stopped to watch. As she jumped into her chauffeur-driven car under my nose, she threw off her top and sprawled across the back seat. She lay there looking absolutely stunning; maybe 'ravishing' was a better word.

Since she could see me gazing at her while I tried to negotiate her departure, she smiled, as she realised I was giving her the very closest of traffic facilitation and personal attention. With the traffic around it was essential that I walked her car for some distance up the road as far as could be justified, enjoying the spectacle.

Another treat was on the occasions when a show was not doing well, or had started badly. To fill the theatre, they would send free tickets to the police station and the local hospital. That was how I came to the Adelphi in the Strand, where I watched a show in which the female vocalist could not attend, as she was indisposed. The compere announced that they had got a young and unknown seventeen-year old girl from Tiger Bay who 'deserved a great welcome.'

She certainly got one. As she came on to the stage, dressed rather revealingly, and looking utterly devastatingly gorgeous, there were gasps all around the theatre. She then began to sing the first of her numbers: we all sat spell-bound and one could literally have heard a pin drop. After rapturous applause, she sang her second number and again the silence was astonishing. The applause was as before, and at the third number there was cheering and deafening encouragement, then utter silence, followed by tumultuous applause.

I had seen the most amazing debut of anyone in any theatre – and at that time we could afford to sit in the gods at most theatres. It must be said that it did appear that we would be seeing more of this girl! Her name was Shirley Bassey.

Now married with our first daughter, we were living in a large house near New Cross. I needed a transfer closer to police accommodation, since travel from New Cross was almost impossible. The downside was that I would have to leave the West End and Mayfair, and miss the hustle and bustle and the round the clock activity which they presented. Piccadilly was a magnet for every sort of activity fuelled by drink, vice, vagrancy and street entertainment, with the appeal of its bright lights and air of general excitement. I always thought an important aspect of its appeal was that it afforded anonymity, and so to those so attracted, anything went.

There would be shoe-blacks, knife grinders and other pedlars, buskers whose performance seemed to lack much musical talent, and beggars, including ex-servicemen. Pedestrians would wander along muttering, or singing or arguing with themselves– so many with mental disorders-- and numerous prostitutes flaunting themselves, with the taxis in which they entertained their clients hovering close by for their custom.

The biggest treat were the three Egyptian sand-dancers in Leicester Square, drawing huge crowds nightly. Whilst they were offending the law, and informal rules of moving on, no officer was going to brave the crowd and bring this to an end – and it was a very professional and entertaining performance.

Another memory was of trying to help a very old lady who appeared utterly incapable through drink. My assessment was somewhat premature, for during this exchange she took a fancy to me. Rebuffing her drunken advances led to an attack on me with her umbrella. The public started to gather round as she continued striking my helmet with surprising power, loving my discomfiture.

The only way I could get out of this, certainly not by arresting her, was to hail a passing cab and bundle her in, and tell the taxi to take her away...anywhere. The driver laughingly agreed, and never even troubled me for her fare. Taxi drivers were often our sole communication of trouble, and were also most helpful to us. The crowd generously applauded.

Royalty imposed duties, too. For a visit by the Queen Mother we had to man every junction along Lower Regent Street. Manning my point, I got the word of her impending arrival, and kept my junction clear in readiness. I was then horrified to see a horse and cart, laden with scrap metal, slowly enter my junction to cross the road. A moving horse was not to be stopped and it just continued making its exit, as the limousine swung round and passed through with a few feet to spare.

The incident was not closed, as the next morning there was some publicity about the theft of some valuable gates from Buckingham Palace. I mentioned my horse and cart to the CID, and looked at photograph albums to point out a person I thought I would be able to identify, since he had had my total attention for some time. Whilst the person I picked out was a well-known scrap metal dealer, who used a horse and cart, and might well have had a gate on the cart, I heard no more of it.

The day came when I received my posting, and a flat to go with it, and moved from the West End to the East End. The posting was to Plaistow, the flat in Barking.

Chapter 5
To the East End and Beyond

Gone were the silver service breakfasts at the Dorchester, or waiter service at Claridge's with the Times. This was the East End, and it was two slices of toast and dripping with a mug of tea in a 'greasy spoon'. Since our sergeant would be checking up on us, we would gather far enough away from the station to make it unlikely for him to walk that far to find us. Needless to say, he never did, but probably because he would have been ensconced in much better surroundings.

Our beats were huge, to such an extent that there were police boxes placed around for us to ring in from (there were set times for us to do so). We were expected to eat meals in the boxes, and write up our reports, as to walk back to the station and return would mean a long absence from one's beat. We had to manage largely on our own, with just a whistle to blow in an emergency. We could ring the station, but only from the police box, and, if so, were expected to cope.

Plaistow was an area of about 8 square miles, the vast majority comprising terraced houses, built mainly to house dockworkers. There were still huge bomb sites around, but it contained main routes to the east and towards the docks. Occasionally we had to police North Woolwich from Plaistow, which was the sub-divisional station. Both the foot tunnel and the ferry across the Thames had to be covered.

At the time there was industrial action at the docks and at Ford's in Dagenham, and we were used on demonstrations and picketing.

Generally, we patrolled our beat on foot, dropped in to the local dairy or cafe for a tea-break, relieved the two traffic points, and got to know the public. As far as most were concerned, they would threaten to call a copper if their children misbehaved, but mostly they were upfront with their policemen, and if they had something to say it was to your face.

An instance demonstrating our functions occurred when, with a colleague learning beats, we two were approached by a distressed young lady. Addressing my colleague (people always spoke to the learner), she asked if we could come to her school and really tell the children off. I thought this undesirable, but my colleague, confronted with a very attractive damsel in distress, and after sinking into her deep blue eyes, strode off with her to the nearby school.

I felt oddly ungracious to have tried to prevent it so we entered the classroom and were confronted by about thirty pairs of very wide eyes behind their little desks: they were about six years of age. The teacher stood aside, and my colleague took over the lectern.

He performed manfully and as his confidence mounted and voice rose he added some mild threats. The teacher was well pleased and I began to feel slightly jealous of his prowess. Further encouraged he moved into pointing, more and more energetic finger-wagging and even an occasional fist-thumping on the lectern. All eyes widened. He turned to the teacher who was clearly delighted and said, "Should I ask if they have any questions?"She replied," I don't think there is much point, they are all deaf and dumb." My colleague had given a half-hour lecture to thirty recipients who could not have heard a word.

I bit my lip as we left, so as not to burst out laughing, realising my colleague's utter discomfiture. He swore me to silence, and I was as good as my word, and never mentioned his name on the very rare occasions when the story was worth telling. Such an occasion would be when, out of the blue, you are asked to make a speech to a suitable audience as a warning against impromptu speeches.

The most regular offence was street betting, in which bets were placed with known individuals on street corners, or in their houses, or more often in public houses. Rather like the vice squads in the West End, there was a specialist team engaged to deal with this offence, and this was a much sought after post, since betting in public houses was a specific and more serious offence. It was conducted in plain clothes, and arrests necessitated long observation and involved much court attendance and overtime.

Otherwise, there were few arrests, but more traffic offences to report, and attendance at afternoon court. At the local Magistrates court lay persons dispensed justice, as advised on the law by their clerks. The appointment of the JPs was strongly political, and they were largely of an unforgiving nature: sentencing was tough. Their support for us was welcome. Not for nothing was the inscription above the entrance 'Police Court'.

It was only once that I heard them refuse to hear a case. It involved one officer whose arrests for assaulting him regularly seemed to feature black eyes and bruises on those arrested, yet no obvious signs of his own injury.

I began to realise that the use of discretion, which was a powerful aid to policing an area such as ours, could achieve much more than an automatic arrest. That items had fallen off the back of a lorry or had been bought in a pub were reasons frequently offered to explain their possession. Without solid proof, the CID would often use their discretion to foster better relations or to obtain an informer.

Another example of the thinking of some of the public occurred at court, on the part of the parents of the accused. I had been called over by a member of the public to an allegation concerning a grassy bomb site opposite our flat. He had just seen a teenager and a very young child disappear into the grass.

I went over and found the teenager lying in the grass on top of the young girl, one hand across her mouth to keep her quiet, with his other arm around her. I arrested him, and he was taken to Barking and charged by the CID with indecency and attempted rape. At court I overheard his mother say she couldn't understand him. He had two young sisters, so why did he need to look for strangers?

Such behaviour was quite atypical of most of the residents, who would have been as horrified as we were, but some family relationships were alarming.

Yet we were frequently abused by one regular who would shout from the other side of the street, mouthing swearwords threateningly, with violent gestures. He lived with his wife and young family in what was truly a hovel, without heat and water, and with little food.

His children were removed to a home many miles from London. Nevertheless, most weekends the children -between ten and six - would travel somehow all the way home to be with their parents. They would be seized and returned.

This constant struggle, with parental love battling a civilised and better upbringing, would disturb me, but wiser heads than mine were in charge. Perhaps, by now, having three young children of our own had made me think more about such conflict between institutional care and love.

Our station had a unique way of dealing with youngsters we arrested. (It was a scheme that I heard praised many years later by a Chief Constable from Wales who was with me in the force at the same time, and who was still ceaselessly attempting to reintroduce it under another name with her fellow Chief Constables – but without success.)

Called the Juvenile Liaison Scheme, it would prevent youngsters from being charged or taken to court. Instead, the sergeant in charge of the squad would visit the homes of the juveniles and meet with their parents. Using his very great skills and commonsense, and with his own charisma, he would advise and then monitor their behaviour by means of more visits and consultations.

Perfectly suited for this task, his results were astonishing, and the re-offending rate became remarkable. It transpired that, of all the efforts to control juvenile delinquency, this scheme was by far the most successful: criminological statistics which I later studied supported its success. I have always been baffled that it was not utilised as a full-blown scheme.

Although the West End must have seen many runaway and delinquent children, none ever came to my notice, although their descriptions would have been circulated and posted up to study. This may have been because such duties were regarded as the primary responsibility of our women police officers.

Interspersed with ordinary duties was the opportunity to volunteer for Football duty at West Ham. It gave those of us who did it mainly for the football - not the overtime - the chance to sit on our rolled up capes, literally on the touchline.

My main memory was of the total hush whenever Jimmy Greaves advanced over the halfway line with the ball at his feet, and the heightened expectation that accompanied his advance. It may seem strange to compare Shirley Bassey with Greaves, but it was the same phenomenon.

The money from overtime pay was another bonus from Upton Park, and came in handy with a growing family. As in the Navy, we queued up for pay, placed in cash in our hats or helmets. As one moved along the queue the overtime would arrive in a brown envelope. In the queue were a number of individuals taking money back out, collecting dues, pension support, personal collections for those retiring or promoted or for other charitable reasons, e.g. the Xmas savings club. It was most depressing, as a fair amount of money would quickly disappear. The system cleverly maximised contribution at the expense (and initial pleasure) of gain.

At times there were tough days. One such was being called to a tenant to await the arrival of the Mental Welfare Officer. As my colleague and I entered, the man was smashing his head against the fireplace. He greeted us, blood running down his forehead, with, "What a game this is." Then, "I'd better get back in the scrum." He turned and threw himself back into the fireplace, mentioning that it was tough for the Welsh to play at Twickenham.

He was utterly deluded, and we both had to drag him back. As we continued to humour him and stop him hurting himself, we realised he was suffering from epilepsy, and, unfortunately the *grand mal* variety. Every so often he would have a major seizure. Then we had to pounce on him to deal with it, and stop him giving his tongue a serious wound. The fact he was built like a rugby player did not make it any easier.

When he calmed down, we told him he had better get dressed to go and to change his clothes. The next few hours were spent restraining him, humouring him by talking as much gibberish as him about the match and getting him to go upstairs and change every item he was wearing, again and again, as it did not suit what he was now wearing.

He next took out his boot polish to clean his shoes for the trip. I did notice that he was using coloured boot polish on my colleague's shoes and socks; my colleague had no choice, in the circumstances, but to put up with it. The fact that he always failed to relieve me when I was on point duty, because it 'was too cold' as he walked back to the station had not endeared him to me. He would then ask the sergeant to be relieved to write something up. I somehow failed to warn him, and enjoyed his concern over the desecration of his beautifully polished boots.

By the time the MWO arrived, we were all exhausted, except for the patient who still had not cottoned on to our tactics: otherwise we would have been hammered.

There were more good times than bad, and good fortune continued to favour me. One quite remarkable piece of luck was when some of us were given tickets to go to the cinema in East Ham for some sort of show that needed a boost to the audience. There we witnessed one of the very few appearances in the UK, I assume, of Buddy Holly and the Crickets. They were little known here, hence they played in a downtown cinema, in a very unfashionable part of the East End. In the US they were becoming legendary.

They went through their full repertoire, with little of the showmanship displayed on film: song after song written by

Buddy Holly, songs which were to become worldwide hits and standards in popular music, all beautifully performed. Early in the following year, 1959, the news broke that he had died in a plane crash, and practically no one in this country would have seen him live.

Some of us were also lucky with our bets at the dog track. When we paraded for duty there, the security would give us our postings, and, to help us enjoy the experience, there would be tips on the first two races. That these dogs invariably won by massive distances whatever the odds made us some spending money and raised some concerns about the predictability of greyhound racing in general.

I brought my mother to the track when she visited London, as, being slightly posh, she had never descended to such a venue. I had to drag her away before she spent all of her housekeeping, and never took her again. She would have become a complete addict.

Things there were pretty basic for the officers at the track, although with more confidence in our tipsters, and more cynicism about the system, we would, as they say, have cleaned up. For our refreshment, we were handed a three penny raffle ticket for one cup of tea per evening. After enduring this for some weeks the situation changed, as a race-goer threw a stuffed rabbit on to the track, and chaos ensued.

The following week, trays of the finest sandwiches and beverages of all sorts, mostly alcoholic, were brought to us in the track's best dining room. It was a veritable feast and made me wonder if the thrower of the toy was wearing very dark clothing, pointed headgear, and carried a raffle ticket. The feasts continued for some time.

Sports days were on Wednesdays, and I would play football in the afternoon, and table tennis in the evening. It so happened that in the Navy, Wednesdays were days off, and called Make and Mend days, where we sat like our mothers, sewing, ironing and mending. For most shops Wednesdays were also half days. I still feel I should not be working on a Wednesday.

I worked shift work at Plaistow, which allowed me time with the family, shopping, taking them to the park across the road, taking each in turn on the front of my bike to the police station to collect my pay, visits from their grandparents– in other words, a full domestic life. Each police station would hold a Christmas party for their children, and there were four police sports grounds to enjoy. Ours was at a palatial mansion at Chigwell, with massive grounds containing sports pitches, tennis courts, a miniature and a 9-hole golf course, and weekly dances for the adults.

With time to study and a need for better pay, as well my ambition to become an Inspector in ten years(four years having elapsed) it was time to start studying for the promotion examination. One had to prove one's suitability and knowledge in this rank to qualify for entry to the examination. At that time there were many vacancies. The examination was hard, but the pass level quite generous.

We had attended learning courts for a week, both in the Magistrates and Crown courts. Court attendance was frequent at both stations, both for arrests and for traffic offences, and experience was gained at demonstrations and ceremonial occasions, where we wore a heavy uniform with studs down the centre, a high collar, and white gloves with a cape for protection.

Hundreds of officers would gather at such events, as well as accompanying marchers, and policing Trafalgar square for meetings. It was during this time that I recognised in their police uniform two of my fellow National servicemen from the Redpole. They too had joined the Metropolitan force, but there was little opportunity to talk.

There was much unrest, mainly industrial, and some from the CND, to which we were assigned. Off duty I would occasionally visit Speakers Corner in Hyde Park, and listen to the finest orators of their day debating and arguing with a very vociferous crowd, handling hecklers and providing great entertainment, absolutely free. They were masterly performers, from politicians and philosophers to senior religious figures, and they had plenty to talk about.

I had learned a great deal early on at a practical level which was critical for every police officer. We all disapproved of the pressure to continue with Lord Trenchard's scheme to bring in officers from the Forces and academics as our senior officers. Being on the beat for two years was now an unassailable requirement; one could see the difference.

Basic law and the subject of evidence had to be mastered; technique and tactics in court needed to be learnt, and watching the performances of other officers and defence solicitors was useful, noting the good as well as the bad. Sometimes such solicitors were fierce, critical and insulting, and giving evidence was stressful. Keeping calm, trying to 'assist the court' when prosecuting, avoiding aggression, considering a question (and where it led), needed all the practice possible – to such an extent that, under challenge by a solicitor in a careless driving case, I agreeably dealt with all of the matters he put in his defence. He finished after securing my apparent support by asking, "So what would you say generally about my client's driving?" Answering that it was diabolical won our case, and left him quite crestfallen as he had, he thought, been doing so well.

Giving evidence was always an ordeal, but could be handled by telling the truth, being scrupulously fair and considerate. The more experience, the better.

In the Crown Court it was much harder. There was the formality of the language and procedure, the skill of the barristers as opposed to solicitors, but above all the realisation that you would not necessarily be believed just because you were a police officer, as in the lower courts. Your evidence would be weighed up by the judge and evaluated.

A police officer's notes could be examined, his notebook handed up for thorough examination by counsel, a judge and even the jury, as well as the proper procedure and powers, examined minutely.

The defendant's answers to you were similarly weighed up, to make sure that he would have said these things, and how. Did what you said in court that he had said make sense? Was it consistent? These were the main issues.

The skills in questioning and interviewing needed developing, but could be learnt watching a suitable mentor or an experienced and capable detective. Fortunately, when I volunteered for duty as an Aide to the CID, I came across the best.

Our first class Detective Sergeant was superb in interviews, and I had many opportunities of watching him in action. If interviewing someone vulnerable, or a sex offender, one could almost see him in a clerical collar. He exuded sympathy and understanding, and confessions poured out. With the tougher he would just sit and look through them for long periods of silence until they could stand it no more and would confess. Others he let run on interminably, until they slipped up on some detail, or put their second account at variance with the first over some apparently immaterial detail. His knowledge of the East End and its population made him truly formidable.

The next was my own sergeant, who taught me a valuable lesson when he suspected I was off my beat, and came in late for a meal in the middle of the night. After hearing my well thought-out excuse, he started to have a long and sociable chat with me. At the end of our chat and out of the blue he asked me where she lived. I answered that I had walked her home to...and he had got me.

It was a technique I came to use on several occasions, and it always worked. When I read about his record in the Force in the war, and his numerous and constant arrests of criminals, I was not surprised. In the cricket match between the ranks, I was determined to knock him for six, but I was bowled out first ball by a diabolical leg break; I remember his satisfied look, as he had again put me in my place.

Finally, I have used techniques seen in Terence Rattigan's *Winslow Boy*. The story was a true one, and in it the QC interrogated the suspect, a young naval cadet. At the end he told the family he would take the case - the boy was not guilty. He explained thus: the boy during his account admitted having done wrong by smoking, which was against rules of the school; he gave some inconsistencies that suggested guilt; and he had not walked into the trap set for him by the QC who suggested he only did it as a joke.

These ploys were all used in interviews and in cross-examining in court. The jury especially enjoyed being told the techniques, and having seen the results.

I had wanted to join the CID and be a murder investigator – a complete pipe dream, yet I did not fancy the CID as it then was. The uniform branch was safer, the hours were fewer, and those they dealt with were less dangerous, less unethical and less corrupting. The macho culture and tendency to womanise (being in plain clothes) had no appeal, and I had family to bring up.

A stint as an aide was always an interesting diversion, providing opportunities for study, more experience in interviews and questioning. 'Early turn' was thus avoided, and public order duty too. I could learn a lot from the opportunity which I was given, as I had a decent record of crime arrests.

I started out by chasing up warrants for those to be interviewed or arrested for breaching bail, for instance. Some were not that bright, and one burglar arrested on warrant had written, on a note left on the premises, next to an empty bottle of spirit, 'You'll never catch me.' His real error was in signing his name afterwards.

I was heavily criticised by my Detective Inspector for leaping on my bike when a message was received -a thief was carrying valuable scrap metal on his bicycle near the station. Though arrested, the DI did not want it known that his smart and sharp-suited young detectives used pushbikes. My claim for eight pence a day for that and future cycle use was turned down contemptuously.

One clever defendant turned the tables on me. Having been arrested for theft of a number of expensive tools, and caught red-handed, he made full and complete confessions, admitting everything. At court, he unkindly pleaded not guilty, and I had not brought the tools to court. The case against him was therefore dismissed as the bench could not see the evidence and his shrewdness taught me not to expect a guilty plea until the defendant had said the words in court.

Another arrest, for pressing indecently against young women in a street market, failed disappointingly. This was called 'bustle-punching', but was normally confined to tube trains. The defendant was a local VIP, but I had no support for the facts, so nothing came of that.

As an Aide to the CID, it was expected that arrests of criminals would feature in the arrest summary in the back of the diary. Since theft and serious pilfering from and around the docks occurred with regularity, stops of suspicious individuals or goods being carried would lead to arrests. Alternatively, the security staff would detain employees and hand them over to us.

Metals were frequently stolen and sold to the scrap metal dealers, and, again, stops of those on their way to such dealers would result in arrests, depending whether the value of the goods made the effort of prosecution worthwhile. Cautioning was not in force.

Finally, a short tour of duty at Ilford brought about yet another such case, which started off when we were walking past a railway yard and noticed a group of men through a gap in the fence. They were just standing around a railway carriage, but it looked odd and, we thought, suspicious.

On entering the yard, we searched the carriage to find a large pile of copper items clearly related to the railway. We brought all the men into the carriage and started questioning them. Whilst all were 'in on it,' we could not arrest everyone, nor could we support all their arrests with convincing evidence. Our instincts would not justify arrests, and the sergeant before whom we had to bring them, and to whom our arrests had to be justified, would not proceed to charge them without more.

After discussing the matter with the group, they offered up the foreman as the instigator and prime mover of the theft. He admitted it, and would plead guilty if we took no action against all the others. On that basis he did plead in court; justice was served, and the crime cleared up.

By now the results of the Sergeant's examination were published. Due to our exceptional promotion class instructor a good number of us passed first time, and soon we would be sent to the Training School for the promotion course.

Back in uniform for this waiting period, I was posted to both the traffic points on the sub-division. The first was at the junction of Barking Road and the Becton Bypass. It was the point where all the traffic teemed west into the city in the morning, and east to go home. The difficulty there was that as one cleared the traffic at my point – a terminus for trolley buses – another bus would arrive. These were connected to overhead electric wires, and my point was where they were turned round to return to their route. The process involved the poles being disconnected from the wires, the bus being turned around, agonisingly slowly, and the poles then being re-attached.

Sometimes this drove the motorist wild. He would be eager to roar off, as though from the grid at the start of a grand prix, when I signalled him on, with nothing for miles but the odd traffic light junction between him and home. The trolley driver blocking his route as his bus was manoeuvred would sit stolidly, arms folded, and sometimes seemed to smirk at the car driver. The drivers would get out of their cars and approach the trolley bus driver and start to climb up to his window, faces working with frustration. I preferred not to notice the altercation that would follow, having some sympathy with the car driver. From the point of view of the trolley bus driver, whilst there was little he could do, the body language was inflammatory.

The other point was at Rathbone Street market, and the job there was to see pedestrians across but keep the traffic flowing, as this was two hundred yards west of the other point. The task was to step out, wearing white traffic gauntlets, point at the vehicles that were to stop, see that they did, and usher pedestrians across. Many were mothers and children carrying their basins, containing hot eels, or pies and mash floating in a green liquid, home from the pie and eel shop.

One day proved of more interest than others. I had stepped out, stopping the traffic to my right, and then pointed to a lorry a safe distance away to the left. The driver shook his head, and waved his hands agitatedly. Noticing that pedestrians had started moving off from the other kerb in anticipation, I turned to the lorry-driver, shrugged, and indicated that I had no choice. He had to stop, which he did. With his head out of his window, he was waving furiously at the pedestrians to get out of the way.

As he came to a screeching stop, a huge wave of sludge and sewage flooded from the rear of his open lorry over his cab covering his head and shoulders completely in filth. His expression and very hard glare needed no further words or description.

My crossing was now a pool of sewage and sludge nearly a foot deep. In total dismay, I looked around and noticed the market street cleaner with his barrow, brushes and spades. He was off his mark, scurrying away down the market. I chased after him, hauled him back and he and I did what we could: the point was unusable for at least an hour. I thought it best not to approach the driver when he was trying to clean himself up in the cafe. An apology would have done nothing to mollify him.

Years later there was a similar incident outside Billingsgate fish market, again worthy of a comic sketch, but that is another story.

After this last short tour of duty, the training school beckoned. On arrival, immaculately attired and keen as mustard, our elation faded slightly on being reunited with our old tormentor - still in charge, but in a higher rank.

The duties of a sergeant were very different, and they came with a welcome and substantial increase in pay. Again, the course was a mixture of the practical and theoretical, but study for the examination had brushed up our knowledge in both: we were all eager to learn and had much more confidence.

My first brush with our tormentor was when he called me out to show him the books at the mock police station we used. This ceremony consisted of a visit by the senior officers on the sub-division to inspect the station books, of which there was a very large number, dealing with every aspect of policing.

He would call for those he was interested in on this visit, and the station officer, usually the sergeant, would present them to him one by one. He would scrutinise every entry, pencil or red pen in hand, for omissions, errors, criticisms and remarks. (This practice achieved a remarkable and an enviable standard of recording, use of correct procedures, and close supervision of all at the station.)

I waited for our senior officer to tell me which books he wanted to see. He sat and glared at me: I waited. He still sat silent, glaring, and I waited, feeling a little uncomfortable. This went on for some time, and then he shouted that I was supposed to show him the books. I replied, a little nervously, that he was supposed to tell me which he wanted to see today. Maybe he had never worked at a police station as a senior officer, and did not know the system.

The awkwardness and silence persisted and the class of some thirty would-be sergeants started to titter at the scene, and my discomfort. He then turned on me, ridiculing my lack of action and my failure fully to address him. This went on for some time, and I realised this was not going to be the end of my tests with him.

Several days later he conducted an arrest for a breach of the licensing regulations, picking the selling of an uncorked container of alcohol as the offence. He called out the participants and nominated himself as the father of the daughter who bought the uncorked alcohol. Yes, I was the daughter.

He called me Phyllis to the enjoyment of the class and made much use of the name. Then the investigating sergeant asked why I was carrying the offending container. Our tormentor said that he did not know, and that it was nothing to do with him. Seizing my chance, I shouted, "Oh yes it bloody was. You told me to buy it, you fucking old bastard!" There was a shocked silence and our Inspector in charge of us looked as if he was going to faint. I had called his senior officer and the Commandant of the college a 'fucking old bastard'. This in front of the whole class.

After staring at me for what seemed an interminable length of time the Commandant threw back his head and roared with laughter."Well done, Forward," he said, and ushered me to my seat. I was left alone for the rest of the course. Still, it was not the last time I was to come before him.

Part of the duty of my new rank was to listen to the evidence given for an arrest, and to decide if it was sufficient to prefer a charge. With criminal charges, the CID would often make that decision. I would be in charge of ten to twenty constables to supervise on the streets, meet them at specified times, and inspect their work at the end of their tour of duty.

In the station, the sergeant would keep the books and ensure that the proper steps were taken, procedures followed and the hundreds of forms that related to the entries sent out. The main books dealt with crime, charges, the following up of missing persons, Property Lost and Found books, and those recording the production of driving licences and insurances that had not been produced on the street when a traffic offence or accident had been reported. He would process all the traffic offences reported by his constables, or by others who brought in work occurring in our area.

This extended to typing all the summonses and preparing the case for court. There he would present the case.

We were told that accidents would have to be typed in triplicate word for word, and, if mistyped, each carbon copy had to be corrected. Some supervising officers would hold them to the light and reject them if they had been altered.

We learnt that they were required for solicitors and other parties, often used in civil actions. Legal aid reports had to be meticulous, as they were destined for the Force's solicitors for prosecution. They prosecuted crime, of course, but in serious vice or licensing matters, the Yard's solicitors would also act and advise and provide counsel. I was to quickly find out that I had not been misinformed as to the precision and accuracy required.

So the important areas were report-writing - since we were told that a station was judged by its books -the supervision of my PCs, and seeing that the cases brought to court were fully and properly prepared.

I was posted to Wanstead, a small sectional station on J Division, which stretched some eight by ten miles, to the edge of the Force's area. For completeness, its borders were set by Stratford, Ilford, Enfield and east as far as Epping.

It was a residential area containing much very exclusive private property, largely middle class residents, two very notable high streets, very successful grammar and private schools, and an excellent golf course, where the force had a concession for police officers. We were also served by two tube stations, at Wanstead and Snaresbrook.

It required a light police presence, since there was no regular rowdyism or vagrancy, and the one arrest which had ever happened there for prostitution was of a music teacher going home by Epping Forest. Her prosecution caused a huge and successful claim for unlawful arrest.

Perhaps more typical was the frequent need to control the cows that were allowed, by bye-law, to roam free, since we were situated beside part of the forest. So there were the occasional cattle drives, where the cows were discovered standing thoughtfully in the middle of our main roads, or chewing up the prize flowers and shrubs in the many well-kept front gardens of the affluent.

I set off to Wanstead from my police flat in Barking. The address was Long Reach Court, so named, I am sure, by some clever member of the civil staff in the accommodation department, who doubtless received promotion for such wit. I need not explain the title. The year was 1960, the day, a Sunday, and it was for a start of 2p.m.

At the station, I got dressed in uniform, and introduced myself to my fellow sergeants. They looked appalled, and treated me as if I was to start a paper round in their area. They had not realised anyone could be promoted so young, and this was a quiet station where no-one rocked the boat or brought in any charges unless serious and where a 'word in the ear' would be the best way of dealing with things.

That being the case with this sort of station, there were only PCs and sergeants. They were all broadly the same age. I was the youngest man at the station and I was the highest rank there. My first parade was due, and I loved it.

My relief ambled into the parade room; time was not of the essence at Wanstead, and my glancing pointedly at the clock on the wall went, it seemed, unnoticed. There were about eight of them, and they shuffled about getting more or less into line.

I was certainly not to be trusted to be the station officer by the other sergeant, but was posted on the section, on patrol. I gave them their beats, and picked up the clipboard containing all the jobs to do e.g. the 'please allow an officer to call', to verify an address for another station's bail enquiry, to inspect documents, to warn a witness for court in the following week, etc. Then there would be the 'please make an enquiry... or take a witness statement from...or have such and such a form delivered... or the forms specifying the details of driving documents were to be completed.

They looked in horror as I took this out and started dealing with the items which related to their beats. I solemnly handed them out to each officer, who took them tentatively with thumb and forefinger and held them out. They then turned to each other and started saying, "what have you got?" to Tom, or Bert, or Paddy. Each would then say he had to see someone at the far end of the High Street, or it was some inquiry about a firearm licence, or something about bail, or he had to take a statement.

The scene reminded me of handing out Christmas presents, and comparing what you all had received. The spokesman then informed me it was Sunday, and they didn't do that sort of thing on a Sunday. Added to that, Tom didn't do writing. Tom nodded in agreement. I said, "He gets paid the same as you doesn't he?"With that they acknowledged I had a point, but told me none of the other sergeants let him write; he wasn't very good at it; and I wouldn't like what I got back.

We resumed the general discussion, with comments like "I've never done one of these, Sarge," or, "the other sergeants don't ask us to do this on a Sunday." I had never been on a parade where we discussed what the sergeant wanted us to do and I was biting my lip and trying to keep a straight face.

They continued looking at each other's jobs and shaking their heads sadly as they clutched their forms and messages. They could not believe it was happening, but I was the sergeant, although not schooled in the ways in which Wanstead operated.

Enough, I thought, and told them for a start that even he who cannot write (it sounded like a Red Indian name) would go out and knock on doors... They nodded, as if to say, you couldn't say fairer than that. Then I got a bit firmer and told them that they would all do so, and that I would go back to the addresses to see if they had called.

I finished by reading out the list of stolen car numbers, local information, and prevalent areas for crime written in the appropriate book for the sergeant taking the parade. They left, shaking their heads, for tea in the canteen. If only I could have been privy to their conversation there. Though things were very relaxed at Wanstead, and they had something of a point ,it was in general a superb performance from them and I did not come out of it too badly on our first acquaintance.

There were three sergeants per relief, one day off, one in the station and one out on the section, sometimes in the wireless car. The police station was adapted from a small house, and is still the same fifty years later. We were part of the Woodford sub-division, from which an Inspector would visit us twice a day, unless he was required for more advanced work, often a drink driver. He would mark up the accidents for investigation, if required, and check the books. He would have to be informed of anything out of the ordinary.

The biggest dispute I recall was when one sergeant wanted the work received at the end of the shift to be passed to the next shift, not kept by him. As would seem obvious, his was the harder working shift, which contained officers who looked for overtime or to bring in unusual work as a challenge. I believe he was outvoted though the senior sergeant.

Generally, it was the dog handlers who were responsible, and they brought in work for everyone. One delighted in the obscure, and his masterpiece was reporting a petrol tanker for allowing its waste pipe to drip at a faster speed than the regulations allowed. To assist the preparation of the summons a top traffic specialist was despatched from the Yard to Wanstead with the only copy of the regulations the Force had. He would not allow them out of his sight before returning. This was a huge feather in the reporting officer's cap!

He would also specialise in offences involving wild birds whilst out exercising his dog. Since he was forever in court, he earned so much overtime we had to visit him at home on many occasions, to tell him that he would have to take the next week off. It still did not affect his work rate, but it created difficulties, as he was an excellent officer; and on our division, dog handlers performed sterling service.

With the job for the first time came stress. Night duty involved hours spent typing as accurately as possible, copy after copy being ditched until it was perfected. The files for the traffic process piled up, but especially the careless driving cases, with strict time limits for papers to be served, the collation of witness statements from persons involved, and from officers from traffic division reporting the accidents, plans from the plan-drawers, and arranging dates of hearing for witnesses and for oneself to prosecute.

The files piled up, and balancing them and keeping on top of the requirements and paperwork, so as not to lose a case, caused sleepless nights.

Night duty still offered the best chance of arrests for crime, especially if posted to the wireless car. One of our best went badly wrong for me, however, when we were called to a factory breaking. On the first floor was a radio tuned to the police channel, and nearby was its operator. He was arrested by me and a fellow sergeant, and taken downstairs to the waiting car, parked by the gates.

He had continually protested his innocence, pleading to be released and whinging throughout, despite being caught red-handed. As there came a moment when we took him downstairs, my colleague took out his truncheon, possibly believing that he was going to resist more strongly. In any event my colleague, six feet five and very powerfully built, lifted his truncheon above his head and went to bring it crashing down on his head. I feared that he might well have killed him, or at the very least split his head wide open.

I pulled at our prisoner, to get him to the car and safely out of the way, but he twisted from our grasp and escaped, while we were all clambering over some metal parts scattered on the floor. His desperation helped him, and despite a thorough search, lasting through the night, and involving other cars to assist, he was not recaptured.

We made statements and we were accused of prisoner escape, which was a disciplinary offence: the offence was made out according to the manner of the prisoner's escape. Eventually we received a formal warning from the Commander.

A frequent burglar was found who fitted the bill. As he was in custody, we were asked to attend an identification parade held in prison. My colleague picked him out: I did not, though I was sure from his body language which one on the parade was the man presented. In my opinion he was not the man we had arrested, and I said so. I had no more to do with the case, so never knew the outcome. The sense of failure over such a good arrest, and my part in it, facilitating his escape, brought about, for a long time, a sense of failure as a police officer, and a loss of face with my relief. Our driver was on my relief and was an ex-soldier. He was the most capable and conscientious officer I had, and he had missed out on a very creditable criminal arrest on his tour of duty as wireless car driver.

This was through me, and could have been considered inexperience. Privately, I felt sure I had probably saved the life of the burglar, or at least prevented really serious injury. Maybe that was why we were advised rather than disciplined.

On occasions like this, when the adrenalin is running high over a possible arrest, officers can get caught up in the drama of the moment and commission of a crime. A somewhat similar instance had been when we had gathered outside the station, when told that a stolen vehicle was being driven our way by a couple of youngsters. A PC standing next to me picked up a concrete parking sign and was about to throw it into its path. When I said, "What the hell are you doing, they are just kids joyriding," he stopped a little shame-faced at what could have transpired.

Such reactions, especially in response to chases involving stolen cars, were particularly difficult, and many cars joined in. There is always the thrill of the chase, but also a need to balance the risk to drivers, passengers and pedestrians, something in which traffic patrol drivers are well trained.

The nature of any other crime committed by a getaway car also plays its part, but with the non-traffic patrol drivers the radio operators would coolly advise care and caution.

One of my other disappointments was that, at the flat at Barking and which was surrounded by lawn, each of us was allowed to cultivate a plot. We could grow what we wanted; it was rather surprising of the service to permit a series of allotments around the three blocks.

I threw myself into gardening, and had a plot that soon resembled many proper allotments located on the Bypass. As some of the residents did not take up the offer, I was allocated a neglected one to tend. To vegetables, I added soft fruits and quality flowers, spending a fair amount of time leaning on the fence like a proper gardener, chatting to the other allotment-holders as they passed by, and picking up tips.

Having invested in tools, etc., the disappointment arose from a fresh review by the Yard. Finding that some of the plots had not been worked at all, they decided the whole area must be grassed back over. There was, of course, no appeal.

I did rent an allotment, having caught the bug, but my neighbours told me the plot I was assigned was entrenched with couch grass. After some effort to clear it failed, as had been expected by the experienced spectators, my horticultural interests were to wait a year or two before turning into a lifelong hobby.

Work and domesticity settled down into a regular and very necessary pattern with three children under the age of three. We had wanted more than two and had at least 'one of each.' The bicycle had given way to a forty-nine cc motorbike, with a double seat for passengers, which proved invaluable on the journeys to Wanstead. A rocking chair became the best piece of furniture we bought, as after 'early turn', with one or more of the children on my lap, we would doze off, listening to Wally Whytton's nursery rhymes LP.

When not in the garden, I would be making thick woollen rugs, while my wife knitted identical jumpers for the children and then churned out other clothes on a knitting machine. We had no TV.

At work, occasionally, I would have to relieve at the other stations on the division, all of which had their differences.

Barkingside was the busiest, and I was mostly occupied there on station duty. The area even had a prostitute problem: street betting had largely been an East End tradition. There were always a number of sergeants who, because of the volume and variety of work, were all far more experienced. Opposite the station were the Dr. Barnardo's houses, and their recreation room, where we played some of our home table tennis matches – hence my greeting from my favourite sergeant, "How's your backhand, Barry?"

We never saw any of the children, but knew they had a 'mother and father', who may have had their own children as well. There were ten or so to each separate house, all set in ample grounds. It is to the institutions' credit that I remember never having dealt with them in any capacity.

One sectional station was at Claybury, notable for its huge mental institution. Most patients returning would book in with me – entirely unwarranted, but they liked it, and it never posed any risk to me.

The main task my reserve officer there undertook was to make tea. This he did lovingly, and with such ceremony as would have qualified him for such a task in Japan. It was the best I had tasted, or ever would taste. Otherwise, there was virtually nothing to do, except take over the station from the previous station officer, check the safe, prisoners (if we ever had any), and supervise the one or two officers out on patrol. Sergeants could bring over their own work and clear some of their files, so it was a pleasant and useful posting.

Then there was Woodford, the main station where the Duty Officer, usually an inspector, would operate from, and make his visits. He too took tea at Claybury, needless to say, as he made his rounds. We always got a good warning when he was getting close to the station, as the officers on patrol did not stray far.

I do not recall a single incident of any interest from the few times I went to Claybury, but do especially recollect a particularly nasty one from Woodford, involving the top CID officer and our own Superintendent.

We had arrested a driver who was over the limit and brought him in. We had the same driver who had taken us to the factory breaking, and there was another sergeant. The man arrested was utterly obnoxious, as well as drunk (many are), and was threatening all manner of trouble for us. When he got to the station he alleged we had sought a bribe from him not to charge him and he had given us some money.

The duty CID officer was called, our car searched and a bundle of banknotes found slipped into the side of the rear passenger seat where he had sat. Cars were routinely searched top to bottom before use and so it could only have been put there during the journey. The fact that he had indicated to the station officer the likely place where officers might find hidden banknotes led to his account being treated with deep suspicion.

The Duty Officer called out the Detective Chief Inspector, who in turn called out our Superintendent. The senior detective started to interrogate him, during which the story he was told became more dubious. Its authenticity was unravelling so obviously that by the end, it was all the DCI could do to keep his hands off him.

Our Superintendent then arrived and we knew he would take this with the utmost seriousness as his career had always been in administrative posts, and, latterly, in the department at the Yard which was responsible for force discipline. It was credibly rumoured before he arrived that he had never actually made an arrest.

He listened to the spurious account, carefully questioning the prisoner. At the end of his investigation he was so incensed he nearly took a swing at him himself in the presence of the other senior officer. Afterwards the prisoner confessed to what he had done by planting the money in the car.

It would have been possible for him to have faced a charge of wasting police time, but as I was not called on to make a statement, nothing more came of it.

Less serious matters were brought in to me at Wanstead, involving arrests for some form of indecency in the forest; another, of an aged shoplifter whose charge I was considering when she told me, "everyone I know is doing it and I'm not going to stop and miss out," so she was charged; a peeping Tom, who, in answer to the complaints of two young women in their early 20s, who had been undressing in their ground floor back bedroom well after midnight, said that he had been in their garden looking for his son's ball, and who was duly reported; and the sort of visit we all dreaded, informing a wife that her husband had been involved in what might be a fatal accident.

I had to inform her that the injury looked terribly serious (a brain injury – which looked fatal to me) but he was alive when taken to hospital. A fatal accident required a procedure of its own, and since I was not required to make a statement, I hoped for the best. I was pleased to hear that it had not been fatal, but knew no more.

Another sad moment arose from the sudden death of my favourite colleague, who told me about seeing the Chief Medical Officer. He had only been given some aspirins, when he knew himself he must be really ill. I sympathised but very soon afterwards heard why he had apparently been dismissed by the CMO – he was terminally ill, and nothing more could have been done.

His funeral took place at Waltham Abbey, and was attended by hundreds of officers in uniform. As a colleague I acted, with the other sergeants from Wanstead, as one of the pall bearers, and felt honoured to do so.

I have said there was no rowdy behaviour, and the nearest we got to it was from a residential care home for the unruly. Situated in magnificent grounds, with a huge lake filled with swans, fish and Canadian geese, depending on the season, with woods stretching unfenced for hundreds of yards, this had once been an orphanage.

In the nineteenth century, it changed into a home for youngsters whose parents were abroad, or were in difficulties, and then into a charitable institution with royal support, re-named the Royal Wanstead School. It now housed a dozen boys rattling around in it. Our job was to return them if they ran away, or have a word to preserve order.

As I shall recount further on, this building was to feature heavily again later, and my future attendance would be in another life and in a very different uniform.

Figure 1. Street party at Leigh-on-Sea on VE Day, end of World War II

Figure 2. My first photo album bought in Germany where we lived in Army Quarters 1947-1949

*Figure 4. At Meropolitan Police training school
at Hendon on Initial Training Course, 1955.*

*Figure 3. Mum and Pop at Grendon Open Prison NR
Aylesbury whilst on home visit from Hendon.*

Figure 5. Sheril and I at her first Christmas Party at East Ham Section House – Police accommodation for single officers - 1960

Figure 6. Left to right: Suzanne, Michael and Sheril at our police house at Leytonstone, 1963

Chapter 6
Putting Down Roots in Leytonstone

Soon was to come one of the happiest days of our lives when we all excitedly arrived at what was to be our new home, a large terraced police house on a corner in Leytonstone, with a decent sized garden. The year must have been 1962. Our eldest, Sheril, was five, Michael three, and Suzanne two. There was a shed for my motor cycle, and a good sized front garden. Bliss!

Still stationed at Wanstead, but closer to it, I had started to study for the Inspector's examination. This was much harder, and the opportunities present more limited, as there were fewer places, and a high mark to pass; it also required gaining a civil service qualification, which stopped some entrants. I had gained the equivalent from my entry to the civil service.

The examination took the form of citing large sections of a topic, word-perfect. This demanded knowledge of practical action, of theoretical and legal procedures, and of the evidence necessary to justify the charge to be preferred. Acts and sections had to be quoted. Moreover, each question added another sub-question on an unconnected and usually obscure matter, to stiffen up the competition: there was some predictability with the main question, as it was an important and common matter, but a good answer to the subsidiary was essential to succeed.

This meant that a working knowledge of the whole of our General Orders had to be learnt, since when, for instance, the main question was on burglary, the subsidiary might be on pedlars' licences.

My solution caused some amusement amongst competitors and others travelling in the area, as I was to be seen walking to work every day – a distance of a mile and a half – reading a handful of pages. This was for the unexpected questions. Promotion classes focused on the main areas, and it was possible to predict the favourites, or those likelier this year. Our excellent inspector and tutor did us proud.

At home, another system prevailed. I would do the ironing whilst my wife sat, book in hand, testing me. Though it proved effective for learning by rote, relations could get strained, as, if I got a word wrong, I would get testy and reply that that word or phrase didn't really matter. The response invariably was "well, you told me it had to be word perfect." To that came, "well, not that perfect," or "that word doesn't matter," or "what I said amounted to the same thing," or some similar defence. But it was a good system overall, and the clothes got ironed.

With Sheril starting school, education became a growing, in fact a never-ending, concern. Our last was soon born, Maria (West Side Story was responsible at least for the name) and we were complete.

Football and table tennis were replaced by golf after I had been taken by a friend to Crews Hill Golf Club and asked how old I thought were the two elderly players who had just walked in from the course for lunch. I was informed that both were over ninety, but played nine holes nearly every day. This would last me as long as I could move, and keep me fit as well. It was the game for me, and I soon became the typically obsessive golfer. I even kept all my score cards, and worked out where I was dropping shots from them.

I passed the inspector's examination comfortably, thanks to all the methods used, without, this time, spending hours on the tube going round the Circle Line.

The next rank was that of Station Sergeant – an SPS – similar to a staff sergeant or a Chief Petty Officer. There was no promotion class, the assumption being that, as an experienced and qualified sergeant, this would be unnecessary. That meant no re-acquaintance with my tormentor at training school, but I still had not shaken him off.

My posting was to North Division, and, specifically, Holloway. There were two other SPSs, all around the same age, and all ambitious for the next rank, as an SPS would generally be based at the station, unless deputising for the Inspector who was in charge of the Relief. Our sectional station was Highbury – in many ways more interesting, containing Arsenal football club, an area well known for street prostitution, and the Astoria theatre at Finsbury Park, which hosted top stars such as the Beatles and the Rolling Stones, amongst others. There were very many public houses and cafes, where trouble could often break out.

We were now on four wheels, though the car was not far from being an antique, if I kept it for a decade or so. It was a 1934 Morris Eight, and was cheap, and my first car. It was reliable and handy, since the engine could have fitted in a shoe box, and repair required one spanner and one screwdriver. For a year it got me from Leytonstone to Holloway or Highbury. We even fitted curtains round the windows.

Again the rank provided a decent pay rise and a better standard of living, and then a much better car could be obtained, with some football overtime from Arsenal. We patrolled the pitch, were amused by the chants of the crowds, especially those from Liverpool, with their allegations of the sergeants' sexual preferences as we stood in front of them, and then listened to the Metropolitan Police Band and soloist at half time.

I loved my football, and to sit on the touchline on our rolled up capes when the game started was the very best way to watch it. Having seen all the greats, the player I most admired was Stanley Matthews. I once saw him, in an international match totally mesmerise two defenders, having run up the wing and then worked his way into the edge of the penalty area, beating both defenders.

He looked up, and found no support (he wasn't renowned for scoring). Turning round, he dribbled back, beating the same two defenders, and arrived at the corner flag. He turned and started making his way back to the box, beating both defenders for the third time. Support had arrived and he laid off a sweet pass to one of his forwards. This piece of sheer effrontery towards two international defenders earned him rapturous applause, intermingled with roars of laughter. He was also renowned for never committing a foul, though he was forever on the receiving end from the opposition, reduced, by sheer desperation, to bringing him down. In those days football was regarded as a sport, and played in a sportsmanlike manner.

The only occasions when I did not enjoy my football were when my mother took me to watch West Bromwich in their heyday as 'The Team of the Century' (coming desperately close to doing the double in the 1953-4 season). She invariably sat us in the middle of the opposition's territory in the stands. Knowing practically nothing about the game, she would start to remonstrate against their players for fouls and unsporting play. The referee took some stick too for decisions against us. This was delivered in her posh middle class voice. The fans remonstrated with her, despite her encouraging them to see these examples of misbehaviour, indignant that they couldn't see it. At first the arguments would get heated, but still, in that voice, amongst a sea of Brummies, she carried on. I would slink away, and had no compunction in doing so: she could manage on her own.

Eventually, the ridiculousness of it all started to amuse the crowd, who then incited her to berate all and sundry. There was, on such occasions, more enjoyment in the crowd than from the players. If I had not refused to go after two such sessions, she would probably have ended up a mascot and crowd celebrity.

Back at the Finsbury Park Astoria, things were hotting up, with the arrival of the Beatles and, later, the Rolling Stones. We had to police these events, and manage the vast crowds of screaming teenagers for the three nights the Beatles performed there. Our other difficulty was getting them into the theatre. The first night saw them smuggled in dressed as policemen. The second night we slipped them in through the rear doors. The third proved the worst, as they were becoming alive to our tricks, but we managed somehow by sheer numbers.

Inside the theatre, it was bedlam. The noise was deafening, and they literally could not be heard. Suzanne and her friend came on one night, and screamed nearly as loudly as everyone else. Her hysteria was also more restrained, and I don't think she wept at all - speaking as a parent, of course. Finally getting the group away proved almost as difficult as getting them in.

On one night I had the pleasure of seeing Lulu at the theatre and, passing her in her dressing room, exchanged a few pleasantries. Her voice and looks told that another big star was on her way. Once again, I never found a true star to be too self-important to exchange a few words with a policeman; in life, only the climbers seem to be too pompous to do so.

The Rolling Stones experience was a little easier, as they could just about be heard. Since the Stones were less well-known, our arrangements, polished from the experience with the Beatles, coped much more easily.

To conclude the name-dropping, we invited Ken Dodd to be the cabaret at our police Dinner and Dance at a venue in the Holloway Road. He asked to bring his fiancé, we ensured she was comfortable, and, as a result, he stayed much longer than expected, despite being due to go back up north the next day.

It was just as well. He teased us dreadfully, loving his chance to do so, but as we were an adult and broad-minded audience he could introduce more adult and blue humour than usual. We almost begged him to stop as we could laugh no more, truly with aching sides. For me he has been our funniest comic, and just doesn't let up. He matched the Crazy Gang whom I had seen years earlier at the Victoria Palace; I had ached with pain at non-stop gag after gag from them too.

My first parade at Holloway was routine, nothing like my first in authority at Wanstead. Its conclusion was also much different for, at the moment they were released, they all rushed to the nearest vehicle and took to the streets. I joined them to find out they were hunting for 'gamers' gambling on the pavement, usually with dice. The rush was to arrest them whilst there was cash to provide evidence.

Oddly enough, this activity lasted only a few weeks and then stopped completely, why one never knew. Once they were dealt with, my constables worked their beats, which, here, were more extensive than before. Radios were at last being introduced, which allowed officers to get support from their colleagues on foot and, even better, to communicate with our cars and crews. Combined with the most efficient of telephonists, our organisation and responses were vastly improved.

The final improvement was that access to the police station was unfettered, so our reserve room, with telephonist, became our control centre. Since she was also the most admired it became our social centre – a must for any efficient police station.

It made for a happy station, especially when coupled with refreshments. An example was one Christmas night, when one of my officers, an off-duty choirmaster, started some carol singing in the room – Christmas was often a surprisingly quiet time in the police station.

We were interrupted by a nearby licensee, who called in to speak to the senior officer. Tidying myself up, I hastened to meet him to deal with his complaint. He was accompanied by two of his bar staff with trays of well-filled pints. He told me his clients in the pub loved it so much that these - indicating the trays - were to keep us going.

Our Division embraced all walks of life, a cosmopolitan mix, with no dominant groups or race, though there were racial tensions elsewhere in London. Certainly there were many Greek cafes, clubs, and Irish pubs. A new business which was developing was that of licensed betting offices. Since they were set up with tight regulations, I steeped myself in their compliance and reported a number of breaches, but these were never prosecuted. My rivals were more concerned with prosecuting licensed premises, and conducting the odd raid with their reliefs.

In this rank arrests were few, since my job outside the station was to supervise and to take turns at patrolling with my sergeants, particularly when visiting the public houses. I would go out with one constable or another to test them, advise them on some matters that had arisen, or get to know more about them to complete their annual reports.

On one such night, patrolling Highbury, one of our number thought he had seen someone duck down in a car as we approached. We stopped, turned, and spoke to the very nervous occupant. A search of his car revealed piles of coins that were obviously the result of housebreakings where the meters had been broken into. It made a welcome clear-up to add to the crime statistics.

It also resulted in a Commendation all round 'for detective ability,' which did no harm in the rivalry battle.

Naturally, with my rank, and deputising for my inspector, the call-outs were getting more serious, and one of the saddest involved the death of son, who, at home with his parents, had choked on his very late evening meal. He had died before I got there, and there was nothing to be done to save him. Their grief was devastating. The police service can throw up the most awful moments, and many years ago officers were retired as 'worn out'. It is a fair description still.

One awkward incident arose with a call for assistance to the station from an ambulance crew at a hotel in Highbury. A patient suffering from pneumonia refused to go to hospital. On my arrival, I spoke to the young woman, who was indeed gravely ill, and tried to persuade her myself. She would not leave without her dog, the sort favoured by models or film stars. It turned out that she *was* a minor film star, and highly neurotic, but she was adamant in her refusal. The hotel staff also failed to get her to comply.

Everyone looked at me, and I felt a decision worthy of Solomon was required. I told her I would ensure that her dog was cared for and brought to the hospital regularly (yes, and every day) so she could see that it was alright.

Had I a little more foresight, I would have given more thought to who was to be the bearer of the dog. Whilst she was a most attractive young woman, her neuroticism guaranteed my objectivity, despite her increasing emotional reliance on me through the dog.

It was a typical show-business pretty poodle type which, contrasting with my serious uniformed presence carrying it at the hospital, caused much giggling with the nurses. Fortunately, there was never any technical or medical difficulty in maintaining visits at any time; my dog-handling status overrode such views. My wife did raise the question of how I had got myself into this. My explanation sounded weak even to me when I went into it all, and she became more highly suspicious on appreciating the nature of its owner, and her occupation and implied looks. (Sad to say, some years later I read of her suicide in the papers.)

The North London Hospital on Holloway Road was the scene of my worst call out. A young girl of about nine had been brought to the hospital dead on arrival. I saw her, and there was a horrendous wound on the top of her head. She had been brought in by her stepfather, who was making little sense to the staff, and none to me, when I spoke to him. I refrained from questioning him, as certain answers could have created a legal problem, and difficulty in remaining calm and objective. He accompanied me to the station, and I handed him into the custody of the Detective Chief Superintendent. Later he was charged with murder.

When making my statement there was much criticism that I had not formally cautioned him and that this might prejudice the case against him. I explained that the Judges' Rules dictated that I only had to do so if I believed that the person had committed a crime. I did not believe at the time in the hospital that a stepfather would have murdered his nine-year-old charge. He pleaded guilty at the Old Bailey to manslaughter.

A difficult judgement arose in the station with an arrest brought in by a young officer on my relief. In the presence of the prisoner the officer gave me the facts of the arrest, as was the procedure. Not once did he look me in the eye. I was far from convinced by what I was told, namely that the prisoner had been with a group of young men walking in the street and all behaving rowdily and in a disorderly fashion.

The prisoner accepted he had been walking amongst a group, but said that he had been nothing to do with them, but had merely been trying to pass. He was polite, articulate, and made no attempt to disagree or criticise the officer. He was older than the others, and was smart, more soberly dressed and a man of substance.

I informed my officer that I did not believe a word of it, especially on hearing the man was a press reporter on one of our national newspapers. I told him I was releasing him without any formality or report, and that I could not prevent him from repeating it in the papers the next morning: I would have to take that chance, as he was innocent. There was no mention of it in any of the morning papers. (My dealings in this incident came to help me in an awkward moment several years later in Pentonville prison.)

In the police service, loyalty came at too high a price on occasions; truth should outweigh it. For my younger officer, he had to learn the useful lesson that a person about to be arrested should be allowed to talk and explain.

Working close to Highbury, one bumped into the famous. On one occasion it was a call to a minor accident involving Henry Cooper who, around that time, had nearly knocked out Mohammed Ali, who, however, had been saved by the bell. You could tell even from his aftershave that he was famous, and he was a true gentleman.

Another was George Eastham, an inside forward newly transferred to Arsenal, whom I had watched play. His clever and thoughtful style of play was new to the swift directness of the team, and he, and they, had to adapt.

Another star of our team (I was by then a fan) was our consistently brilliant Scottish left winger - Robertson. His intricate dribbling and speed tended to leave some of his own team standing. Any foray of his up the wing was greeted with huge applause and expectation: he was deservedly capped for Scotland.

I have mentioned police schemes that existed and operated with great success –one being juvenile liaison, in place of immediate arrest and prosecution. Another, at Holloway, was the issue of licensed premises cards to each Inspector, for him to visit and supervise his premises. The thinking behind it was to make the licensee responsible for the behaviour of his pub and its compliance with the law. No notice was given of a visit, and being reported for prosecution could ensue for any breach.

Attention was to be paid particularly to afterhours drinking, or allowing prostitutes or drunken, disorderly or under-age drinkers on the premises. Even betting and gaming on the premises was reportable. Since the practice ceased, binge drinking and drunkenness at and just outside licensed premises has totally escalated.

Despite this safeguard, I had to report one licensee for a breach of the Licensing Act when I was fairly new.

That evening a brown envelope appeared on my desk, where only authorised persons would be allowed. It contained a wad of banknotes, was addressed to me and for services to be rendered. It could have been put there from a number of sources, the CID, and a senior member of it, the most likely; or, possibly, Mounted Branch, Special Constables, or even traffic patrol. I was undoubtedly being tested for my reaction to being approached.

I thought carefully about my next step. I could prove nothing, and might be disbelieved as making such allegations could bounce back. Secondly, I needed to establish my integrity. Thirdly, the matter had to be brought to notice at a high level, in case the perpetrator should come to light and expose the whiff of corruption. The licensee had to be put in his place.

My solution was to deal with this as an unauthorised donation to a police charity by a licensee. I countersigned each note in the presence of my sergeant, and we dated and initialled each. I then recorded the matter in complete detail in the

Occurrence Book, for all to see. This entry would have been initialled by each officer up to Commander level.

A full written report prepared by myself was then sent through all the channels to the Commissioner. That would include the offence by the licensee, and the police regulation that laid down that donations from licensed premises were expressly forbidden. I was never approached again.

In this rank, my traffic files were not building up so much in my locker with the deadlines to be met. Admin units were introduced, with huge numbers of civil staff recruited to add to police enquiry officers in the unit. The advantage which this provided to the sergeants outweighed the variety of some of our more unusual and interesting work, such as, for instance, the renewal of firearm and shotgun certificates, or other character enquiries for licences.

Much more to our advantage was the taking over by the unit of responsibility for the recording and calculations involving overtime worked and taken off. In the middle of the night, we would assemble the time off cards of our twenty or so PCs - small buff cards the size of an average diary -and then came the torture of adding and subtracting amounts like 2 ½ and 3 ¼, all in the one column. As it involved an officer's entitlement, their card would be scrutinised closely, so they could only take off time that was on the card. The quarters of an hour used to drive us mad.

There was more time to initiate my own work, and other interests. One police subject I had thought about a great deal was our power of discretion, and that year a national essay competition offered that very subject for its Gold Medal. I really enjoyed working on and researching the subject, its principles, its legal aspects, the opportunity to introduce more flexibility into police work, and to mitigate the power we were granted. As was becoming apparent, I needed the academic and the pragmatic at work, and this filled that gap. This mix is probably why it was so difficult, when I was younger, to find a career.

There was also more time to devote to the children, as I still worked mainly in shifts in this rank too. The children were starting school and approaching senior school, the comprehensive system replacing grammar schools. Accordingly, I joined both Parent Teacher Associations, in the all girls' and boys' schools, and gradually got more involved in both. The situations in which I became involved threw me into the deep end time and again. I had promised myself that I was going to support my children every way possible, as my parents had assumed that I would succeed in everything, and so needed little support.

The first job I was given was to assist on a school trip to Boulogne. This turned out to be a real shocker, as we disembarked and traipsed in a crocodile along a wobbly gangway over a dry dock. The sides were made up of planks, held together vertically to head height. When I describe what happened to others, they tend to shake their heads in disbelief, but, as we trundled along, I noticed two planks were missing. Again, it really did occur to me that this was so dangerous that a child could fall through. Lo and behold, the boy in front of me tripped, and promptly did so. I managed to grab his ankle, and clung on as he dangled upside down, maybe a hundred feet above the concreted dry dock. With some assistance he was hauled up, and scampered off.

I had taken the job on to polish up my schoolboy French, using which I would chat to tourists and other French speakers in the West End, until it came to street directions and everyday language. The opportunity to have a decent meal in a restaurant would also lead to some improvement, though the more I tried the more English they all spoke.

Being baffled by a question involving the size of my cup of coffee made me realise that I did need the practice, as I heard loud bangs coming from the town square. My heart sank, as I recognised fireworks, and guessed who was to blame. My group was setting them off, and causing mayhem. I grabbed two of the biggest boys, and told them explicitly what was in store for them if it happened again. My bluntness and police-like tone and presence was instantly effective, as was seizing those fireworks left – again, probably an ill-advised course of action, though school staff had more authority in those days.

There was more to come, for, on our approach to the customs office to embark on the ferry for home, one of the boys slipped into my pocket a most evil looking knife in front of the customs officer. The officer dived into my pocket and took it out and, without more ado, disposed of it. In England this would have constituted an offensive weapon possessed in a public place.

I breathed a sigh of relief, after I had given the boy a serious telling off; we got on board the ferry and sat in a group round the table inside. Out of their pockets came tumbling a wide assortment of toys, cheap watches, car-keys and other trinkets which I was assured were gifts from the good Burghers of Boulogne.

I was at first inclined to write a semi-humorous article in the school magazine about the trip, but, on reflection, decided it was not a good idea. Not a word was said about the incident on the gangway, and the more I thought about revealing it, the more I realised that there could have been serious repercussions. It made me most cautious when considering school trips for my own children, and the risks that may and tragically do occur.

A much happier moment came with Michael at school, and his selection for the football team in a cup final. As a treat, I bought him a pair of George Best football boots, of which he was as proud as punch. Everyone was so jealous of him, and he got to play in them. That his team won, and that he supplied the pass that was tapped in by one of his team, was the stuff of dreams, and it was something he always mentioned when he reminisced about his youth.

Our family's favourite trips were to the Southend area, where I had grown up. At first the first port of call was the Kursaal with its Wall of Death – a motorcycle travelling at speed round and round and up and down a circular wall. Then came the scenic railway, several times, and some similar rides, a bit lower, and, finally, a scary ghost train. It was a sad day when the Kursaal closed: its replacement never seemed so much fun. Finally came the slow drive home past all the lights on the sea front, as the children struggled to keep their eyes open.

Other times there were picnics on such beach as we could find at Southend, the food always scoffed by eleven in the morning. Alternatively, we could visit Westcliff, and walk along the front to Southend, or drive to Leigh-on-Sea and its cockle sheds.

Another essential activity at all these resorts was wallowing in the thick black mud, and the warm shallow streams that traversed it. They would all come out black and filthy – that being the point of it, and the proud boast of such resorts was that the mud was good for the skin and general health.

Turning back to family life back in Leytonstone, I threw myself into gardening. The first step was to test the soil for its pH content. Armed with the kit, test tubes and beakers and indicators, under the fascinated gaze of the children, I tested just about every square yard. Even the front garden came under scientific scrutiny. We were going to start on a sound foundation, as this was to be for life.

My tools from Barking were intact, and I started subscribing to gardening magazines and, on hire purchase, bought the three volumes of the Popular Gardening Encyclopaedia (still my Bible). Even a compost heap was created on scientific principles, despite the rear garden's size being no more than half an allotment. This approach was typical of police officers. The times they start a new sport or venture, and purchase immediately the best equipment their money can buy! So, after a few months, an advert often appears in the police broadsheet, called The Job, selling an almost new set of...

Similarly, my half set of golf clubs arrived, bought from a club book, the usual means of purchase. At least it was only a half-set, so I had bucked the trend, and it is still in my garage, with a few other clubs separately obtained as presents. This hobby or obsession was again to be for life, so I bought six lessons from the professional at Wanstead, which was my local course. In that way I would be able, when practicing, to correct myself and improve.

Wanstead was one of the Metropolitan Police Golf Society's clubs, but, being local, they were quite relaxed with their police, especially as we played off-peak. The Force had put down a large deposit many years before, which allowed our use at six clubs around London for discounted green fees. It was a most prudent move on somebody's part, and they were all good courses.

I took over as secretary of the divisional golf club, and we arranged some matches with other Forces and private clubs. One of the most memorable was against the Kent Police, on a course that wound its way round Hever Castle, surrounded by its moat on a historic site near Maidstone. This was fascinating, because it had only nine holes, but each had two tees. Thus the approach was quite different, and it was the equivalent of playing a full eighteen hole course. The nineteenth hole provided a spectacular evening, though we were made very welcome at all our venues.

Holloway had seen my police competitors promoted to Inspector, and I had to wait for the next board to see my name on the list. Previous ranks had needed only an examination, and I was better at those than at boards. I would have to agree that, as far as some senior officers were concerned, I was not their cup of tea.

Chapter 7
My Further Education

The next phase of my police career took place at Shepherdess Walk, perhaps an odd name for a station next to the City of London. Certainly I never saw any shepherdesses, although City of London councillors did have a right to drive sheep on bridges across the river.

The police station was just off City Road, and was the divisional station for G Division. The local authority was Islington and Hoxton, and it bordered Camden and Hackney. I was most surprised to learn that Hoxton was regarded as being the true East End, with its street market, its dark and dreary square, with equally dismal and dingy streets, and, the more one moved away from the City, its workshops and small factory buildings.

There seemed little of interest to police, and even Petticoat Lane was over the border. When an interesting call came over the radio, it was frequently the City of London police car that got there first – they too were looking for work.

The station was largely staffed with administrative offices, a host of senior officers, the divisional admin unit, Mounted Branch (for ceremonial duties), the CID and a large Special Constables contingent. Uniformed officers on reliefs were considerably under-represented. They were much younger than I was used to, and urgently wanted to get involved. My SPS and I were very keen that they should do so. He was close to my age and was a rugby referee when off duty. So he was not only fit and dynamic, but also as keen as mustard.

On parade for our first night, I sent half of the relief home to get changed into plain clothes. They looked, at first, startled at this strategy, but returned bursting to go. Leaping into whatever vehicles we had, we went on the hunt. Backing us up was my station sergeant, metaphorically licking his biro ready for action. It paid off from the start, and the other reliefs were a bit jealous.

One of our first calls was to a flat in a block that was suspected of housing IRA sympathisers, practicing manoeuvres. When we searched the premises we found rifles, an anti-tank gun, leaflets and posters, machine gun parts, and ammunition, confirming our suspicions. Statements from the neighbours revealed that the occupants would march around with rifles to Irish anthems, and so the occupants were charged and prosecuted. Due to the seriousness of the charges, it was dealt with in the Crown Court.

I was the officer in charge of the case and, as such, was able to liaise with prosecuting counsel, assist him generally with the police side of things, and learn some of the procedure and language used in the Crown Court. Contrasting with the Magistrates Courts, everything has to be proved: nothing can be taken for granted. To a police officer used to having his evidence accepted by the lay justices, this comes as a shock.

In this rank, there were spells of relieving the court inspector at Old Street and Stoke Newington Magistrates Court – a welcome chance to perfect addressing the bench, and to note their idiosyncrasies. Much of the work there was to offer the police view on licensing applications and other matters, and the bench, despite being licensing justices, would place heavy reliance upon their Inspector. Accordingly, he had to know his stuff, and the locality involved.

I still had my licensed premises to visit, one of which, in Old Street, included a venue for professional wrestling bouts, with many TV wrestling stars involved. It was no chore to visit them and check those premises.

With more time available to me on the street, and a strong back up in the station, I could supervise our responses more widely. One such response to a call witnessed some fifteen to twenty police cars pouring down City Road, two abreast, in answer to a call to suspects. It was like a scene from a US car chase movie. I watched them rush through the front of the premises, waited till the suspects were found, and then ordered the crews to report to me. They were given a dressing-down for leaving North London almost devoid of response cars in their excitement. The lesson, as so often when the adrenalin is pumped up, was that enthusiasm sometimes needed tempering with wider judgment.

Keeping Information Room fully posted would have precluded such over-reaction, and ensured the proper management of resources. As an aside, I also mentioned that none of them had the sense, as far as I could see, to go round the rear of the premises to seal off possible escape.

Still out and about, we received a call ourselves to a suspect with a sack full of music tapes. Arriving hotfoot at the scene, we were told that he had gone 'that way', indicating the street ahead. We hurtled on, but found nobody, nor anywhere a person could have gone. Having been well tricked, a thorough search of the area for our informant took in a number of shops and a small cafe. Inside was the odd customer having a meal, the owner behind the bar and a waiter at work cleaning the surfaces of the tables.

The owner was nodding at us, rolling his eyes and grimacing but saying nothing. He would look pointedly at the waiter, and start winking at us and nodding. The waiter scrubbed away with increased enthusiasm, and the owner continued this strange behaviour, again in total silence. Throughout, the waiter kept his head down, engrossed in his task, and kept moving towards the door.

At this, the owner became even more animated, face getting redder and contorted, the nods now directed towards the waiter and then the door. The waiter had a last energetic polish, head down, and shouted 'goodnight' to the owner, intent on leaving: the owner almost went berserk, by which time we eventually got an inkling of what was really happening, and got to the door first.

Just around the corner was a sack full of music tapes. We heard a loud groan from the waiter behind us.

As a pantomime, it was delicious, but we all felt quite stupid over our lack of nous in what should have been obvious. In the car, after his arrest, we had a good laugh with the waiter, admiring his performance which had again nearly fooled us. His remark that 'you have to give it a go, don't you, guv' was a fitting end.

My time at City Road was to come to a swift conclusion with the news that I had been selected for the Inspector's course at the Police College at Bramshill, Hampshire. The course was to last six months, and was residential except for weekends. Some Forces had their own colleges, but the Metropolitan officers went to Bramshill. The less ambitious, or more prosaic, could opt out, and did so. The rest attended and mixed with the Special Course, run in parallel, but for the bright young sergeants who had been recommended and selected after very testing interviews with the most senior police officers and civil servants. They were predicted to achieve the top posts in the service.

My Commander never enlightened me as to why I had been selected, appearing quite baffled by the decision. I never was to understand what had prompted my good fortune. But it was one I welcomed, and was an opportunity to be grabbed with both hands.

It seemed to have come out of the blue, and was to prove a brilliant personal experience for me. Once I arrived, I was determined to impress the academic staff, in particular, though I was not on the Special Course. There were also to be lectures and practical exercises in police work, which were very well thought-out and challenging.

The first day of the course was mind-blowing. We were sitting in the main hall staring at a long strip of blue paper, maybe four feet wide, that stretched from the entrance right up to the edge of the stage. Many there were sceptical about this 'knife and fork' course we had left our families for, but what happened on that one day removed our doubts.

A very distinguished looking man strode onto the stage, dressed in the comfortable clothes of an academic, clutching a sheaf of papers. He told us we were about to learn about what was probably the most important period of history – the time of the Ancient Greeks. The content of his lecture was superb, the delivery immaculate and the enthusiasm compelling. We were stunned, until another voice took over, this time from the entrance. Another professor came onto what we gathered was the River of Time. With identical enthusiasm and brilliance, he set about making sure we appreciated that the one lesson in history not to be missed concerned the Roman Empire.

And so it went on all day. Lecturers were popping in and out from all sides, taking up the historical baton smoothly, tellingly, and with complete sincerity. We sat bemused and fascinated by this battery of brilliance.

Instantly we were gaining knowledge about matters which none of us had spent time studying, or even seriously reading about, for nearly two decades. From then on our discussions moved up a gear, with knowledge and the sort of reasoning that would have raised many an eyebrow in our police stations. We knew we were being educated and would be the better for it.

The signs of the regaining of youth were growing around us. Opportunities were seized for sport, squash and volleyball being the main activities: the increasing number of bruises, injuries and arms in slings at the College after a few weeks testified to this. The numbers reduced after these novelties, and we started to get better. I loved the volleyball, a game totally new to me; I never missed a game, and, as a result, it played a large part in every holiday thereafter.

The opportunity arose for activities of an entirely different nature, and made me appreciate the accomplishments my fellow officers were capable of achieving. There was a move to see if we could, between us, muster up some music. On a call for volunteers, I was amazed and proud to see hands going up, mentioning the instruments they could play. There was even a part-time conductor and top class pianist to go with them. Never again was I tempted to stereotype my fellow travellers.

Whilst we went home most weekends, there was little to stay for, except for one magical Saturday, when the World Cup final was screened. The only way to watch such a match was to be surrounded by a large crowd of your peers, glass in hand and shouting vociferously till the voice just went. It was 1966 and we had won!

Home I went at every opportunity, to be regaled, the first time, by Sheril's immediately asking me how to spell penis. I was taken aback as she was nine at the time, but on reading her journal – a favourite task – found that in answering a question about where babies came from she had delivered a long treatise on every aspect of the whole process. It showed she had well exceeded her news to her teacher that, for instance, we had once bought a new bathroom mat. Clearly, to her, this was the most significant event in our household that week.

I believe our next car was an ex-police car, very spacious, quite powerful and ideal for all of us. A local favourite outing in it was to Chigwell, where the District Sports club was situated. It was like a private holiday camp, with putting greens, a nine-hole golf course (on which I would go to practice during the week), several grass tennis courts, football and cricket pitches, a decent restaurant and club house, and snooker tables and weekly dances. It was at one of these that people noticing Maria doing her disco dancing got her up on the stage, from which, after some ten minutes, she had to be dragged away. Sue was just as good, but not such an extrovert.

There were four such sports clubs in all, placed in the four districts of London, and all built on the same principles; but Chigwell was ours, and the best, and all the officers and families I knew went there.

With the sea-side, my parents at Maidstone and my wife's at Symonds Yat near Monmouth, we were spoilt for choice. I was especially fond of Symonds Yat, not just for its beauty but for the honest decency of our relatives and its strong community feel.

Going to town with my wife's father on a Saturday, I loved the fact that he would stop every ten yards or so to chat and catch up with half the people in town, whilst buying a couple of tools and some plants and seeds.

The rich appeal of Monmouth or Ross-on-Wye contrasted so much with Leytonstone or any part of London. My father-in-law had been the local Squire's gardener, and had his own garden, three times allotment size, with rows of prize-winning sweet peas. From his wife, who had been the cook, I learnt her specialities, and was well spoilt, even on one birthday having her cook me a pheasant in the 'big house' style.

Going back to college, my tutor was looking for a project. Discovering that I enjoyed biographies he set me to write a thorough review of Robert Graves's *Goodbye to All That*. It was a great choice, being a subject on which I had strong opinions, and about which I knew a fair amount. The disasters, the behaviour of the generals, the stupid jingoism that prevailed even to the point of dreadfully underestimating the length of the war and its strategy, the failure of equipment and lack of understanding of its effects on the troops, had always appalled me. I gave it my best, and it was well received, despite the patriotism of my tutor.

The atmosphere of the college, and its prompts for quality reading, saw me spend a whole evening in bed reading Rudyard Kipling's *Kim*. It was unadulterated luxury to read it from cover to cover, tucked up cosily in my room.

The only difficulty I had was at the social functions and parties thrown for us to mingle with all our teachers, the Commandant, his family and the police staff and the eminent guests whom the college entertained. I had no small talk. Conversing about specifics proved easy but to chat saying nothing of any consequence whilst having a few amiable words with everyone, smoking, balancing a glass and a plate of canapés at the same time, was not my style. I'm sure they must teach it at public school, but I never got the hang of it.

A regular social event was to invite guests to dinner one night a week. I think this, remarkably, was on a Thursday, though Wednesday was still sports day, or, in my case, golf match day. On our table, we decided to try a different wine each week to improve our dining skills, so gradually we went through the card: red, white, expensive, quite cheap and dirt cheap. We found out that the ladies thought the expensive reds were too bitter, as with dry whites, but the cheap went down very well. The lesson learnt was to drink what you like, despite the snobbish connoisseurs, so ready to put people down, that wine readily produces.

It was during a guest night that I came across an extremely bright young sergeant, who may have dined with us on occasions. He was to become the Commissioner of the Metropolitan Police. His name was Paul Condon, and he was obviously destined, even at that time and in such limited circumstances, to make it to the very top.

Another of our guests was my own uncle, who was then the cinema manager at Basingstoke. He had been a Chief Petty Officer in submarines, and loved the wardroom feel of our dinner, its tradition and ambience. It was perfect for our re-acquaintance, as I had not seen him for years.

Naturally, a free visit to his cinema followed, from which it was apparent that his profits stemmed mainly from his sales, as its warmth made several ice creams essential. He readily admitted his strategy. He invited me home once, and we toured his well-stocked garden, devoted largely to vegetables. It was about the size of two allotments and a picture.

We never met up again and missed a real opportunity to do so. According to his son, he had noticed my name on the front page of a national newspaper about a male brothel which I had prosecuted and apparently remarked "that couldn't be Barry, he's in the police force." Such a real shame, as we had so much in common

My other work earned me praise, and there was talk of the possibility of my going to university whilst in the force. There was no precedent for an inspector to do so, just the sergeants from the Special Course. My tutor discussed it with me, and I told him I was still ambitious to go, as I had missed my chance whilst at school, and had always regretted it (though it had been impossible then). He said that I should drop a line to the college. I did just that, one line, and submitted it. I could have composed a long application, but thought that, as I would have to be the first to be allowed to go, I would not get the chance.

On my return to City Road, my Commander was taken aback by my report and stared at me, in complete disbelief at its tone and contents. It was as if I had perpetrated some fraud on my tutors. His astonishment grew that I had made such a request, as I would be the first inspector to make it to university from within the service and at full pay.

Nevertheless, a reply came back asking me to pick which university I wished to attend, which degree, and to specify my subject. The choice was not difficult, but none of the subjects I was to pick had been available at school.

I wanted to stay in London with the family, living at home. The subject I fancied was Sociology and at the best university in the world for it: the London School of Economics, in central London. Furthermore, it was a centre of radicalism, very left wing and controversial. If I was going to have my mind blown open allowing my tendency to rebel, in an intellectual way, this was to be the place.

The subjects I wanted to study were as wide-ranging as could be wished for, and some turned out far better than I had ever imagined. These would consist of a number of modules in Sociology, with the main subject of Economics. There was Economic History, Political Thought, British Constitution, Criminology (which included Penology, making it doubly fascinating and career-bent), and finally Statistics. That was the killer. It was fifteen years since basic Maths, so I would need to brush up, to put it mildly.

The interview did not go as expected, but I did not have to play any role: for once I could be myself. The professors lay back virtually horizontal in their chairs, and stared at me with real curiosity. The first question was how might I set up a new police force in an area that had not had one before. I liked that and they seemed satisfied with my response. Within minutes we had wandered into religion, and did not quite know how we had got there. I held up my hand and confessed that I was getting out of my depth. They smiled with relief, and said, 'Thank goodness, so were we.' We all laughed, and that was it, more or less.

Within weeks I turned up for induction, and about twenty students called me 'sir', and asked me the way to places. I saw one grown-up near me who was my own age, and latched firmly onto him. We were both pretty disorientated, and wondering why we were even there.

I was wearing a dark suit, looking as if I needed directions to the High Court, while he looked like a well-to-do estate agent, which he was. We looked each other up and down, and realised this would not do, and went home for some old clothes, golf or gardening gear preferably. We returned and sat at the back of the hall, looking like caretakers taking a break.

The alienation lasted some time, but John was doing much the same course as I so we continued to cling together until the others started to talk to us. They were still very polite, and did not ask why we were there. John had just had enough of his job and the sort of life that went with it, such as responsibility and duty and politics (he was also a councillor), though he did run an old-time music hall at Lauderdale House.

Our maturity did lead to being part-time mentors, though more so with John. We could help and discuss life's problems like sex, the lack of money, their parents, the job market and how Marxism was not the answer to everything. In turn they kept trying to persuade me to smoke pot, to which I said that I would, if they could logically provide me with a good reason.

I was sought out by three of my colleagues, who were from the Special Course. They were reading Law, Economics and Social Psychology, and in their second year. They, in turn, mentored me about the new world I was entering, and I attended a lecture in which one of them attacked Marxism, quite bravely I thought. I was impressed by his argument that, if capitalism contained the seeds of its own destruction, then Marxists should press for more rather than oppose it. They did not seem to come up with an answer, but went back to the dogma apologists for the 'correct' answer.

As I had thought, Statistics was proving virtually impossible, and every weekend was spent on Maths. Fortunately, Sheril was having difficulties with the subject, so I started with the basics with her, and we learnt together. As I progressed I turned to Statistics, and the weighty tome our tutor had written and supplied to us as our text book. It didn't help.

In a second-hand bookshop I came across a thin paperback titled Teach Yourself Statistics. It used examples like football league tables, cricket moving averages and it did not take long to grasp the subject purely from this cheap book. Once understood it became easier to make some use of the tutor's book.

Economics, they say, is the second hardest subject. Parts of it were graphic, like supply and demand, with the clearest of diagrams; others were a nightmare, but perseverance and excellent tutoring got us through. My favourite was the Economic History, which could be compared with Geography, dealing as it did with the opening up of the United States and Japan in the nineteenth century, and the reasons for their economic success.

Criminology was naturally of great interest, and at least I knew something about it, so could spend more time on other subjects. That it embraced Penology was a definite bonus, and the principles involved, and the systems and means adopted to resolve the problems, were familiar to me. It was here that I learned how successful the Juvenile Liaison scheme adopted at Plaistow had been in controlling recidivism.

As part of this course we went on a number of visits to three custodial institutions. If we learned anything, none of it related to penology.

The first was at Grendon Underwood where we had lived when my father was a prison officer (cook and baker). I went for nostalgic reasons. Mental treatment had very little appeal and by the time the visit was over it had none at all. Every patient I talked to would weigh up his answers to every question, however innocent.

I could see their brains at work to give the 'right' response. Everything had to be worked out to establish their sanity. It was all deeply depressing. The staff acknowledged the problem when I raised it with them but, reassuringly, they stated that the patients could put themselves into solitary confinement for three days to chill out from the mental pressure.

The second visit was to an approved school, for youngsters aged ten to twelve or thereabouts, who had to be confined. It was run by an ex-naval reserve officer, as far as I could tell, and definitely under a 'ship-shape and Bristol fashion' regime. He asked us at the end of our tour what we thought of it. I spoke out and told him I was appalled. I didn't like him or his smugness.

I told him I haven't seen a spare sock or single piece of clothing in all of the dormitories: There were no personal items whatsoever, and nothing to suggest they even had parents. Not a single photograph on any locker, by their cots, and certainly nothing to express their personality was to be seen - nothing visible but sanitised furniture, no belongings, and total depersonalisation. I was livid, he uncomprehending.

Finally, our third trip was to Pentonville Prison. Our team was made up of the criminology tutor (also my personal tutor), a young female student, and myself. As we arrived, the young student handed packets of 20 cigarettes to the first five prisoners she came across.

In one stroke we had not quite wrecked the economic system at Pentonville, which, as with all prisons, is based on the currency of tobacco: we had thrown it into complete disarray. How or why the prison officers came to allow this was beyond me, but at times, to my knowledge, they had a very black sense of humour.

Next we were ushered into a large room with forty or more prisoners and a light scattering of prison officers. We all started to converse, taking the line that but for a stroke of luck, we too could have ended up in trouble. Then out came the sympathy line that it must be very hard here...to which they responded by saying how hard it really was, and that some prisoners had even committed suicide because of it. A number of them started to drift away, having doubtless heard these sentiments often. If this was going to be of any use - and there must be some purpose for such visits to the inmates - I was not going to have them walk out on ours. I wanted it to be really constructive. I interjected that people outside prison have problems, and they commit suicide too. The leavers stopped in their tracks. I added that the prisoners had less to manage or worry about than many outside, and their basic needs are or at least should be met. There was more I could have said, such as that they were themselves mainly responsible for their being there, but I don't think I got that far, because already they were coming back. They all came back to see who this was.

As they did so, my tutor and the student sat down in the corner, a little alarmed at the way this was all beginning to go. The prisoners came back at me quite strongly, and I replied. The mood worsened when one of their leaders, a huge man (as prison leaders often are), reacted immediately with the claim that most of them were actually innocent, and had been fitted up by corrupt policemen. He spoke threateningly, fists clenched and face working with anger, and said that that was to be expected, as we were all living in a police state. I was not going to let this pass, and took him on again. He made for me - furious partly because in prison he was not used to being contradicted. I expected him to hit me.

I talked him down for some time as the others went silent watching the exchange between us. He stood his ground as did I and the tension lessened. One or two failed to support him. The more I answered him with calm logic the more he started off again, and I was once more very close to a possible punch on the nose. By this time all the prison officers had left the room, and the number of inmates had doubled. My tutor and the student were huddled in the corner. Petrified would not have been too strong a word to describe them.

It occurred to me that if I continued to argue along these lines, as I was, without admitting being a police officer, and it were to come out, things would turn even uglier.

I took the plunge, and told them so. My opponent virtually exploded and really came for me this time, and I was on the way to being flattened. A small voice piped up. 'Weren't you at Holloway, guv?' I said I was. He said, 'you once charged me.' I said, 'Well I hope I was fair to you.' He replied, 'You was a fucking gent, guv.' My opponent stopped in his tracks, the others muttered approvingly of me, the two in my group slumped with relief, mopped their brows, and the tension largely evaporated. Not quite, though, as one or two put other situations to me about police actions, ending with, 'what would you do if you came across a bent copper, or one who you knew had fitted someone up?'

I was able to recount the case of the articulate press reporter whom I had released, as I believed my officer was not telling me the truth. This was greeted well by the inmates, and the further discussion came shortly to an end in a more reasonable and peaceful tone. Their leader had sat down, mollified as things went on, and the meeting broke up. The prison officers returned.

The trip finished with a quick tour of the prison, which I could have done without, as I have never been comfortable with disturbing prisoners' privacy. As we were leaving I could hear whispers following me from the metal grill walkway above and dreading something being 'accidentally' spilled. My concerns were unnecessary.

On our way back, my tutor admitted that he had never been so frightened in all his life; the young student was still speechless; and I was eternally thankful for the man from Holloway. It did not surprise me when I was told that the leader was part of a very nasty and vicious London gang.

Good fortune does seem to have followed me on important moments such as the above, and more was to come. Once again I was fortunate when it came to my turn to read a paper in my Sociology seminar. Our tutor allowed us a free topic, and since she was a brilliant young professor and very much imbued by the LSE political philosophy (and was no supporter of the police) I wanted to impress her. Of course there was a need to do myself justice in the class as a whole as well; but she was the one who needed convincing that I was not out of place at this university.

A few weeks before my turn I had seen a film about Helen Keller, called The Miracle Worker. Keller was deaf and blind; the film starts with her in her middle class home, running round the house, totally out of control and manic. The blindness means that she grabs at anything she smells or comes across. She can do nothing for herself, fights and struggles with everyone, and is quite uncontrollable, comparable with a wild animal. Being deaf, she is also mute. The family cannot cope, other than by pulling or dragging her around, and their life is a complete nightmare. She is housed mainly in a small outhouse, resembling a kennel, in the garden.

The desperate (but well-off) parents hear of a teacher from a local school for the blind and deaf who may be able to help. The 'miracle worker' arrives, and starts to enforce discipline without any understanding from her charge. Her firmness alienates her from the family, especially the mother, but she carries on undeterred.

She starts to teach deaf and dumb language by forming letters on Helen's hand with her own fingers, ultimately bringing them together for simple words like 'food', 'bed', etc. Noting her success, the family are encouraged to copy. More complicated concepts are added: mother, father, brother, teacher and napkin. The latter word is symbolic for the mother, whose criterion of social etiquette is table manners, which, in her case, is particularly centred on the proper use of the napkin.

The main highpoint of the film is when the word tapped out is 'water'. She learns to pronounce 'water' herself, and, if thirsty, runs to teacher and taps out the word, letter by letter. It is when the teacher runs water from the tap in the garden through Helen's fingers, whilst tapping in the word, and getting her to pronounce it herself, that understanding dawns. It is a magic moment, and she knows how to talk. Communication exists, and now she can learn and start to live fully. Of course, thereafter, she runs round the garden ecstatic, saying aloud all the words while touching and spelling them, like, for instance tree, grass, the well, table etc.. Then she goes into the house, and the process is continued with all the persons and objects indoors.

For the mother, dinner is the highpoint of the day, and it becomes a triumph, since Helen now arrives at the table, washes her hands, sits, takes out her napkin and carefully folds it and places it ready for dinner. The meal then follows in a civilised fashion. This is the second highpoint.

It is still my favourite film (both Helen and the Teacher won Oscars for their performances) but it was its applicability that fascinated me. I used the concept of socialisation for much of it, but it also lent itself to another central concept - that of internalisation – the water moment. The film epitomised other concepts, for ultimately Helen goes to University, becomes a famous lecturer, broadcaster and author, and wins the Congressional Medal for Freedom.

My opening in class had everyone wondering what I was doing discussing a film in a sociology seminar: had I gone mad? My professor sat silently, but as I warmed up, she started to see the light. So did the rest of the class, and they were all fascinated as I developed my theme for the best part of an hour.

There were two reactions, the first from one of the class, who complained bitterly that he had to follow me, and that there wasn't anything for him to talk about, because I had said it all. The second was the one I wanted, my tutor saying that it was the best presentation she had heard in any seminar.

My studies carried on satisfactorily, despite the political unrest at the time over the Vietnam war and powerful industrial and CND disputes. Our own university attracted much newspaper coverage, and made headlines for its place in the turmoil that was to occur, especially in Grosvenor Square. In the university, the conflict between staff and students affected the atmosphere, and some of our studies, and led to a widely publicised demonstration. Many staff members were certainly not in tune with the students, and the higher status they had, the less so they were.

The fervour came to its height early in 1969, and a large meeting in the hall discussed the proposal for a sit-in. After the vote, the strategy to be adopted was for the building to be surrounded by all the students, shoulder to shoulder. The intention was to prevent strike-breakers entering. Prior to this I had experienced and policed unrest at the Docks and Fords at Dagenham, and we had come to know the rules about demonstrations and picketing.

Hearing what was proposed I had to object, and addressed the chairman by asking if he, or anyone else organising the demonstration, had any knowledge of the law on picketing, and particularly the concept of 'peaceful picketing.' I was shouted down immediately, but persisted with my question, to the baying of most of the audience, who knew my background, coupled with, "sit down, Barry" and "shut up, Barry." For easily 10 minutes I persisted, surrounded by some 500 students.

Eventually I began to gain support, as nobody ventured knowing anything about the law or the practice on the subject. Allowed to speak, I explained the law and practice that was held to constitute peaceful picketing, together with actual numbers held to have made it lawful.

I told them if their actions were adjudged unlawful, many arrests could follow, and many careers blighted, by a conviction and a restriction on visiting or working in the USA, for instance. Finally, their proposals would be seen as provocative at a time when the LSE and its rebels were something of a target: violence could ensue, with arrests for more serious matters than political protest.

Their plans were swiftly amended in compliance, and numbers, in single figures, permitted at each entrance were agreed, in order peacefully to persuade. The agreement to go on strike was massively supported; and the sit-in passed without incident, and achieved the desired media coverage, despite some staff opposition.

A significant contingent was from the anarchist group, and once given the go ahead they joined with the other students to plan the event. There were enough young men in white mackintoshes inspecting our notice-boards without my demonstrating any more police interest in the details of their tactics. I could not resist teasing them on hearing they had set up constant patrols throughout the building in shifts for security; to contain rowdy or disorderly behaviour; protect property; prevent theft or criminal damage; or any other crime. I ventured to suggest that their first step was to set up their own police force. They did not appreciate the paradox.

One of the pleasures of being at the LSE was its position of being at the centre of radical thought and public order events. Policing such events required a number of strategies, and the more flexibility there was, the better. The diversity of non-university speakers, from all walks of life, increased with their notoriety; and some graduates, such as, for instance, Tariq Ali, became celebrities, much sought after by the media.

Graduation was a non-event for me and many others. For such an anti-establishment institution, the choice of the Queen Mother to make presentations and to smile sweetly with a few easily anticipated words was crassly inappropriate. Background music from Bob Dylan that the 'times they were a 'changin' ' would have better fitted the bill. It was in keeping with the failure of the higher echelons of the LSE to have made such a selection, and so to fail to understand their students or to appreciate the political and social climate at their own university.

We were told to line up and to receive a blank roll of paper at Her Majesty's hands, and, sometime later our certificates would be sent through the post. They couldn't get that right, and the ceremony smacked of farce.

Even my first interviews were 'off the wall' and indicative of how things were done at the LSE.

My first mentor was world famous in his field and hugely respected. I sat at his feet in awe. He asked whether I had seen the TV last night, and then discussed the usual TV programmes watched in most homes. Absolutely nothing of any consequence, no sociological or economic documentaries were screened, nothing of any consequence. I thought 'maybe this is how it should be done,' but I was most disappointed.

The next commenced with his asking me how I was, and I returned by asking how was he. He then started to tell me his troubles at home, his health, worries about the everyday stuff of his life for, possibly, half an hour. He thanked me for coming, and said he felt much better: my contribution amounted in all to less than a sentence.

1969 was an important year for me in the light of personal and unexpected developments. After my university studies that year, the family had their first holiday away, in a roomy chalet in a private holiday site at Falmouth. We had travelled all day in our spacious Ford Zephyr, arrived, opened the chalet door and let the children loose. It matched the sheer delight of entering our new police house, and remains an indelible memory for all of us. The children, screaming with excitement, ran from room to room, picking out their beds and wardrobes, exploring every cupboard, picking up all the utensils, cutlery, every pot and pan until everything had been examined and wondered at.

Their next target was the grounds, and finally the club room and cafe that provided for meals and snacks and music from the juke box, which was never-ending. I still need just one burst of "Sugar, Sugar" to re-live the whole joyous experience. The views over Falmouth, and its numerous bays and beaches, were reserved for the next day. In all the resort proved a perfect holiday, and a novel experience in a part of the country we had never visited.

Since I do not remember doing any reading during that holiday, I suspect it followed graduation. I do recollect that, on completing my examinations, I threw all my books out with feeling, and an intention never to read a book again. Similarly, never to attend an academic lecture: except, of course, to watch the 'first television don', A.J.P. Taylor, giving, off the cuff, his brilliant historical talks. That resolution may not have lasted forever, but just saying it felt good enough.

The other personal development arose with my election to the committee of my daughters' school's PTA. Its regular activity was the weekly Bingo session which it ran for the local population, most of them at least middle-aged. It was not long before I was asked to be the caller. Getting the language right was a crucial part of the set up. To confuse the numbers, of, for instance, 'two little ducks, all the twos' with 'two fat ladies, all the eights', would prompt catcalls, many quite animated, as winning at bingo was a serious business. The experience eased me into speaking in public. After golf dinners, there was a ritual of the telling of well-loved and familiar tall tales or new jokes by favoured speakers, at which I would never have tried my hand.

Around this time, the PTA was approached by a fireman who had made his own DJ equipment, consisting of turntables, tape players and two boxes of painted light bulbs. With this came two milk trays of records. The PTA was in favour of buying these and setting up our own Discos for the schoolchildren. My enthusiasm talked me into acting as DJ. The fact that I had acted informally as such at times on the HMS Redpole was no help at all, even when I had to put the right weighted coin on the turntable arm when the school floor started to bounce.

Sheril would always come and help with refreshments, as she also enjoyed being with older people and loved the music. Sue and Michael were more likely to be with friends, or at home with Maria, doing stuff. Our two dogs helped to keep them occupied.

Not only were the Disco nights very popular with the youngsters, a fixture, but the task was not any easy one, as my young audience were quite loud in their demands for the choice of music to be balanced between white artists and black, (for example, the Osmonds and the Jackson Five, etc.).When we ran one for the parents, at their request, it was very well attended, and became a regular event.

It was not enough to know the records making it in the Top Twenty; they wanted the best 'exports' from the Caribbean. A new and lone white face started to make its presence felt in the local West Indian record shop, where their chart had to be consulted. By then they had got used to me, and were very willing to help in my selection. Knowing my day job provided them with extra amusement.

I enjoyed the experience of playing and introducing the records or tapes made up at home (courtesy of the local library). Occasionally I would play Big Band records, such as Glenn Miller, to give them a taste of our musical heritage. This went down quite well and, of course, the parents would enjoy the nostalgia, mainly at their dances.

Finally, in this phase, I started to get booked for weddings and private parties, even with my home made equipment. As the success of the function rested entirely on my shoulders I was exhausted at the end. The right music had to be picked to allow friends to meet and chat, then something suitable for a sit down meal and finally, when the feet started to tap, to let rip with the right music to get everyone up, and staying up, till a romantic LP closed the event – usually Max Bygraves.

Chapter 8
Leman Street – Yes,
L e m a n S t r e e t– a Miscellany

Each year that went by, the Connaught girls' school's PTA saw a new wave of parents who were keen to participate. Our Bingo and Discos were drawing in the locals, youngsters and parents, more so once parents' evenings caught on. The school had a high reputation, and the annual fair spread the word. The Head was most enthusiastic and proud of her PTA, and the staff fully supported our taking an active part.

At the time of joining, the fair was making a profit of some £200, but it felt like a church bazaar held in a church hall. Yet we had a large playground, about the size of half a football pitch, with unrestricted parking in the street alongside. There was also another building, an annex with its own playground, so there was plenty of room to grow.

We decided to bring the Fair out into the open, and so increase the numbers attending, as we would have the scope, and plenty of helpers to run it. We kept the same stallholders, with their own stalls, allowing them to bring in improvements as they saw fit. A major change was to have all the prizes donated, even from local shopkeepers, and to make winning tickets end in a 5 or 0. Other innovations were brought in, and nothing was ever set in stone, as had been the custom. Once this was working well, we set about attracting a celebrity to open it.

In the first few years we started by obtaining the Hackney Speedway Team, complete with equipment and a few speedway bikes. Then I rang Kenny Lynch, just as easily as that, and persuaded him to attend by telling him he would be a first class role model for our students. He agreed instantly and stayed all day with us even though he had a performance up north the next day. Another was a local TV personality, Bobby Crush, who was making his name as a singer and pianist. He was a very good looking young man, and the girls, and their younger mums, turned up in droves, and he had the idea of selling kisses to swell the take.

It was not long before we were reaching over £2000 on a regular basis. So that I could have some fun, rather than just oversee things when everyone was perfectly capable of running their own show, I designed a putting game which featured a ramp with a revolving green (a turntable) and the cup. Its short fairway was painted with bunkers to make it look authentic.

Since I offered a five pound note for each successful player holing even on a slowly revolving green, we were going to lose money. I could, I suppose, have spun the green at 78 but it was fairer to offset the hole. Though a high -speed moving golf hole would have been much funnier. The queues for it lasted all day and many were so determined to hole they came back time and time again. I gave away no more than £10. I have the feeling it is still tucked away in some dusty corner, with the new caretakers pondering over that ancient contraption.

A walk round the school allowed the new parents readily to see what had been bought by the Head, and doubtless she told them where the money had come from. She had the pleasurable duty of spending it, without any recourse to her Committee.

Maybe our proudest accomplishment was that the members of the PTA, and the Committee, teachers and the Head, had become friends. Since the school was set off the main road at the centre of five residential roads (with two well-kept 'pre-fabs' - thrown in for historical detail) grounds for a community existed. The relationships between school, parents and locals led to the further development of a strong sense of community. For London that was a great achievement.

My efforts as a private DJ for the occasional booking added to the funds, and they remained in a very healthy state. We did so well that I commissioned a console from a musical engineer, which he designed to order and built for us. It came with a twin turntable that allowed one record to fade out and the next gradually to fade in. He provided two tape decks; very effective in-built lights; and a disk-player for oil wheels, which were all the fashion in commercial discos, to reflect pretty moving patterns on ceilings and walls. I felt quite professional going into a disco emporium to choose such items. The console was pushed to its place on wheels, and with one plug into a socket, we were off and running. It had cost some £900, but was a real investment. There was no more struggling to balance coins on the turntable arm when the dancing got lively.

My garden was fine and thriving, and I was putting so much into it that I decided to keep an account, as enthusiasm in a hobby can outweigh common sense, all the more so with gardening. I also grew to enjoy the maths, and although my produce could be bought more cheaply, of course, it didn't taste as good. The final lesson was to grow only what you can eat. The best compliment was from my father-in-law, the professional gardener, who was truly astonished that a London garden could produce such great cauliflowers, when he had the best looked-after soil in the Wye valley.

My mother bought two fruit trees as a birthday present, one that produced three different varieties of apple, and another two sorts of pears. Whilst they were bred to grow at the right height to pick, and were supposedly self-pollinating, the practice failed to match the theory, and only a few apples of one variety came to fruition. No pears pollinated then!

Indoors, our dining table resembled a battlefield with my studies, my help to the girls (Maths still, and then French), and their own work and preparation for one examination or another. The younger two were taking ballet, as well, but ceased to enjoy it once lessons were to be doubled to practice for grades – another economy.

My posting came through, and it was to a station I had never heard of, namely Leman Street. Yes, Leman Street, a street that when you pronounced its name people shook their head and said that they had never heard of it. What had ever happened in Leman Street, nobody knows. Where was its drama, its history, its excitement? It was not even named after a district in London that anyone had heard of, like nearby Bethnal Green, Hoxton, Whitechapel, or Wapping.

There was not one building of any note in Leman Street, and yet it is within a stone's throw of The Tower of London, Tower Bridge, Spitalfields and Billingsgate markets, The Royal Mint, The Customs house, Cable Street (steeped in vice, they said), Wapping and the river front, Wilton's music hall (the world's first music hall - still surviving and putting on performances), Petticoat Lane, the up and coming Brick Lane and the London Hospital. As a street, Shepherdess Walk was just as mundane, but at least it sounded interesting.

It housed most of the senior officers on the division and all the departments that had been at City Road, except that Leman Street had a complement of women police officers. How it was that the other stations I had served at had managed without them, I could not understand, for such officers had essential duties relating to women prisoners and sex cases - there being no domestic violence units - and assisting with arrests or observations; and they were very welcome, to soften our image. Yet, as it turned out, Leman Street gave me the best time I ever had in the Met.

I well remember the arrest of a sixteen-year-old youth for breaking into a dress shop for a pair of high-heeled leather boots to go with the outfit he had on. His face was burning with embarrassment when he appeared before us in the station - probably his worst nightmare. He had expected a male officer's typical reaction, but not one of my relief was anything other than considerate, gentle and sympathetic, as if he were their own son. I was inordinately proud of each one of them.

In 1970, the dustmen went on strike, and the Army were called in to clear the rubbish. It very much affected the City, with which again we bordered, and my Commander called me into his office to help him compile the report for the Commissioner. We sat together at his desk and wrote it. I was starting on the right foot this time, and he at least that thought my education would be of use: many senior officers thought the opposite, and graduates were having a hard time on division. Conversely, it was at headquarters that it was recognised as an asset, and a qualification for progress. Out on division, it is my belief that we were thought indecisive in giving more wide-ranging thought to an event. To be positively decisive was always seen as a virtue in a senior officer, and promotion boards seemed to enjoy such attitudes: time spent thinking made the interviewer uncomfortable.

My loyalty came under pressure when I was called out to a serious fire, at which my Commander attended. Striding into the centre of things in plain clothes, he started advising the senior fire office on his duty. This so offended the Fire Brigade officer that he called me over, and told me that if I didn't get him (my commander) out of the way, 'he would probably plant one on him.' Having to assist a Fire Brigade officer, and prevent a breach of the peace involving my senior officer, was difficult, and he may have expected my total support. The situation demanded more tact, and a step backwards in letting the man do his job and fight the fire, which was also my function. It may, however, have proved a backward step in the relationship between my Commander and his subordinate.

One of the advantages of wearing plain clothes, as opposed to uniform, is seeing what is happening on the ground and, on occasions, to take action. Not only to spot offences and make arrests, if appropriate, as it is best that senior officers do not tie themselves up in ordinary duties. To see how officers behave on duty can be revealing, and I remember a friend telling me that his father, then a Superintendent, made a practice of patrolling alone in plain clothes to spot any corruption.

Petticoat Lane was difficult to police in terms of unlawful trading, as lookouts would be used by the traders. That required plain clothes officers, but it was not a job for the CID. Women police did the job well, but usually with a male officer, and I went on occasion. Certainly on one occasion we tested our street credibility by standing as part of a crowd around one such seller for some time until he remarked, "I'm feeling real lucky today", to which came the reply, "Not that lucky I'm afraid, you're under arrest." At least they would always plead guilty.

Such actions would put a brake on illegal activities, but often, with crowds, would come other offensive behaviour, and knowing the practice of using officers in plain clothes did have a deterrent effect. It is surprising what does go on in the streets when there is the time to watch, and doubly advantageous if combined with the power to act as necessary.

One dramatic deployment for the WPCs, as they were then called, was the prosecution of a woman for an offence in relation to her young family under Care and Protection proceedings at the local Magistrates Court. The Act provided a useful power when a specific assault could not be proved, but the child as a result could be removed, and the behaviour by its mother stopped, or controlled by a non-custodial order. On this occasion we required the evidence of four of our female police officers at court and it provided useful experience for them.

Furthermore, this particular prosecution had a far greater significance than would appear, as, in court, I was astounded to see my old Superintendent who had conducted my promotion class to Inspector, and who in his own exam came top of all the candidates. Wearing a very smart suit, he was conducting the defence to a criminal charge in a most impressive and utterly competent fashion.

To see him operate so capably and persuasively in favour of a defendant, having been 'on the other side,' left a lasting impression with me. I could not ever forget such a demonstration of fairness and forensic skill from an unexpected source - without injustice to his intellectual ability.

In most groups or service units, there is one member who becomes the unofficial leader. In the Navy, he would be a leading seaman; in the army, a corporal; in a prison, the toughest; and on a police relief, despite being the same rank as the others – there being only constables and sergeants – the one who is accorded such authority by maturity, wit and strength of character. He will bring the relief with him. Mine I will call Tony.

Whilst many days and nights are routine, there are some which are particularly memorable, and on the following occasion, Tony surpassed himself. It started when a prisoner in the station escaped as far as the front office and was trying to climb over the counter, pursued by the charging sergeant and Tony. Despite a fierce struggle by the prisoner, they put him down, and started to pull him back into the charge room. As they left Tony turned to me, in front of the shocked members of the public transfixed by the spectacle, and in a stage whisper, panted, "That'll teach him to come in here and ask the way." I kept my head down and briskly attended to the callers: nobody mentioned what had just happened.

Later that same night, Tony took me and two others out on patrol. As we arrived at the cobbled area outside Billingsgate Fish Market, there was a market porter washing it down with a large hose. He had a crumpled uniform, a battered peaked cap and wellington boots, with a Benny Hill look about him.We stopped to let him finish as it was quiet and after midnight. It was not proving easy for him, and the water was not washing away. The hose was proving elusive, and his footing was insecure, causing him to splash around struggling for control.

The hose was thick, with a powerful jet, and beginning to writhe around, putting him also under pressure. He was evidently losing the battle, the hose now had a life of its own, and the water was rising well over a foot deep. It was not long before he lost the battle and fell with a huge splash into the pool the hose snaking around him and thrashing up and down. His cap was knocked sideways, and he was now a Benny Hill lookalike.

He was floundering in a sea of water, with an out-of-control hose, when a colleague came from the market and waded in to help. They both fought for control of the hose, and to retain their balance, but were unequal to the task. We now had two Benny Hills, the second's cap similarly dislodged, splashing around in the pool, fighting the hose.

Throughout, none of us said a word. Eventually the hose was subdued; but it had put up quite a fight. As Tony drove off, he spoke for all of us with "did anyone else see what I think I just saw?"

The way he dealt with our next call was pure genius. The caller alleged a rape was occurring at an address we knew to be a squat for vagrants. The allegation was that the male partner was raping his female partner there and then in their flat.

Arriving swiftly, we noticed both were out of breath, reeked of drink, legless and completely incapable. She trying to demonstrate that he had been chasing her round and round the bed to get at her. His ardour certainly could not have been aroused by the virtual rags she was wearing: they were as unlikely a pair of lovers, or rapist and victim, as could be imagined.

Tony took over. He sat them down and, addressing the male, told him that this was not the way we did things these days. The chasing round and round the bed until pouncing was out. "Have you tried chocolates," he asked. He was met with incomprehension. "What about a nice bunch of flowers?" he suggested. Another blank stare was the response. I was beginning to bite my lip.

He moved on with, "a nice bottle of chilled white wine, two glasses, and the lights turned down for the right ambience?" At this I had to turn away, as did the others but he continued with his rules of courtship as to the tender and loving removal of clothing that would allow foreplay. Ambience, their clothing, and foreplay was too much for us, and we had to withdraw. The result of the call was written up as Advice Given, which was both truthful and unconventionally appropriate.

Another caller at the station posed a difficulty with a crowded foyer late at night, and demonstrated the effectiveness of another unconventional approach.

This was a persistent character who had harmless delusions, a condition regularly demonstrated by many of those with whom we had to deal. Her first words were that, "they were at it again through the wall." I asked what they were doing this time, and she replied, "It was the rays again... always the rays, but through all the walls now...and what are you going to do about it?"

The other callers waiting their turn (as they did then) looked at me, expectantly. Inspiration was called for.

I turned to my reserve and ordered him to send out two PCs and a sergeant in the squad car, plus a van and two specials. If there was a dog handler, too, that would be useful. Then I raised my hands, shrugged and said, "But today's Wednesday." She said "Oh, sorry," turned and left. A ripple of applause greeted my effort and the next caller stepped up, smiling approvingly. There was no privacy at the counter for the caller or the officer in those days so it was a task that demanded experience and ingenuity.

Before turning to the other part of our area, Wapping, there was one final scene in the front office to provide some colour to a quiet New Year's Eve. There was a commotion at the swing doors to the office, as one of my officers arrived with Long John Silver in tow, complete with crutch, parrot, and a wooden leg. Equally determined to get in were two other officers, plus two authentically dressed pirates, and Robin Hood. All were passengers from a party, and strongly inebriated, according to the officers. Testing on the street had proved impractical and, as in most cases, they were arrested to sort it all out.

Swaying before me as the evidence, as far as it went, was given, there was very unseemly hilarity and total confusion displayed, not least as to who was driving. I was secretly hoping to create a legal precedent by adding a charge of 'lack of control of a motor vehicle by virtue of a wooden leg and restricted vision' - added to the usual 'under the influence of drink'. The press report the next day from court would have made for good reading, and great photographs, since the driver and his witnesses would appear at court in fancy dress, but the court played it safe with a change of clothing.

Our sectional station was in Wapping High Street at the centre of Wapping, a narrow strip of land running alongside the River Thames for about a mile, and half a mile wide. To the East was Limehouse, and to the West the City, starting at the Tower of London. It comprised of a string of four-or-five-storey warehouses with huge hoists on the fronts, allowing deliveries to be hauled up to the floors from the barges and other ships and boats in the Port of London. They had been largely disused because of the demise of the port, but were gradually being transformed into workshops, studios and storage units.

A yuppie invasion was beginning, and several elegant apartments and penthouses had been the result of expensive renovations. At the same time there were blocks of tenements in the side streets, where the older residents lived with their families and children. There was, in all, a strange mixture of buildings, from the decrepit through to the ultra-modern, but with the potential for exciting development.

After dusk, this area was mostly dark, and the atmosphere mysterious, with the sound of the river lapping gently across the main road for most of the street's length. The darkness was punctuated occasionally by the brightness from the well-lit windows of the more opulent dwellings, which were often un-curtained.

More localised patches of light were afforded by the numerous public houses in the centre of Wapping, with their warm cosy interiors and quiet saloons. Along the riverside were Wapping's main attractions for visitors, a number of famous old traditional pubs much frequented by tourists and by young Londoners wanting a night out with character and something very different.

These provided all that was missing from the rest of Wapping, and more. Good, traditional, and largely British food served at candle-lit long oak tables, all the drinks for the discerning, a wide range of music from folk to jazz, antique furniture, naval paraphernalia, genuine artefacts and plenty of history in an area that, as the tourist guide recounts, was the haunt of sailors, smugglers, thieves, footpads and pirates.

These pubs, from the Prospect of Whitby, the Captain Kidd, close to Execution Dock, through to the Dickens Inn, were full of nooks and crannies, galleries and bars that felt like a stately galleon's cabins with massive windows which overhung the inky waters of the river a few feet below. Despite their constant popularity, and bohemian customers, there was little need for police action, and most visitors arrived without cars, or with sober drivers. The revellers there were the sort who had turned up in fancy dress at Leman Street.

Moving through the High Street along St. Katharine's way were situated more warehouses, but these were the property of the Customs and Excise, and housed valuable cargoes of contraband. They stored much of the evidence for their cases and operated with a very high focus on security, precautions and the requirement for instant responses and road closures.

This road opened up into a truly magical spot, which was also responsible for the presence of most levels of society and their cameras. As one approached via the car park at Thomas More Square and Wilton's Music Hall, one came across the Dickens Inn, which took up one side of St. Katharine's Dock by itself. This huge pub had been transported whole with its original structure, and was presented like a literary venue, but with long tables, candle-lit, both inside and outside. Its lights were reflected in the waters of the dock, and the mood was set by its floors, deep in sawdust. It was always jam-packed.

The dock was bristling with river craft of all types, but mostly high value speedboats and tall and very expense yachts. Opposite the Dickens Inn was the splendid Tower Hotel alongside the river and, across it, the spectacle of Tower Bridge, bathed in floodlights.

Behind was the Tower of London, resplendent in its floodlights, and between the hotel and the Dickens Inn was a row of more warehouses, which had served St Katharine's Wharf, and which had now been largely modernised.

They housed similar sized rooms and studios occupied by artists and their installations, some daunting in size and in the prices being asked for them; sculptures abounded, and more expensive works, with other music and artistic workshops. They were presented like art galleries, but the visitor could see the work in progress, talk to the artists, enjoy the varied music being played, or background music, or maybe even discuss a commission for some work. Clearly, that side of the dock was affording good light for its tenants.

Of particular police interest were the Tower, with its Crown Jewels, and the Mint, where the highest security was required. Whilst public order was a necessary duty with the crowds as they were, especially at nightly ceremonies such as the handing over of the keys, this mostly took care of itself. More important was to ensure immediate attendance, and a watchful eye was cast over our response times, and those of Information Room.

For anyone with a sense of history, social, naval or literary, a love of art, music or good food in convivial establishments, where the famous and infamous had trod since before the sixteenth entury, a complete tour of London excluding Wapping would, in my view, be unthinkable.

Any problems with the Tower response times, or even tickets for the ceremonies, were in the capable hands of the Admin. Inspector, named Sydney. He was my favourite at the station, for his ready advice on matters involving the senior officers, and he was also the aide to the Commander. He also had a great sense of humour.

Since he had been responsible for a number of events at the Tower, I felt the following report should be delivered to him by hand, for his eyes only. It was titled 'Disorder at the Tower of London' and read very much as follows:

"On (day, date and time) at the Tower of London a festival was held at Tower Hill Terrace where a very large number of spectators gathered. Present was the customary entertainment with street vendors, several members of the City Mounted Branch, three special constables and a contingent of the St. John's Ambulance service. A forty-one gun salute by the Royal Regiment of Fusiliers commenced proceedings, but had not quite concluded by the time the Morris-dancers started their performance. Unfortunately, one of them was so startled by the concluding volley (exceptionally loud, I must report) that he dropped his stave, which allowed his opposite number's stave to strike his head, which was unprotected. The injury required medical attention, but the ambulance called was declined by the St John's ambulance service, and all seven immediately undertook first aid. So enthusiastic was their response that the ambulance had to be recalled. Due to a number of minor injuries, and a panic attack by the said Morris Dancers, he was conveyed to the City Hospital A & E Dept.

"Meanwhile, the other dancers pointed out that the stave had been seized as a memento by a visitor, who had decamped with it. He was being pursued by other dancers, with special constables Smith and Jones. At Petty Wales the mounted officers were exercising their mounts, and joined in the pursuit of the thief. A number of Japanese tourists followed filming the incident, in the belief, as they said later, when accused of unpermitted filming at the Tower, that it was part of a police demonstration.

"It was during this incident that police horse Sydney, becoming excited, kicked over a container of roasting chestnuts, which set fire to the easel of a street artist sketching a most attractive Japanese child. Her two younger sisters became alarmed at the fire, and were in such evident shock and distress that they were conveyed by police transport to the said A & E, the offers of first aid by the St John's ambulance having been declined.

"More was to follow as Yeoman of the Guard, Corp. Sanders, showed initiative by seizing a fire extinguisher to quell the blaze, but failed to notice that his Chief Yeoman Warder was in the line of fire. His Chief received most of the contents of the extinguisher in the face and on the front of his uniform. He was immediately transported by ambulance, and detained for impaired vision as a result.

"It was therefore my duty to inform the Resident Governor, in the presence of the Constable of the Tower, of his Chief Yeoman Warder's predicament, since it would be touch and go whether he would be able to fulfil his central role later, in the Ceremony of the Keys. In a most intemperate tone the Governor shouted 'Touch and go, Inspector?' I was tempted to ask him to calm down, when the Constable of the Tower repeated, 'Touch and bloody go?' About to explode, he continued to inform me slowly, word by word, almost spat in my face, that for every day of the past seven hundred years, the Ceremony of the Keys had been performed before the public in a time-honoured ritual, with the main part played by the Chief Yeoman Warder and his escort, every sentry on every door making totally prescribed responses. This would end with the Chief Warder doffing his Tudor bonnet with, 'God Preserve Queen Elizabeth.'

"Whilst the Constable was shaking his head and muttering 'seven hundred years of tradition, and on my watch,' the Governor ordered a leading guardsman to be despatched to the Queen's House, for the keys and a clean uniform for his Chief.

"Some delay ensued, as the guardsman had apparently slipped on the cobbled walkway and dropped the keys into the moat – regrettably, the scene of a jousting display the previous day. Nevertheless, with the aid of torchlight, afforded by the Governor and the Constable from a latticed window overlooking the rather soiled moat, the keys were found, cleaned and conveyed to the A & E unit for the Chief. It remains to say that after considerable pressure from all involved, an eye specialist was able to resolve the Chief's difficulties, and the ceremony went ahead, you may be assured, exactly at the pre-ordained time.

"The following action is required. A letter of thanks is to be sent to the A & E Department. There is a claim for compensation by the street vendors involved, to be settled by the City Mounted

Branch. A report is sought by the Japanese Embassy dealing with the shock and distress suffered by the two less attractive children of the family involved, who were not placated, it seems, by allowing their elder daughter to sit on police horse Sydney as a gesture of goodwill. The theft from the Morris-dancer will be reported in the Crime Book with his oral statement that, 'It was a complete farce,' and the twenty-seven verbal warnings respecting unpermitted filming will be replaced by 'the giving of proper advice,' in the circumstances.

"Commander H has received a message from Buckingham Palace, from the Duke of Edinburgh, stating that having counted the cannon salute he is unaware of any authority for a forty-two gun salute by the Royal Fusiliers. He asks that their Commanding Officer explains this serious error in royal protocol in writing to the Commander's Aide, for transmission to the Palace."

Sydney had hugely enjoyed my practical joke, and, despite my having written that it was for his eyes only, had passed it around for full appreciation. In a bid to demonstrate its popularity, he said that it had reached the very top. I was not inclined to ask him 'the top of what?' but waited for a caustic note from the Commander stating that the Yard advised giving Forward more work to do, if that was how he deployed his time and effort.

I did receive an unusual call from Sydney on his Commander's behalf, but it was to inform me that the training school had requested my presence on a new course being implemented for recruit training.

In 1971, a social studies input was authorised in recruit training for Metropolitan officers, to add to their initial training. The force chose to implement it with their usual pragmatism, by not employing their own graduates to teach, but to teach their own police instructors. This is where I and the others with me at the LSE came in.

Since we were the experts and experienced police officers, we were very much left to organise the instruction ourselves. Our teaching took about four weeks, and comprised Economics, Law,

Sociology and Social Psychology. The aims stated in a subsequent report were to train interpersonal skills to develop self-knowledge, self-awareness and community relations, focussing on race and cultural awareness.

As far as I was concerned, basic sociological concepts were discussed accurately, for the little time available to our class of enthusiastic sergeants. Certainly, we recognised that this should be directed to attitudes, and to formal and informal behavioural training, but without lacking academic credibility. An example was a lecture on Weber's model of bureaucracy and its application to the Police. This ideal combined the practical with the theoretical structure of the model, and still allowed a broad and useful discussion of police behaviour.

Another experiment I stole from Social Psychology was that in which a recruit is chosen to return to the class after three lines of varying distance are drawn on the blackboard, and the rest of the class asked to nominate the shortest. We ensured as far as possible that the toughest and most independent recruit was chosen.

The test is carried out by each recruit in turn, answering by pointing out the longest. As each answers, one is able to focus on the chosen one who, after squirming and struggling in his seat, as in every class, picked out the shortest. This result came as a complete shock to the school, and caused genuine alarm. It tended to validate the intended course and the lessons I was hoping to instil, about loyalty, independent-mindedness and truth. Canteen culture was often discussed, as the idealistic recruits may become hardened under the influence of their more experienced peers.

We all attended a conference with the Commander of the school (my old tormentor) and all those involved. He was looking for the recruits to gain from such teaching some concrete answers in these more sociological areas. He was addressing me, looking for such certainty for the young officers, as imparted by their sergeants. I had to explain that the discursive method I suggested was best-suited to my subject, as opposed to set answers. If academic content or methodology had to give way to practical certainty, the training school could be open to criticism.

The Commander listened intently, accepting what I had said, but insisted that we were training new entrants to be police officers. It was not long after this that reports indicated that the social studies were thought to be too academic, as they were thought to have clashed with the law enforcement image maintained by the school. The input was developed further and the subjects spread over the whole course, which retained Sociology and Social Psychology. Social and Public Administration elements were added, all to be 'related to appropriate police duty.'

Whilst at the school, I was approached by the Cadet School tutors and asked to give a talk on race relations. They were particularly anxious that someone of my rank should give it. Whilst in the Navy, I had been much influenced by a police cadet, as mentioned before, and, once in the Force, many officers came through via the cadet school. My rank, it was felt, would give me more credibility (and interest) than their own academic teachers; and I would not be dismissed by being thought impractical, or unrealistic, or challenged by the more vociferous or dogmatic.

Expecting to speak to a group of listeners informally, I found myself in their main hall, with a semi-circle of all their tutors ranged behind me, and, in front, about a hundred young and eager teenagers in cadet uniform. I had been asked to come in uniform and had no notes whatsoever.

I started by asking them whether they had been, for instance, to Brixton. I moved on for them to shout out in a few words what they had seen there, or how in a word they would describe them.

It was not long before the usual stereotypes were forthcoming. They became more extreme, and I allowed them to continue. I am not sure what their teachers made of it, but it carried on, and at last one or two voices from other cadets spoke up to object. I remember all the cadets appeared white.

More spoke up, and all the stereotypes were advanced, together with more and more objections. I let the arguments range widely, noting that the 'canteen culture' (even among cadets) was breaking down, and that the more right-minded were speaking up more positively and constructively. It now needed a finish.

My conclusion then distinguished prejudice from discrimination, and what could, and needed to, be done about both. I had greatly enjoyed the session, and so, I think, had most, if not all, of the cadets – none showed any lack of interest – and there was great enthusiasm from their teachers. It had been a fruitful and instructive afternoon all round.

It was not long after returning to Division that it was suggested that I could take on the post of head of Social Studies at training school. Whilst I was flattered to be considered, there would have been constant conflict between the senior officers and the Commander who was still in charge, and my firmly held views and opinions. In addition, it was not the path I wished to pursue, side-lined into academia or bureaucracy.

Lord Reith, in a lecture in 1952, had said: 'the recruit is taught everything except the essential requirement of his calling which is how to secure and maintain the approval and respect of the public whom he encounters daily in the course of his duties.' Little appeared to have been done in my time to remedy this, and the Social Studies was an attempt to address his view. Such studies would always clash with the law enforcement image, and that image would prevail. That the course did continue indicates the recognition of the value of such training; its delivery, however, was always modified to fit in with the predominant image.

I was asked next by the Detective training school to deliver a lecture on social attitudes to a class of experienced detectives. Presumably some schooling in social behaviour was thought necessary, as per Reith's view.

I arrived in class to be faced by some thirty obviously experienced detectives, many staring deliberately out of the window: a few others were looking at me out of curiosity, and two took up newspapers, and read them under my nose when I started to introduce myself.

They were offended that they were thought to need any such lecture and reacted accordingly. One or two I knew, so their disrespect was not personal, but addressed to the subject. Being from the uniform branch did not make my reception any easier.

I ordered them to put away the papers and pay attention. Sullenly, they did so; few met my gaze, but their reaction came as no surprise. I had joined the CID as an aide whilst at Plaistow so knew the department well. Despite a strong interest in the detection and prosecution of crime, the CID had not been for me.

A lecture never would have got off the ground, so I handed out a questionnaire on social attitudes, one well-recognised by social scientists. Although I stressed that it should be completed anonymously, some defiantly signed theirs, and started reading. Gradually, as they moved through the questions, they became engaged, then animated. They were comparing their answers with those of their colleagues, and, I noticed, were amending or crossing out and replacing their first answers, and looking to see my reaction. I sat and just observed their behaviour.

There was a great deal of whispered discussion when they compared their answers. Some were taken to task by their colleagues, and others changed their minds on listening to others' answers. Some of the questions were open-ended ,and covered apparently innocuous behaviour, whilst others were more cultural, with racial content; and others I could relate to their perceived self-image. A correct answer was not obvious.

As with the cadets, after initially dogmatic opinions were expressed, these were then moderated by peers, and positions would be retracted, or hard-liners made to look bigoted or inconsistent. The class had livened up, as intended, and, to a man, they all participated. It ended with appreciation for what I was doing, and the value of the discussion and the examination of their own views, positions and behaviour, without criticism or preaching. They all seemed to have enjoyed it, and I was even thanked for my session.

I mention this experience because it indicates some of the thinking on the subject of Social Studies, and the opposition to it. Nevertheless, it points up the advantages it possesses, if introduced more widely to any police officer in his dealings with the public, and not just recruits. Reith would have approved.

Chapter 9
A Change of Pace at Management Services

Back at the station, I was distressed to hear that, in my absence, Tony had been suspended and was about to leave the force. There was nothing to be done, matters had gone too far, and any withdrawal was impossible. From what I learnt, Tony had come into the station a little early to finish his late shift, and was asked by his sergeant to take the car out and deal with some routine task.

He had asked why the oncoming night duty then arriving at the station could not do it. He was ordered to get on with it, and remonstrated again that it was unfair, and that he was finishing his shift. I knew no more of the details or conversation between them, but gathered that the sergeant saw this as a challenge to his authority, a dereliction of duty, and a refusal to obey the order of a more senior ranking officer.

Tony was suspended, and the investigation that followed was, as is usual, the detailed account of every minor aspect of his duty; infractions were revealed, such as not booking out his car properly, coming into the station too early (normal to hand over and complete his paperwork) and possibly others. The investigating officer 'threw the book at him.'

Tony' s character, status at the station, and experience as a valued CID officer before transferring to the uniform left him, it appeared, with no alternative but to quit. He was as adamant as was his sergeant.

He left shortly afterwards, taking up almost immediately a position in security. In a matter of months, he was running his own business, and it soon became an impressive organisation, thriving under his management.

Not knowing the details of what he was asked to do, the nature of his response, or the possibility for discretion, there is no more to say other than that the precision of police disciplinary investigation, and attention to any minute transgression to complete the papers, would have precluded any compromise in this situation. It meant the loss of a most competent officer, with great leadership potential, yet for whom promotion was not an option. For many officers, promotion comes at a heavy price, despite their capabilities.

This deserves explanation, as in many walks of life promotion has social disadvantages: upheaval from the work place and one's team-mates; further expense ; re-arrangement of domestic matters; and keeping distance where rank is involved.

In the police service it becomes more problematic: at first, there are months if not years of study to pass rigorous examinations up to Inspector rank (the pass level is set higher where there are fewer opportunities).Transfer of station or department will follow, since the loss of valuable local knowledge was always outweighed by the policy of a fresh start. Loss of overtime versus twenty-four-hour responsibility played a part, as did the increasing likelihood of a desk job, the avoidance of which motivated most in the service.

The benefits were mainly personal: satisfying one's ambition (though money helped); but the downside is always the baulking of further steps, especially in the Station Sergeant rank, which would tie one to the desk in the station. So rarely does it provide the freedom of a sergeant, or being in charge as an . Inspector. In higher ranks, for the very ambitious, being blocked so often provoked bitterness, and induced a philosophy of playing it safe and time-serving.

On my return, after some time, it was depressing to find that the workload was still the same, and there was no possibility of the Vice section's being re-instated. The significance of such work was that it was carried out by the uniform branch on this division too, and enabled us to detect, investigate, collate the evidence, and pursue a criminal allegation, without recourse to the CID. In higher ranks such experience rated highly for promotion.

We must have dealt with the last prostitute on our section, as she attended Wapping to make a complaint of rape in a parked car. The essence of her allegation was that he had failed to pay after having sex with her. That immediately sounded odd, as it would be ingrained for her to demand payment before sex, even if drunk. If completely incapable, her lack of ability to consent would need proving by the prosecution.

The fact that she was already drunk, abusive and uncooperative when asked to take forensic tests made our decision to proceed no easier. Her account changed continuously as it went on, and included further allegations that she had had to perform acts with which she would not have consented. The vital question was whether she was willing to support a prosecution.

To dismiss a complainant in these circumstances and record No Crime had to be considered, weighing all the factors in the balance, and resisting being influenced by her occupation. The lack at that time of rape units and clinics made an immediate decision imperative, otherwise we would face a serious complaint of neglect.

There appeared to be no witnesses available, so it was only her word which could back up an arrest of the suspect. We insisted on taking a full statement from her, including every detail or matter that impinged on the consent issue (and possible defences): another indication of her credibility and physical and mental condition.

Having played our parts, there was no follow up required from any of the officers involved. No prosecution statements were called for by the Yard's Solicitors, but, also, there was no criticism of police action.

What was remarkable was the cessation of street prostitution in the whole area, after decades where its reputation was well-known to any punter in the East End. Continuous efforts are always being made in London by officers and squads to move them off the streets, yet on our Division their demise appeared without police intervention. One could only make assumptions about changes: in the building of many huge tower blocks surrounded by their estates; the replacement of dark and narrow streets; the influx of a different cultural mix, prompted by Petticoat and Brick Lanes (and a cinema devoted to Asian films of the 'Bollywood' type); and really well-lit main roads bringing in speedier traffic, necessitating traffic patrols.

It was clear that it was going to be some time before I came into the frame for further promotion. Sydney, with his experience, contacts and all round competence, was obviously preferred, and I only had two years' operational experience to offer. Despite a degree, practical experience counted for more, and some of that time had been spent at training school, and on Social Studies work. Being a senior officer's protégé led to a strong recommendation, which I lacked.

An open advert to become the chief officer for the Alberta district in Canada was published, as the country was seeking to recruit experienced officers from the UK. I saw this as an opportunity for an objective assessment of my potential in the police service, and applied. Obviously Canadian officers had applied, but I nevertheless reached the short list, and found that there were not many contenders.

My interview went well, and I felt I was being treated as a serious prospect. The last question was whether I would only accept the top job, or would agree to be the Deputy Chief, and I saw that this was a serious proposal. It was also a practical offer, since many Chief Constables had been promoted after experience as a Deputy. In a different police culture, in a different country, such experience would prove invaluable in a much more senior rank. I said I would accept such a post, and then felt immediately that it was the wrong answer. Nothing materialised, for it was unthinkable seriously to bring my family over to a completely different environment, climate, conservative and rural culture, as well as cutting ties with family, relatives, and friends. Finally, I could see no prospect of re-joining if it failed and if we lost our police house, but I was pleased at the result of this venture in increasing my self-esteem at a low moment.

I was becoming restless generally, too, as well as unfulfilled and under stress at home. Despite the appearance of a happily married man with a loving family, good job, a wide circle of friends and relatives, and wide fulfilling interests my relationship with my wife of sixteen years was becoming stale. It was all on my part, and it was unfair to, and undeserved by, her, yet it was obvious that I was becoming more distant and, as time went on, the children would feel it.

It did not help that, apart from Sheril, my other three children were much occupied with their friends, school work, and exams; and, with my pre-occupations, I was having a hard time being left with my wife. To continue without satisfying my emotional needs made the future a grim one.

One of my best friends had died, and the other, a close neighbour, was living with his wife and two children in what seemed a very cold existence. He worked extremely hard to keep everything together, to support and provide a high standard of living for them, and he gave in to every one of their demands. The emotional return for him from his investment, to put it this way, was absolutely minimal, and he was simply the provider.

There were, of course, family pleasures: Sheril and I, and our stamp collection; Michael, the only son, and teaching him chess, so that we could talk about serious matters without his being preached at by his Dad. His lack of ambition or interest in school indicated that he was destined to be a stereotypical teenager, and difficult conversations would ensue in the future. My younger daughters were a complete delight, and doing well.

All my children were my saving grace, but there would come a time, inevitably, when they would leave home, and leave me and my wife together and that thought was becoming unbearable.

It may sound selfish, but I considered that I had a right to a loving relationship, provided that the children would not suffer, and I had recently seen how such a life was possible.

All the time spent on thinking about the future led to some necessary decisions on my part, and, to fit in with my new resolve, around the same time I decided to apply for a post in the Management Services Department, operated by Scotland Yard.

I liked the look of Management Services, as it contained scientists, mathematicians and IT specialists; an Organisation and Methods team, and another for Research and Development; a psychologist; and a number of Inspectors, topped by a Chief Inspector and headed by a Chief Superintendent. The Department had its own computer terminal, and, though contained on one floor of an eight-story block in Vauxhall, it was part of Scotland Yard.

In order to be accepted, there was a battery of tests to complete, comprising the usual educational tests, but also tests new to me then, involving word and non-word based knowledge, and reasoning problems. They were totally unfamiliar at first, but the first few questions were set out helpfully, and became enjoyable once you started to cope. The whole battery was very different to anything I had experienced, even in entering the Navy, and felt challenging. To succeed would feel like a very positive achievement.

Somehow I got through, and I was accepted immediately; though it meant travelling to Vauxhall from Leytonstone, the working conditions, and the social and intellectual mix, were exciting. Its ultimate sponsor was the Commissioner, Sir Robert Mark - a legendary figure, whose main claim to fame was to have cleaned up the corruption in the force's middle ranks. Other sponsors were the next upper echelon, usually Assistant Commissioners, who ordered the studies and kept them under their watchful eye.

Certainly there was the opportunity to shine, but the transparency required involved a great deal of consultation and input by the sponsor and his aides.

I was pleased to find that the Department had some autonomy, deriving from its direct link with the Commissioner; also, that my academic attainment proved of no direct use whatsoever. The projects were very practical, and had force-wide application, and all the skills on offer from the whole staff, including its top officers, were used wherever necessary. Advice was always available whenever sought, and provided clearly and expertly. The atmosphere and ethos of the Management Services Department (MSD) was responsible for its high reputation, maintained by the successes of our projects.

The only difficulty was that the very senior civil servant brought in that organisation's written style, and precise use of the grammatical meant that our telling phrase,and persuasive imagery or examples,were usually blue-pencilled. There were endless arguments over semantics, which spoilt the pleasure of writing a report one had spent months on, so as to present to a sponsor in the way that would be most effective.

The first project I was given was a study into wastage in the Metropolitan Police. It was commissioned by the Commissioner himself, and my function was to assist the psychologist with her report. Not only was my sociological qualification of no interest to her, but it was actually a hindrance. I had to keep my sociological nose well out of what was her business. The study involved questionnaires to be completed to throw light on decisions to leave, and my role was administrative, in getting them back, carefully completed and in proper form. There were initial interviews by my leader, and my rank expedited their completion and return.

We used punch cards, which were sent off to an agency for putting into a program for statistical analysis of the results. This proved unreliable, and too time-consuming, so I put in the data, and we ran our own program on the department's terminal, unconstrained by another programmer or his staff. So often the programmer came to control a project because of his design of the program, and, accordingly, he might override the sponsor's requests by raising difficulties which they would cause for the program.

On one of my programs, I had asked the designer to put in an extra loop to solve a problem; he was first astonished that I could know such a thing, and then aghast at having to do it and to amend his own program.

Compiling the data ourselves from the cards ensured one hundred per cent accuracy, for, firstly, this was an important study into the recruitment and retention of police officers, and, secondly, as a psychological study, it involved original research which would be published in the psychologist's name, and affect her reputation in her field.

We travelled widely to get the material, and the Commissioner himself attended MSD, and discussed the study in our room, with great interest. He then left the building, and, as we caught the lift, we found ourselves alone in the lift with him. His personal charm did nothing to reduce my leader's embarrassment, and as we were walking back to the bridge, his limousine stopped by us, and he leaned out of the window offering us a lift. This was too much for my young colleague, and a stiff drink was called for, as the Commissioner drove off, smiling broadly.

The results of the study were complex, and assessed with statistical probability. When asked at the next promotion board what was the cause of the force's wastage, in a ten minute slot, I took some time to think where to start with an answer that would satisfy my interviewer and be true to the study.

He found my thinking time awkward and odd, since I had been working on the study for months; but then, I was not the person to ask, in my subsidiary role. Since he was renowned for his bluntness and practicality, I felt that he was unimpressed with me because I could not come out with a simple one-line answer. Of course he may have had better-supported candidates, as I was relatively new to my Chief Superintendent, and she knew little of what I had been doing.

The next project involved the problem of getting our traffic prosecutors to court in the Magistrates Courts around London. Punctuality was their byword, and they would remain at court all day, prosecuting. Using their own cars had been sensibly rejected, so they had chauffeurs in the force's cars, but these were then unavailable for other uses. Travelling through traffic at peak hours was not all that faced them, for they then had to find a place to park and bring them back.

A pick up and drop service around the courts, as with other police transport, would not solve the punctuality problem, which could cost them their job.

The obvious solution appeared to me to be to allow them to use taxis, funded by their department. Such a solution would resolve traffic and parking problems, whilst avoiding tying up police drivers and their vehicles, as well as providing flexibility if papers were missing at court, or if the courts were switched.

The prosecutors thoroughly approved of the idea, but the provision of such freedom needed justification in the somewhat bureaucratic environment in which they worked, governed by civil servants. As our department liked cost-benefit analysis, I proceeded on this basis, and produced a compelling and popular argument. The fine tuning of the submission of bills, etc. was left to their supervisors to implement.

It had been most enjoyable to work on a practical project, and to please those most involved. The next I was given was also practical, and involved every police officer, and every police station and its civilian staff. It was to solve difficulties that had bedevilled sergeants particularly. With the advent of administration units, the problem remained, but for our civilian clerks. For the individual officer, too, it was a matter that needed revising.

If overtime was incurred it could be taken as time off or paid. To the officer, the accuracy of its recording and correct disposal was crucial. It could almost be said that the system was not fit for purpose, and I considered changes that were thought almost revolutionary by those who had struggled with it for so long.

The system required one A3 size form, called the 'Duty State', and the time off card, three inches by one inch, on buff card, with boxes to be completed giving the current time in hand. The column was a single figure, arrived at by adding or subtracting time worked or taken off, measured down to quarters of an hour. The mathematical difficulties involved in their addition or subtraction, with other more urgent duties intervening, speaks for the stress and the likelihood of error and of consequent argument.

The cards were filed in any order in trays, were far from ideal in size, colour or design, and created a great deal of time-wasting in the station, when the emphasis was on getting out on the beat.

If it were not for the scale of the foregoing, the problems could have been dismissed as petty, but since they happened in two hundred stations, involving thousands of men and supervising officers, the very scale of even a small improvement was worthy of consideration by an Organisation and Methods section.

The Duty State recorded all the hours and the duty worked by every officer of Chief Inspector rank and below, taking the norm of eight, and then scribbling alongside the time duty ceased. The card had to be completed when there was variation from the norm. They would be taken out from a tray, completed and returned. A return was made for payment.

Separating the overtime from the Duty State led me to the introduction of a single supplementary sheet filed with it and which only dealt with time off. I devised new A4 white cards, which dealt only in whole numbers. Both the 'time off' and 'worked' columns were totalled by addition only: deduction and fractions were a thing of the past.

The supplementary sheets were detached, and worked on away from the front office, where the Duty State was always needed as it was in constant use. The scheme seemed fool-proof, but doubts were expressed by every practitioner over a new system from some 'bright spark' at the Yard, when the old had been with them for decades.

With everything printed, the scheme was introduced at a few stations first, each of which I attended, to sell it, monitor it and consult those who had to use it. Amazed, the clerks took to it like ducks to water. I waited for examples of its impracticality or lack of foresight into some special requirement affecting an individual branch. None was forthcoming, and it was a universal success, though, for some time afterwards, I kept in touch with the clerks to make sure there were no unforeseen problems, or improvements which they had come up with off their own bat.

Certainly I could not complain about my projects so far, and my next was to be even better. My sponsor was the Commissioner, and the task, to prepare a study on the case for tape-recording interviews at police stations. The recipient of the study was to appear before a Parliamentary Committee on the subject, reporting to the full House of Commons, as interviews with defendants had become a widespread press concern.

The present position appeared favourable to the defendant, according to the judiciary and the prosecution, but unfair from the point of view of defence lawyers, and that of public perceptions arising from some of the cases in court or heard on appeal. Defence lawyers argued that the reality of the practice contrasted powerfully with the theoretical and procedure rules set out in the Judges' Rules, amended in 1964.

I began with a critical analysis of the present system, and its possible defects. The Rules provided that there was a duty to answer questions about an investigation; questions could be asked to assist in an investigation, with a duty to answer. The answer given was recorded in the officer's notebook. This could happen on the street, in an officer's car, in the station yard, or in any room at the station.

If arrested, the suspect would be cautioned, and his replies again noted. Only when he was presented to the station officer should the facts of the case be given, and he would then learn what he was being accused of, either in detail, or summarised, as felt necessary to police.

If there had been no admission he would be interviewed, usually by two officers, who had to write down everything he said, but should not ask questions of him. He signed to the effect that the court would be told that he was answering freely and truthfully, and, at the end, he could ask questions or add to his statement. Each page needed to be signed, which established that the statement had been made in accordance with the Rules and was therefore admissible. Special rules should be applied to the mentally ill, and children.

Interviewers were untrained, and were usually the arresting officer, and, often, his partner. The clear purpose of such an interview was to provide prosecution evidence and little, if any, attempt would be made to present any defence. Once there was an admission, the purpose was achieved; there would be no need for further matters unless developing a suspect's admission.

The Rules contained exceptions to the procedure, implying the exercise of good faith, such as: if a procedure was not practicable; where there might be undue delays; where another reasonable arrangement was made; where to follow the rule would allow a hindrance to the investigation; the effect on the prosecution of complying; or, even, proceeding where a caution had not been given. Though this was a mainstay of the procedure, courts, including Crown Courts, would exercise their discretion, and allow admissions where a caution was not given.

Respecting the Rule that officers were not to ask questions, even that was watered down, and an exception permitted to obtain clarity, or clear up ambiguity, or to ask about some other crime committed.

For the unscrupulous, the gate on the restrictions laid down had been opened wide. There was a strong view that matters were too favourable for the defendant, which, according to commentators, led to the inclination to accept the exceptions readily.

Then it was for the defence to argue that the admissions were untruthful, or made unwillingly, or after intimidation, or with the offer of an inducement, etc. The defendant was generally unsupported by tangible evidence.

It was presumed that the defendant recited the whole statement on his own initiative, in his own words, from start to finish, whatever his condition or state of literacy. If important matters in his defence were not stated by him, the assumption made was that he was lying. His accusations would be given little credence in the uneven contest of giving evidence and being cross-examined by a skilled prosecutor.

He was told to sign here, and here, and so on. His scope to disagree, or to add to or change the content afterwards, in the interview room, would be in the hands of the interviewers. It was most rare for a court to accept that officers did proceed by asking questions yet this was completely normal, as was leading or obtaining agreement to facts which only they knew. Subtle inducements were offered for a suspect's co-operation, for example cigarettes, or meals. Sufficient sleep, and the question of fitness for an interview, were matters at the discretion of the police.

Finally, and most importantly, every effort would be made to avoid calling a solicitor, and every exception justified.

In court after court, case after case, these issues were argued at considerable length, the same points being taken in the unequal battle. In the Magistrates Courts 'their' police officers would frequently receive the benefit of any doubt. The Crown Court was much persuaded by apparent compliance with the Rules and by the permitted exceptions, despite the fact that commentators on them had come to regard them as ineffectual.

The word 'verbal' was becoming recognised widely even in judicial circles - when a defendant purportedly made a complete and apparently unsolicited admission before reaching the station officer. Banal examples referred to being 'bang to rights', or that it was 'a fair cop', and reduced the need for further questioning in a formal interview. All that was needed was evidence of it given from the officer's notebook: no other procedural points provided for its admissibility. It cut short an interview and the calling of a solicitor, and prevented the exercise of the right of silence.

A more sophisticated 'verbal' was that in the famous trial of Derek Bentley, which highlighted concern throughout judicial circles, and has increasingly focussed attention on them in the Press. It also provided instances of other unfairness in courts.

Both defendants were convicted for the murder of a police officer in 1952. All in the profession were familiar with that trial, and its unfairness. That such a complicated joint trial for murder was concluded in two and a half days was itself truly remarkable, and indicates the strength of the prejudice held by the judge against the two defendants, and his total support for the police.

The committee would also have been aware that subsequent expert analysis of their interviews indicated re-writing; and they were conducted by questions and answers throughout. Finally, the force of the verbal, 'Let him have it Craig' utterly dominated the trial, despite denials, by both defendants and a witnessing police officer, that it had been said. Even Bentley's own barrister believed him guilty because of it. That the youngster was hanged has only encouraged more debate and criticism. (Later studies have exonerated them and cast doubt on their convictions, focussing on the irregularities and the 'verbal').

Any student of the old procedure, and of what should replace it, could not fail to see the benefits of tape-recordings. The advantages of interviews being tape-recorded could not be gainsaid. They removed many of the objections immediately and persuasively, and were, in principle, the straightforward answer.

Other specific advantages of tape-recorded interviews could ensure requests for solicitors were made on the tape, or assistance for the vulnerable or mentally retarded sought. Any complaint of unfitness, lack of sleep, or oppression could be made during the tape by the defendant, and would be on the record and made contemporaneously. It ensured transparency in the process, in its protection of both sides.

How to deal with a contemporaneous complaint of assault or another impropriety voiced on tape bothered many: wordless intimidation could still occur. To preclude such incidents a visual recording would guarantee total propriety, although an overbearing manner would be apparent on the tape.

On the same subject, visual recording could also negate the 'verbals', if positioned within the precincts of the station, but could not possibly cover any inducement, intimidation or threats. This I discussed as being necessary to provide complete protection for the defendant and the officer (against false accusations).The huge cost of widespread installation of cameras did not find favour at this stage, especially as there were still gaps which such procedure could not close effectively.

In the report's conclusion, the cost of total control was thought prohibitive, in view of the suggested infrequency of such incidents. However, there was to be a trial in the Metropolitan Police area.

The immediate task was the straightforward approval of tape-recording within the police station at a few selected police stations. Highlighting the other problems may have helped to pave the way for oncoming legislation, but my role was practical. It was for those better qualified in the law and practice in court to prevent other abuses, and ensure that evidence be obtained to assist the defence (specifically written into the legislation) as well as the prosecution.

Within a decade, powerful legislation in the shape of the Police and Criminal Evidence Act was to be brought in, with massive changes which not only restricted interviews, but affected all procedures and conduct between police and those processed by them.

I was flattered that my report was regarded as a primary source by the Committee, but had no doubt that the lawyers amongst the Select Committee had considerable expertise, where courts had considered the ineffectuality of the present Rules. In its study, the Committee would have been well aware of decisions on appeal, giving rulings on the conduct of interviews, and the exceptions prayed in aid by Counsel.

From this project arose another related to tape recording, but specifically directed to the transcription of the tapes. It was brought to the attention of the very senior officers that middle rank detectives had to write themselves off duty to transcribe tapes obtained surreptitiously. These were mainly CID officers, in cases where they or their officers were fitted with concealed recorders to eavesdrop or to record conversations with a suspect. Often such procedures occurred in high profile cases, where the recording took place, for instance, in a pub or restaurant, or a deliberately selected spot, to avoid recognition or detection.

The officers that were struck off used domestic tape recorders, writing down all they could hear in the most difficult circumstances, with constant re-winding, often struggling over each word. As with all evidence, its accuracy would determine its admissibility.

The delicacy involved, and the need for confidentiality, required them to transcribe themselves. Something certainly had to be done to remedy this situation.

My task was to devise a tape transcription service to deal with these tapes in a professional, yet confidential manner, and to produce an acceptable result that would satisfy the stringent conditions that would be imposed in judicial proceedings. Since my role was limited to the establishment of a suitable unit, I ensured I had no knowledge of the cases involved, as some would surely have involved disciplinary investigations.

It so happened that I had come across a typing pool at Shooters Hill station, where some twelve or more typists were housed in a very large suite in a comfortable police station. Their supervisor was extremely capable, and frank enough to recognise her staff were under-employed, and morale, as a result, very definitely needed a boost. They were happy in their conditions, car-parking and relations with the police station itself, which made the thought of their being transferred elsewhere most unwelcome.

As may be imagined, it was not long before my return to discuss, and then submit, my report. The unit, in its entirety, became my transcription service, headed by their own supervisor. There were exciting times ahead for all of us, and their notice board told of all their cases which had made the press. In 1974 they started with the important case of John Stonehouse, an MP who had faked his own death, to avoid fraud and other allegations. The enquiry had also involved his position in the House of Commons, and was a very prestigious start for my unit.

It was fitted with a large number of state of the art transcription machines, enclosed in separate booths. Audibility was excellent, and there were controls especially for reducing background noise, as well as for re-winding with consummate ease and efficiency.

Knowing how its customers would behave, and realising as it went on the extreme difficulties which the girls would encounter, I drew up a scheme for its operation. Left to themselves, the CID officers would have dropped in a tape probably directly to one of the girls, and which one could be readily guessed. That would be accompanied by a bunch of flowers or a box of chocolates; probably a bottle occasionally for the supervisor. The staff would be then left to themselves.

That was not going to happen with this unit or this supervisor. After much discussion, the supervisor would allocate the tapes, which would be presented with a summary of the essential features of the case. The roles of the speakers needed particularising, the context where meetings were held, and the names of those involved had to be spelt out.

A liaison officer was to be supplied, so that, if one of the girls had an important query, it could be resolved swiftly. The more help they were given, the better the result. With no lack of enthusiasm on the part of the girls, it was for the police to afford the time and trouble to make the scheme work. Nor was it long after that that prescriptions for sedatives in the area had increased. Or so they teased me.

One small incident brought home the reality of their difficulties, and indicated that there would be ongoing difficulties for the girls which could not have been foreseen. On one visit I found several of the girls in the booth, re-winding a sentence over and over again. They loved a challenge but this was too hard and so I was asked what 'khazi' meant. None had heard that it was slang for lavatory; but this instance indicated that slang, police phrases and even initials – often used in police conversations -as well as criminal jargon, would arise for translation.

Ongoing improvements in practice were always going to be required, hence the necessity for liaison and resolution, preferably by the speaker running quickly through the tape in advance to spot such stumbling blocks. The taking for granted of their work and appreciation of their needs would, I felt, lead to a running down of the service when officers in charge of cases ceased to provide sympathetic but time-consuming assistance.

Such future problems had to be left for others to continue the work, but it had proved an interesting assignment. I heard afterwards that the unit was having problems, but that came as no surprise.

Finally, still on the same subject, I noticed that the passages in our instructions on procedure, and the law on the subject, and on the admissibility of tape recordings and transcripts, were quite fragmented and unclear. Use in court was by no means easy, as it was all new to judges, magistrates and the lawyers. I compiled a handout for use, which put together all the instructions and legal issues to make sense of it all, and improve the use of the new technology.

Instructions have proliferated for tape-recording and for visual technology, which now features in just about every case in the courts.

My final project looked to be a real challenge. It stemmed from one of the Assistant Commissioners who was ultimately responsible for the manning of the divisions' complements of uniformed officers. In particular, there was an excess of officers left over from the training school's allocation of recruits throughout the Met. Their disposal was at the root of the project. I was asked to help our Research and Development manager, though it was very much his baby.

Some hundreds were allocated to the four districts into which the Met was divided; from that allocation the divisional Commanders received their quota, which was distributed by him, either on his own initiative or as advised by his subordinates, to his sub-divisions. The criteria were not made plain, and were probably considered a local matter. This prevented me, certainly, from knowing much of the thinking behind the proposal, other than the ideas brought back by my manager. The reasons for the postings from the training school, or the local postings, may, again, not have been considered to fall within my manager's remit. Yet this was, for him, the heart of the project. Simply put, the project was based on the concept that the busiest stations needed the lion's share of available resources.

If the project came up with an answer, it would provide a scientific and objective basis for another allocation of mobile resources, in the shape of the Special Patrol Group, a large unit with numerous transit vehicles, each of which were equipped with eight PCs and a Sergeant and were under the control of an Inspector.

They were utilised as and when thought to be required, regularly on public order duties; but when available, they would tackle local problems on division such as burglary, drugs, motor vehicle crime, etc.

Again, I had no knowledge of what the deciding factors were, or even who decided on their deployment, but there could come a time when such decisions were put on an objective basis, depending on our progress. The resolution of such decisions, I considered, would be as a result of intuition in what might be a bidding process between senior officers. It would be true to expect that results on divisions affected would improve their prospects. Comparisons may be odious, but reputations can be created by statistics.

Whilst, as stated, my understanding was that these processes were based on experience on the ground, no evidence was forthcoming from my manager to the contrary.It may well have been that subordinate officers, or civil servants in the branch would have used crime figures, etc., to justify arguments over allocations.

It was hoped that our project would introduce a scientific and objective basis for the deployment of substantial units of additional police strength.

The project therefore begged two questions. Firstly, how to measure which were the busiest stations - the statistical factor. Secondly, was it right to divide the work by the number of officers doing it, so that it could be regarded as their workload factor? Man-management considerations held that the share of work should be equalised as far as possible, and provided further support for the desirability of the project.

Obtaining all the figures for the output of stations showed that Kilburn and Deptford were the outstanding achievers. These two stations were off the scale compared with every other station in the Met, and I remember that Kilburn accomplished this position with forty-nine officers. So the second question, at that stage, did take into account the number of officers who had produced the work. My manager had satisfied his man-management concern, which indicated, to those in charge of resources, where to put extra men.

This could have been the end of the project, and would have led to objective assessments. However, we were concerned that the tool of totalling crimes, for instance, did not reflect the 'quality' of the crime. Theft of milk, a newspaper, minor shoplifting, and arrests for prostitution, to cite a few examples, gave the impression that the busiest stations were in the West End, and that they deserved the most officers. That was the opinion of most of the officers who were asked.

Areas where vagrants were prevalent, or which contained cheap and poorly run shops, for instance, would further swell the figures for crime. Could such figures be validly compared with the work regularly involved in other areas dealing with high quality thefts, valuable housebreakings, smash and grabs, gang activity, frauds, or public disorder and violence, to name just a few?

Similarly, we had taken into account traffic accidents in different areas, but the same problem arose where an area included major roadways and multiple vehicle crashes.

On what basis could a realistic assessment possibly be made, since major multi-vehicle crashes affected a number of officers on various necessary duties, re-routing, reporting, and removal of vehicles and obtaining evidence? The more we looked at a qualitative breakdown, the greater the complications.

There would be considerable divergences of opinion involved, and there was a subjective element, to complicate matters further. Our efforts over what appeared insuperable difficulties felt overwhelming. So theoretical were its possibilities, and so complicated its unintended consequences, that we achieved only a partial result, a host of figures, and, maybe, food for future thought.

With the few resources at its disposal, and the vast amount of complications, as well as its potential size, refinement of the study would have to wait, since two of us had been selected for promotion. Being selected for the Branch had paid off, and we were to be transferred. My destiny was Holborn, as their Chief Inspector, and a complete sea change in this and my next life lay ahead.

Chapter 10
Back to Police duty at Holborn as Chief Inspector

Promotion to Chief Inspector required a successful interview and the fact that I succeeded was, for me, a most pleasing outcome. Previous promotions were by competitive examinations, which allowed me to forecast how long it would take to get to Inspector, the first officer rank in the police.

I found interviews difficult, and I had little confidence that I could handle police interviews in particular. Senior officers seemed to require a tough, positive and immediate response from the candidate, who was almost pre-selected by his superiors. On this occasion I had received strong backing from my Chief Superintendent, but on a number of issues my views were sometimes controversial, and this type of interview did not suit a thoughtful answer.

The previous board provided an instance of this. The question put was that of whether women officers should patrol the streets and act in a similar way to their male counterparts. I answered that having had the same training, and being paid the same rate, at a time when a women's capabilities were being recognised without discrimination, I was in favour, generally, of such equality. The Board appeared horrified.

I tried to add that there were situations in which the approach of a capable female would not provoke the aggression brought about by a forceful approach by a male officer, which often led to avoidable violence and confrontation. I did not get as far as developing this, by pointing to the number of arrests for assault on police, or of obstructing police, that often follows the male approach. Women attract respect, and have other weapons to

160

mollify or talk down, with charm if applicable, so as to defuse such situations, gaining support from other males in altercations.

I had in mind my experience as court inspector in Stoke Newington, when the lay bench stated in open court that they would not entertain any more charges from a particular officer, which always contained an assault on him in the execution of his duty, where the only person with facial injuries and the usual black eye was the 'offender'. They noted that this always contrasted with the unmarked face of the arresting officer.

My thought processes were possibly too complicated and controversial for many senior officers. A short-term practical approach did not suit every problem, and one problem about which kept my views to myself, unless I felt that I was in enlightened company, was the 'war on drugs'. I often needed time to develop my argument, but, in many situations, hostile attitudes did not permit it.

When I met my new Commander, the fact that I had served at Management Services gave me little encouragement for my future under him. Added to that, my degree did not help, and the fact that it was in Sociology convinced me that I was in for a hard time. My predecessor at Holborn was very much like the Commander, and with the Detective Chief Inspector, they made a solid team supervising the sub-division. By outlook, approach, habits and socialising, I was not accepted into this circle. My place was in the office, I felt.

This became apparent quite soon when I went through the books in the front office which dealt with the operational side of my duties, as opposed to the other part, running the Administration unit. Immediately I noticed a huge file in the Missing Persons folder, one case being well over a year old and which had been updated with the need for further enquiries, specific steps to be taken and checks made. These entries had been countersigned by every senior officer, (including Inspectors) and all further countersigned by the Commander.

In my experience this was most unusual so I dug into it, starting with the first entry. The person missing had disappeared at night, was well into her sixties, absent minded and quite frail. When reporting her missing from home, her husband described her closely, and added that she had been wearing night clothes, but had had no shoes or anything on her feet; and yet it was a cold night. Other than this there was no clue as to her whereabouts, and every enquiry yielded no result.

It seemed beyond belief that she had not come to notice at a very early stage, given this description, so I rang the Missing Persons department at the Yard, and had a long conversation with a very able and sympathetic member of staff. I asked her to make a thorough search for any person admitted to hospital that night, taken in at any refuge or institution for the homeless.

I got the answer the next day that a person of that description had been admitted to hospital suffering from loss of memory. On ringing the hospital, it transpired that she was still there, and in the same ward.

I contacted her husband, and sent a fast car to the hospital, where he identified her and took her home. I wrote the result up in the Missing Persons book, and thanked the department at the Yard for their help. Their delight (and possible relief at the lack of any comeback or press interest) evoked a huge thank you (and the promise of a bottle or two).

The point of this story is not to claim credit for myself, nor to point up the need, on occasions, for a fresh pair of eyes on longstanding or historical crimes or incidents. That, then, was not a process adopted, and officers in such cases would have resented such reviews of their case.

When my Commander found out the result, when he next inspected the Missing Persons book, he called me over, and asked me what was I doing going through the Missing Persons book. He went on to reprimand me, his view being that that was not my job. That was not the reaction which either I, or anyone else in my position, would have expected. My flabber was most definitely gasted!

There was more to follow later, leading to important changes career-wise and, indeed, significant personal decisions as to my future.

Whereas nobody seemed to have heard of Leman Street, everyone knew of Holborn, and it was to become my second home. Any national rail user would have trudged along our northern border between Euston, St Pancras and Kings Cross stations. The border with the West End and Soho would be well known to any theatre goer or tourist, as it made its way from Tottenham Court Road, through St Martin's Lane, and down to Trafalgar Square.

From there, the tourists would mix with the sharp-suited barristers, solicitors and judges frequenting the High Court and other important legal buildings in the Strand, continuing into Fleet Street, stopping at Farringdon Road close to the Old Bailey, the central criminal court in the country. Turning at Farringdon Street, on the way back to Kings Cross, one would encounter the gold dealers and members of the jewellery trade, recognisable from their ethnic mode of dress and religion. This whole district around Hatton Garden was devoted to this trade, with its tiny workshops, high security and kosher eating places.

Tube travellers would crowd the Piccadilly and Central Line stations through the centre: roads like Chancery Lane (solicitors and silversmiths), and Gray's Inn Road, with the adjoining squares of Lincoln's Inn and Gray's Inn reinforcing their legal history as two of the four Inns of Court. Both were totally occupied by barristers' chambers, and the legal libraries and dining halls that serviced them. Yet this occupied the south side. Diametrically opposite, however, around Kings Cross, were the brothel-ridden hotels of Argyle Square and drug-dealers and abusers, with prostitutes in droves crowding the pavements of each of its dark and grubby streets.

I doubt if any area of the size of Holborn had so many disparate, prestigious buildings: hospitals, universities and academic centres of learning (my own LSE), museums, and the registered offices of leading insurance and massive commercial institutions. With all its history, it kept up to date with all the 'new' music, as well as jazz and traditional music, supplying the best instruments and sheet music for any connoisseur or artiste.

Known as Tin Pan Alley, this street was just off Charing Cross Road, a border we watched constantly to avoid the growth of the pornography industry and the proliferation of its book shops.

I dealt routinely with the administration at the station run by a well organised and competent staff, thanks to my predecessor. He had become more interested and involved in other duties, once he had set up a firm base for the unit. This was run by his deputy with the lightest of touches. One of his main concerns was the operation of a well-staffed team for vice. He had a keen eye on all licensing matters and liaised generally on crime patterns with the Detective Chief Inspector, with a special interest in Hatton Garden.

His deputy, Ron, was well versed in these operational duties, knew each licensed premises and their licensees, and he became my right hand man, too. He kept a close eye on developments in the Charing Cross Road, and we were able to shut down the bookshops as soon as they materialised, by seizing all their books and paraphernalia.

We had our first student sit-in near Russell Square, but, with a heavy police presence it fizzled out, and was nothing compared with the student demonstrations at the LSE. The flower power I was greeted with on leaving university - i.e. presented with flowers on the street in uniform - had given way to a more confrontational radicalism and a variety of marches and demonstrations, for many different causes were initiated and organised at Holborn.

The Queen's Jubilee walk-about in 1977 was our biggest public order event to organise, but it went off without the slightest difficulty. Our main problems were the marches through the West End to Kensington by protesters from the Middle East, and often, mainly, Iran, as we were told by the organisers who saw me at the station to make arrangements. Unfortunately, we only saw them once, to complete the application and to make the arrangements over routes and dealing with the opposition. On the day of the march someone else would take over, and insist on changes to all the matters upon which I had agreed. This was the usual pattern and a strategy was devised, since each demonstration followed the same pattern.

Picking my two fittest and most experienced and positive officers, they led the march from the front, and physically escorted them swiftly and directly through the shortest route at something close to a trot. It was not long before applications for such marches were not made to Holborn, and other routes were used.

I took over the vice and licensing work, since it was my name that went on the charge sheet as the arresting officer.

Reading the papers in advance, assessing the evidence and making the arrest was not without its challenges, as inevitably the success of the prosecution at the Magistrates court was in my hands. Once all the material had been obtained, and the case properly presented, only one defendant failed to plead guilty - an achievement that went without notice.

Since the kudos appeared to be mine from the records, it was appropriate that I had to play my part. My unit came to learn of a particularly cunning brothel manager who had been operating with impunity in the heart of a very respectable part of Holborn. The difficulty was gaining access, but we were determined to catch her and to maintain our record. The stigma attached to such an allegation against a woman of her skill, acumen and untouchable respectability led to my role in gaining entry.

I did manage to gain entry, in mufti (appropriate attire, again inherited from the Redpole) to such an extent that she pursued me down the corridor to her bedroom coaxing me with her whip for an incredibly expensive bondage session. Demurring successfully, I was able to get out without injury – I think the lack of funds did the trick - and she pleaded guilty once we went through the formalities.

With the small sleazy hotels in Argyle Square, the evidence of entry was obtained by our observations, ensuring that the keeper was on the premises and knew what was happening with the client, who was caught in bed with one of her girls. Such cases were very straightforward, and again all were convicted, except one.

In that case our unit took on a new sergeant, new to vice work, but with very considerable police experience. In court, giving his evidence, he had to identify the brothel-keeper on the premises when the clients were with the girls. This seemed straightforward, though she had pleaded not guilty. My sergeant was challenged on his identification of the keeper, and, producing his notebook, gave her description. The bench asked him if he were saying that the woman he had spoken to was supposed to be the woman in the dock.

As I looked at her, I could see that the description was utterly wrong, but he would not admit any mistake, and blustered that it was the same. There was no chance of anything other than her acquittal and a total loss of face (and trust by the bench) so the case against her was withdrawn for lack of evidence. At least the award of costs against police was averted, with her solicitor's assent. He never explained how this had come about, and still tried to insist he had not made any mistake. Nevertheless, our unit's one hundred per cent record was spoilt.

The unit continued, but had the odd situation that, in successive weeks, the same client was found in two hotels with a girl, in cases that we brought to court. His remarks to the police involved no shame; he had experienced extreme bad luck, but no recurring impotence as a result of entertaining a uniformed police audience for the second time in a matter of a few weeks.

I was pleased with the staff I inherited, and operated the unit with the same light touch as had my predecessor. Terry was my enquiry officer, which he combined with teaching first aid - compulsory for all officers. He had a special technique – to stand behind the examining doctor as he asked his questions and if the officer was unsure Terry would, with a subtle hand movement, give a hint as to the correct answer, e.g., which sling was to be used. His final duty was to run the property store, which contained prisoners' property, property found in the street or in recovered cars, all of which was held until restored or sold in auction.

Prisoners' property was held until the case to which it referred came to court, and was then taken and produced as evidence. Failure to deal with it properly and get it to court with the arresting officer could lead to the loss of the case with no evidence offered. It still had to be either restored to the loser, or dealt with at auction. The property return was one of the most important indices of the efficiency of a police station, and this rested on the shoulders of the Admin. Chief Inspector.

As with most of my staff, they had all received lukewarm annual reports, describing them as competent and satisfactory, listed in a few sparse lines and ticks in boxes. The exception was Ron, the deputy to the old Chief Inspector, with his useful knowledge especially of our neighbour, West End Central's, licensed clubs. He was very popular and universally respected, a man whom I very much liked.

The reports were compiled and sent through the Chief Superintendent to the Commander. Being matter of fact, they received a cursory scan, and said very little of the individual. The preparation of the staff Annual Quality Reports was not one that seemed to require a great deal of time or care in preparation, or even enquiries about the clerk in question.

The clerk in charge of overtime and time off was another modest, competent and conscientious officer, who would never bring himself to notice, but went quietly and carefully about his task.

What brought him to my notice was the pattern of his own holidays. With the allocation of twenty-eight days, plus Bank Holidays, weekends and overtime taken off, he managed a large number of weekly holidays. When I inspected his application I noted with great interest that he was holidaying around the world in one exotic place after another. The most frequent venues were South America and the USA, but he also managed to take shorter holidays in interesting parts of Europe and the UK. After chatting with him about himself and any hobbies he had he mentioned that he 'was into dogs', visiting dog shows around the world.

I was a dog lover myself, and when I drew Peter out, as it seemed no one else had, his particular favourite was the Miniature Schnauzer, of which I knew nothing. It was not long before he brought in a pup to show me, tucked in his jacket pocket. We all fell in love with this pup, which was the cutest I had ever seen, and which was clearly the reason why this was the central interest in his life, as I found out as we talked more.

I could not take my eyes off the puppy and was totally fascinated by it, but clearly I would have to prove myself fit to own and care for one before I would be allowed to discuss ownership. Our early conversations revealed he was one of the country's leading breeders, was a world-wide authority on the breed, and was asked to judge them in the most prestigious dog shows around the world where this breed competed. To say that he was world-renowned for his activities, expertise and handbook on the breed, and its major development in the USA through breeding, was no exaggeration.

I mentioned this in his Annual Quality Report, and it astonished all who read it; he became something of a celebrity.

No longer was Peter the faceless, nameless clerk who looked after the time off cards at Holborn police station, but someone to be looked up to, even by the Commander. His self-effacement did not change, and I had fortunately not been responsible for anything other than the esteem in which he was now held.

*Figure 8. Pat and Gary on our first holiday
in Tenerife.*

Figure 7. Both of us at Madeira, for a change

Figure 10. Our wedding at Barnet, 1980

Figure 9. Dressed in white tie for my call to the Bar and a magnificent dinner in Gray's Inn, 1981.

Figure 11. Taken outside 'Sandrevin', Bernard and Molly's hotel in Exmouth on holiday in 1981. I was the brother (step) Molly never had until her mother married Pop. Bernard was also a Metropolitan Police Officer before retiring to become owner of a small hotel

Figure 13. Left to right, Sheril, Maria and Sue get together for the wedding in Wales, circa 1984.

Figure 12. Altogether, with Michael and joined by Katherine, so she gets to spend some time with Sheril,

Chapter 11
"I am going to get into trouble with this Young Lady"

It was at this time that I received a call from a young lady who was running the social club of the Ear, Nose and Throat Hospital in Gray's Inn Road. She wanted to obtain a licence to provide a full bar in the club, and was seeking advice before making an application. We chatted on the phone, and I suggested that I should visit the club, look around, and foresee any difficulties or problems that might arise. It is better, certainly, with any form of licensed premises, to get everything right first time, than to encounter problems that could have been anticipated, and which can breach the law and its regulations.

More informally, those who use the premises need to control their own behaviour, noise, and generally act without offence or exuberance, protecting the licensee, who takes the risk, and who is totally responsible for the conduct of the premises, and of the customers in and around the premises.

So Ron and I visited, and inspected the proposed site from every standpoint, bringing to bear all our legal, local and general knowledge from many years, to make sure that the club would operate successfully, giving us and the licensee no problems.

We spent a long time on this first visit, not least because Pat, the would-be licensee, made a distinct impression on both of us with her looks, character, poise and maturity. As we walked behind her from the site, I remember saying to Ron that I was going to get into serious trouble with this young lady. He has since confirmed that this is exactly what I said on first sight; and this was before we had discussed her proposal. That this was prophetic was a huge understatement.

Pat was the supervisor on the telephone exchange at the hospital, and, even from our first visit, it was obvious she had gained the respect of all those whom we passed and with whom she exchanged words. These included top consultants, registrars, the office staff, and everyone down to drivers and kitchen staff. It was readily apparent that this was indeed a very special lady.

I was very much looking forward to her return from a holiday which she was about to embark on, and hoping that the early indications I had received of what seemed to be her interest in myself would be unaffected by it.

In the meantime, work went on, as did life at home. Now my eldest were teenagers, immersed in studies, romantic liaisons and career choices.

The next problem to be sorted out was a troublesome licensed premises, just our side of Charing Cross Road. Tucked away in a quiet backstreet, it was off the beaten track of patrolling officers; but suddenly, it became almost a criminal hot spot on its own, with very late opening, wholesale damage to vehicles parked around the nearby streets, and rowdy and drunken behaviour by young drinkers in large numbers. Local residents required strong action, as their lives and property were being seriously affected.

A check of the details of the licensee and staff indicated that they had criminal records, and were not the approved licensees; there were suggestions of indecent behaviour and offences associated with the staff, widespread breaches of the closing hours, and drunken behaviour inside the club, as well as on the streets and pavements outside. We raided the premises, and closed them down without delay.

Our local Magistrates court was called Clerkenwell Magistrates court and was, like the other courts, both a remand court and a trial court. Attending a remand court with one's cases was something of an ordeal. The stipendiary magistrates there (those with a professional background as barristers, unlike the lay justices) always seemed more difficult than at any other court. My impression was of a disposition to bullying from one, unpleasantness and nit-picking by another, and, from the third, a tendency to remoteness, with a tone implying little knowledge or appreciation of the life style of those who appeared before him.

It must be accepted, of course, that ensuring precision and overall competence from the police officers was a proper task for these courts. Standards were upheld, fairness maintained, and regular procedures known off by heart. The Magistrates Courts were familiar to the officers attending, and they expected to find a friendly tribunal, where they would generally get a just result and favourable treatment. It is right to say that the results of the proceedings were mostly unassailable, otherwise they would all have been appealed. It was the manner of getting there that was unattractive.

This particular triumvirate appeared to have set themselves the task of forever criticising and correcting the uniformed branch, to such an extent that, when we brought in some twenty prostitutes for soliciting outside the Wimpy bar opposite Kings Cross station, they were treated with charm and something close to flirtation, whilst the arresting officers met with disdain and unspoken hostility.

This contrast was not infrequently the case, but, on this occasion, it was the sheer numbers that made the occasion memorable. If those judging had had to make their way, with their families, through a large group of prostitutes actively engaged in soliciting outside the Wimpy bar - the usual haunt - and other shops, in a busy thoroughfare, with travellers also using the station opposite, they would have approved of police efforts to avoid these scenes.

Their cases had to be remanded for further steps to be taken, papers served, and pleas taken: those who had pleaded guilty were sentenced after receiving their probation reports, if required. The courts teemed with all manner of persons, all involved with their own cases, jumping the queue, and there was much giving and taking of advice, all at loud whispers, with the court staff being hurried on by the magistrates and their clerks. Mostly all the cases were dealt with, as far as possible, in each session.

Whilst the emphasis had to be on alacrity, one could see many a first time defendant sitting bewildered at the pace and brusqueness with which they were treated.

To an impartial observer, the meting out of justice seemed to be lacking, and rudeness was often encountered, as well as, frequently, a lack of patience or consideration. Sometimes an advocate would be deterred from making an application for bail or for a longer style of hearing just by the presence of one particular magistrate. Regular users of the court anticipated which decisions could readily be expected before the hearing; or which orders sought, e.g., for a defendant to be bound over avoiding a conviction.

Solicitors and barristers were regularly exasperated and put down in court, despite their competence and experience, so it became a real pleasure for a high-flown barrister, occasionally a QC, to be engaged in initial proceedings in an important case duelling with one of our more difficult magistrates. For those so minded, it was a learning experience, and where such contests took place the court was full of watching advocates, keen to learn how far to go with a difficult magistrate and yet be successful with their advocacy. At least if they were not asking for more time they stood a chance. Skilful bail applications, or difficult mitigation to sentencing, were huge learning opportunities in the lower courts.

It is only right to say that, in some courts, the magistrates operated differently, with dry humour, kindness and extended help to those who clearly needed it. It was obvious in such courts that the magistrates knew their clientele, their history and problems, and what they had been told, or warned about, on previous occasions at that court. They would usually start with the drunks, prostitutes, and beggars, and progress into the more serious cases, but it was not uncommon for a defendant entering the dock to be asked how he was, and how he was getting on with such and such a problem, etc.

That was unheard of in our courts, in my experience, and it was a real pleasure to hear justice dispensed before the public to its customers, however unworthy they may have been thought. I was full of admiration for such magistrates, and it was a pleasure to come before them and give some helpful evidence, or sound mitigation, in the defendant's favour.

The moment I had been waiting for arrived, when I was told that someone from the hospital was downstairs, to see me about a licence. To ask whether it was a young lady was tempting, but revealing. We went to my office and talked about the licence, perfunctorily, but we had eyes for each other, and we both realised that this was to test our feelings and the possibility of a relationship.

We would meet up locally in the park, or for a lunch, and the matter of the licence was not pursued, as the hospital had only floated the suggestion as a possibility, without realising the complications.

It was not long before we went on a date; I was invited to her flat next to Alexandra Park, and met Gary, her seven-year-old son from her first marriage. If she would have me, I had found the perfect mate; she felt the same way, and we were now a couple with a long-term future in mind.

Of course I was still married with four children, three of them grown up, and all living in a police house. I would have to leave my wife and family in the house, and live with Pat and Gary in her flat. There would never be such an opportunity for a full and happy life with an ideal partner, but there were going to be heart-breaking times ahead, and enormous difficulties put in our way, by the force and some of its senior officers.

From the family's situation, things could have been worse, as my son and second daughter were about to get married and leave home: both were independent. My wife stayed in the house in London with the others, the youngest at school, and the eldest also in a fairly strong relationship; but since she did not intend

177

ever to have children, she would not be so settled as the others, but would remain with her mother, unless I could persuade her (and her mother) to let me see more of her. Whilst that happened a few times, leaving after a short day-long visit was torture for both of us, and it was best avoided so that she could get on with her own life less painfully.

My son Michael wasted his time at school, and his school career came to an end with no qualifications whatsoever. I remember that we sat at the table and discussed what he should do, and started by deciding whether he was any good at anything, or particularly enjoyed any activity that could lead to a career. This may sound insulting, but realism was called for, and, despite the fact that we sat in silence for quite some time, it proved productive.

I remember that he had tried baking at home, weighing and labelling each ingredient in a small separate container in a most organised fashion, and finally produced a virtually professional cake as a treat. He liked the idea of cooking, his grandfather was a cook and baker, and so we took steps to enrol him at Westminster Catering College. It proved difficult to sustain a college course, so the college offered him a course partly at college, and partly working at a hotel. He was fortunate to be placed at the Selfridge Hotel in Oxford Street. The pay was good, and he managed to stick to it.

His proudest moment was receiving his first certificate, and he was the more easily able to get his second; with talent recognised by his head chef, he was set up for a career.

Sue, my second daughter, and her boyfriend, had made up their minds to get married, and work in Germany, to raise enough money to live in Canada, and that plan came about. The family split, but Michael and Sue remained broadly as my supporters, though, as it turned out, I saw little of them. My long term destiny was with Pat and Gary, in a relationship that was as perfect as could be.

Leaving a marriage that had lasted over twenty years, and with four children, was a monumental decision that required as much certainty as could be mustered. We had known each other for so little time, and yet the step had to be taken, or the opportunity lost. The marriage was irreparable, and had no future.

We planned a holiday together in Tenerife, a favourite place for Pat. This would determine whether we did have a future together, and the decisions taken, with all those involved, were neither capricious nor unrealistic, especially as I was fifteen years older than Pat. They had to be founded on a deep love, total compatibility, and trust, to provide both of us with a life-long commitment and marriage. We even went to various functions together, to cement this compatibility and gain further reassurance. All was confirmed by our holiday, and we have never looked back. (It was not for many years that my children agreed that it was the best decision I had ever made.)

As I have mentioned before, police officers had to register their addresses, and have them approved. I notified my superiors that I wished to reside with Pat at her address.

I was called to see the Commander, who then gave me a lecture on showing the sort of self-discipline that a Chief Inspector needed, and said that I should stay with my wife. There were times when he couldn't stand his wife, but he had the self-discipline to stay and behave properly, as a senior officer. Affairs were not unknown, and could be conducted clandestinely, but someone of my rank did not leave his wife. The fact that I would be seeking a divorce, and marrying Pat, was dismissed out of hand. The upshot was that my request was not allowed.

I would have to live with my wife in the house and that was that. Whilst we had a caravan in the garden at Leytonstone, this came up as a suggestion. Not only was this unthinkable for me, but, foreseeing the reaction of my wife, and her opportunity to wreck the potential relationship with Pat, it was a complete insult to Pat and to our future together. I turned it down, and went to live with her, being classed as of no fixed abode, according to the police record.

The next skirmish I had with the Commander would have been ludicrous, except for the manner in which he conducted it. He had called for officers' time off cards, and when Peter sent mine up, it was full, so he had put, on the top, a fresh unused card. The Commander accused me of trying to deceive him with a blank card, and had his deputy sitting alongside as he interrogated me. The interview had the feel of a formal disciplinary enquiry, but his deputy was especially dismissive of any allegation of deception, and that matter never progressed.

It indicated that I was the subject of something of a witch-hunt, and that was soon confirmed when my Chief Superintendent kept coming up with jobs for me to take, well away from him, Holborn and the Commander. Apparently he was constantly at war over me, though other senior officers were uncritical, though they were not openly supportive, so as not to upset the Commander. My own Chief Superintendent was not a very strong leader, and was suffering under the constant pressure from his very tough Commander.

I felt that anything I did was subject to criticism, and though my personal life was all I had hoped for, I was getting as low as I could be, with pressure all round. My determination to carry on with a regular, natural, and open relationship with Pat was a commitment for all to see – this was not an affair to be hidden or maintained in secret. She deserved better.

The last straw came with an allegation that I had stolen money from the marital home. This was an official complaint made to the Commissioner by my wife, who had added that it had occurred at a time when I was not providing any funds to maintain her and the family. That was unjustified, as she was getting all that I had.

The truth of the matter was that I had rescued my coin collection from the house, from a well justified fear that it would continue gradually to be depleted, as had been happening for some weeks.

Shortly afterwards, a Detective Chief Superintendent arrived with his assistant at our flat to search it, and both of us, for stolen property. I knew them both well, but the embarrassment was as nothing when compared with the physical search of our property, and indeed ourselves, in pursuance of this false and deliberately wicked complaint. The fact that I was residing without permission at the address was noted but not pursued, there being some sympathy, I believe, at the situation in which I had been placed.

I do not doubt that this all went on my record, but in what terms, other than (probably) as being unsubstantiated, I was never to find out. It would not have made pleasant reading.

Since it was obviously malicious, it did not further worsen my morale, which was still at its lowest, until the arrival of a new Chief Superintendent.

Chapter 12
Farewell to the Fuzz – the Bar beckons

With one word the new Chief Superintendent was able to boost my morale. When he first arrived we had a long conversation about Holborn, his expectations, and my domestic situation. He told me that he had been in the same situation himself, and understood how difficult it could all be. He asked the name of my 'paramour'. That was the word.

It signified a total acceptance of my relationship with Pat, and that it was to lead to marriage, rather than an affair. He was happy with the situation, and continued to refer to Pat as my partner openly, and in a friendly and supportive manner. I did not doubt that with his firm and fair stewardship of Holborn, I would receive his support in dealings with the Commander.

I was soon back to my usual self, and worked well with him, earning his trust and appreciation. My style of management was not all hustle and bustle, forever clutching a sheaf of papers and making much of the tasks given, functioning instead without fuss or confrontation, and getting the desired results unobtrusively. My prosecutions, apart from that mentioned previously, all succeeded uncontested, as did the closure of the bookshops and the licensed premises which were in breach of licensing law. The administration unit and front office functioned with their usual efficiency, and my new boss was well pleased.

My next task there was to school four of our young sergeants who had passed the examination, and were candidates for the Special course at the Police College. I was to coach them in a week long course to pass the interviews, which were extremely strict and testing. Two of them were strong candidates, but the other two were not sufficiently outstanding to make it. At least I got two out of four through and onto the course from our division.

Having stayed with Pat at her flat for some months, we then started to look to buy a house. We found an ideal property in the Whetstone area, which we loved straightaway, just by walking through the living room and looking out onto a lovely garden. For a London house, it was a huge garden, and it had belonged to a gardener, so it was in good shape, with many plants and fine shrubs. We were well pleased, but still said we should at least look upstairs. We agreed his price without hesitation. Though the seller's chain broke down, some months later he rang me again and asked us whether we still wanted the house, as we had not quibbled over the asking price, and would get the first offer. Indeed, we did, and bought it at exactly the same price. Our status as a couple was now utterly beyond doubt, and we knew from our first holiday (pictured below) that we were meant for each other, and could get married when free. We married at Barnet in 1980, and, after a year, our first daughter Katherine was born in April 1981 (see later).

The holiday was particularly memorable for two events, neither of which Pat was able to catch on camera, to my disappointment, as it was my first trip abroad, and we threw ourselves into everything on offer. The first was on a cruise in a galleon around the coast, where we stopped off for a swim. In the circumstances, I performed my best swallow dive from the deck, high above the sea, and, surfacing, found that she had totally missed it, so I got my rightful comeuppance.

The second was more disappointing, for, on an organised trip out to a mock-bullfight our table, which contained a group from Liverpool, all volunteered to fight the young bulls. I was dragged in too and soon we stood in the arena waiting for the young bull, expecting something the size of a St Bernard dog.

Not so. The bull was the same height and size as a full-grown bull, with the same horns, but a little slimmer. The group promptly leapt the fence, and disappeared. I was left, given a red flag, and faced the beast. I managed a few passes, greeted with applause, but, on the last, the bull caught the flag on a horn, and stood looking menacingly at me. I ran, and he chased me; and as I ran, I remembered something I had heard: that bulls are very quick running in a straight line, but not if they have to dodge or zigzag. I zigzagged for all I was worth, and just made it to the barrier, a yard before the bull sank his horns in the other side.

When I got back to Pat and Gary they were still practically crying with laughter, missing the point that this had all got a bit serious. Of course neither of them had taken a photograph between them. Whilst it would have been most unflattering, it would have shown that for one night I had acted as a matador, for the attendants had been armed with swords to rescue other volunteers, and were taking it very seriously, as my friends from Liverpool had recognised instantly.

The only memorable event that occurred during this period, whilst still at Holborn, concerned a member of the public known as Jimmy, who then would have been described as a dwarf. He was a complete nuisance, and had, for years, been allowed to direct the traffic at the junction of Hatton Garden and the Clerkenwell Road. He was part of the scenery, and tolerated by all, although his efforts would cause mayhem for the traders.

On this particular occasion, he came to Holborn and stood at the front office, where I was checking the books. He was utterly rude and arrogant, and thought he was untouchable by any of my officers. Since he was being totally objectionable in his language and behaviour, in the front office of a police station, attended by members of the public, I had to have a word with him. He launched himself at me, and started kicking me violently in the leg.

I was about to arrest him, as I would have arrested anyone else, when I imagined the Press getting hold of and publishing the story of this diminutive member of the public, who was allowed to assist police, being manhandled by a Chief Inspector. The prospect for ridicule was all too apparent, and I could imagine what my Commander would have made of it, since, in his many visits to Hatton Garden, he would have been well acquainted with Jimmy. Discretion was the better part of valour.

The intensity of his kicking certainly would have deserved the description of valour on my part. However, his arrest, and any attempt at containment short of formal arrest, would have needed several officers, each of whom he would have assaulted. Containment is the most difficult option for officers, especially given some vulnerability on the part of the contained; and viewing members of the public can be guaranteed to present a critical view of police action.

My new boss was soon transferred back to the Yard, for which I had guessed he was earmarked, and another arrived in his place. He was a very experienced officer, his main virtue being his firmness, laced with humour and pragmatism. He would certainly be able to stand up to the Commander, but in a conciliatory way, with an eye on his own future, as he could be transferred to far worse stations than Holborn, should he incur the latter's wrath. I also got on well with him, and things were now becoming comfortable at work and at home, the prospect of which was becoming more certain.

I well remember a social occasion, to which most of the senior officers were invited, at the Catholic Church, opposite Hatton Garden. I took Pat, as it was for a special dinner for the priests at all the London prisons. The food was voluminous, quite delicious, and the starter was three large portions of lasagne; the rest of the meal was on the same scale.

It was memorable for the jokes and stories that were told that, being from the priests' working environment, were mostly scandalous, hilarious, and so unbelievably rude that we were all in tears. The second memorable part was seeing my new boss riding up and down in the lift with an angelic smile on his face, and in a daze as to what was going on or even where he was. After a large number of ascents and descents we rescued him, and got him into his car. It was an unforgettable night for both of us and my wife maintains that it was the best Italian meal she had ever had, plus lasagne that was totally unforgettable.

I had to see him about my Annual Quality Report, which he was to draft for the Commander. Thoroughly embarrassed, he asked me whether there was some failing or fault in my performance that he could include in my report. He said his report was too good, and that the Commander would include some criticism of me that would blight my future, unless it was watered down to match his view.

Astonished, and, at first, disappointed with my new boss, I could see his pragmatism, and concern for my future. I cannot remember how we dealt with this, but I am sure we both decided on some aspect that would prove harmless in the long term, but would get the rest of the report – which was very complimentary –on my record, to stand for the future.

Apart from the highlights I have quoted, and the routine work that had to be done, the rest of my time thus far had been to investigate complaints against police. Each of us was given a number of files, rather like the driving cases which I had had as a Sergeant, and these took up most of my time. As one concluded. another arrived, and I regarded this work as a nightmare.

They had to be meticulously prepared to pass through all the senior officers; every allegation dealt with, and full evidence obtained from everyone concerned; the paperwork faultless, down to the numbering of each page, exhibit and piece of evidence on any matter however related; and all completed by the Chief Inspector, without any real assistance or clerical help.

The Sergeant allocated to assist did so as an evidence-gatherer, but stopped short of helping with the compilation of the paper work, the completion of which was the root cause of the nightmare. The re-numbering of hundreds of pages after a fault was found was mind-boggling, and a real headache.

Whilst the Yard had its own branch for dealing with complaints, those were the more serious ones, and ours were allocated in Division, and inspected and adjudicated upon by the Commander. The scrutiny with which mine met can be readily imagined.

The system itself has been widely criticised, and has been held to be unsatisfactory and unfair to the complainant, whilst quick to support the accused officer.

Whilst this may not be the place for a lengthy discourse on the police complaints system, it featured heavily in my duties, as with all in my rank. That the fundamental fault was that policemen were investigated by policemen had always been the case. In practice, there was no other body to carry out the investigations. Then, too, files were assessed and judged by policemen, albeit of very high rank. Nevertheless, it must be recognised that the higher ranks had all joined as constables, and could not fail to be influenced by that experience.

Eliminating bias, often implicit, to achieve complete objectivity was the difficulty, and to do so by strict rules of procedure never had produced a fool-proof system. However, the rule, and especially that which governed our local divisional complaints, to which we divisional offices were allocated, had to be substantiated from an independent source. This would prove a higher standard of proof even than that in a criminal case, in which reliable evidence would suffice to establish a case. Effectively it nullified most of the work we did on each complaint.

Many complaints involved the word of the complainant versus the word of the responding officer. We knew therefore, on receipt of the file, that many, if not most, would end in this category, the complaint quite unresolved after months of paper-gathering. Expediency – a favourite police tool in such situations - would allow warnings, a finding of inappropriate behaviour where established by a breach of regulations or, for instance, in the case of a complaint of bad driving by an officer, that he was accident-prone and should be taken off driving duties.

The papers produced would be voluminous, and details of every aspect of police procedure involved fully dealt with, many introduced to find fault to be held against an officer, rather than deciding on the actual complaint. A massive file was built up (to show a full investigation), and six to nine months could easily be spent on building it up. Whilst I would have a sergeant permanently assisting me in the investigation, the collation of the papers and the re-numbering when a fault was found, or an extra statement or exhibit was to be inserted, was utterly tedious. With my Commander on my case, my work would 'bounce', especially if I were critical of an officer's performance. My Commander was, as I have shown, very much a policeman's policeman.

I hated this job. My effort to be scrupulously fair and totally objective was certainly not appreciated, but continued, despite its often being obvious which tack the Commander would have it take.

Knowing and accepting the inherent bias which arises when dealing with officers in trouble gave me a particular problem when a medium ranking officer was arrested and brought before me, for driving in excess of the prescribed alcohol limit. I promptly called in another senior duty officer, much to the disappointment of the arrested officer, who, on seeing me had thought that his chances had improved considerably. So many offending officers had been assisted, to the ultimate detriment and ruin of their friend's career.

It came as a real pleasure to learn that our Commander was being transferred to another division in the East End – a much less salubrious area. I hoped that it was to do with the treatment I had received at his hands, especially being registered as of no fixed abode, but there were no rumours about such an odd posting. To uproot him at the end of his career, and to be made to take over a new area, and to be given unknown subordinates, with unfamiliar problems to solve, was odd, and I believe he did not stay long after that: perhaps that was the reasoning behind it. Certainly, the emphasis was for younger and brighter senior officers to take command.

Our new Commander was totally different, in that, firstly, he had always served with the CID, rising through his anti-terrorist activities, had modern views, and got on well with the highest officers at the Yard. He operated with a light touch, a good sense of humour, and his man-management skills were readily apparent. A safe pair of hands, he took control easily and effectively, and was universally liked as well as wholly respected. He enjoyed the skills his officers brought, especially those with academic qualifications, who brought in fresh ideas. In fact, were I to have been promoted, he would undoubtedly have been my role model.

He asked me to take charge of the complaints team at headquarters for a while, and provided me with a strong team of sergeants and an Inspector. That was where I first met Paul Condon on duty, who became our Commissioner in remarkably few years. It was a pleasure to see him at work, and he was widely regarded as a 'coming man.'

My team consisted of a very experienced Detective Sergeant and a uniformed sergeant, equally experienced, and both admirably reasonable and fair in their dealings with the complainants. Their treatment of the officers complained of was clear-sightedly objective, coming from their combined experience.

I remember us all sitting in a student's room, each of us squirming about on bean bags, taking statements, to the not inconsiderable amusement of the deponents. Such an occasion was typical of their informality, which led to less exaggerated and more reasonably held allegations.

Our most difficult investigation concerned allegations about the treatment which the members of a lesbian club had received at the hands of our uniformed officers. There was a saga of complaints of sexist behaviour from every visit, much of which seemed unnecessary, and amounted to harassment, incivility and deep-rooted prejudice. Much of the treatment they had received was plain spiteful and nasty.

We were determined to rectify this by our belief in their complaints, and the way we operated to fully record and set the tone for proper police behaviour, which would be something they surely were not used to receiving. My sergeants were just the type to perform this task.

On entering the club with its manager I made the natural mistake of holding open the door for her, receiving a shoulder charge in the back which sent me almost headlong into the club room. Perhaps I should have been ready to modify my behaviour to avoid male patterns with these particular complainants, but it soon became apparent that the three of us were going to receive the hard time which they had received in the last year at the hands of their male visitors.

It was not long before both my sergeants interrupted me to say that they couldn't take much more of the treatment which was being meted out to them during the taking of statements. They were being personally abused, disbelieved as to their objectivity, having faces pulled at them, being scorned and vilified; and both attested to being deliberately kicked under the table. I could have addressed the members generally and asked for more respect so that we could do our job more satisfactorily to their advantage, in having a full and truthful account recorded as the basis for our investigation. Not only would that have invited ridicule and derision, but it would have set us up as interfering with the process of evidence-gathering: the reaction to such a speech by them would probably have caused a complaint against ourselves and did not seem, putting it mildly, a good idea.

We persisted with our investigation, and made a full and fair report outlining the extreme unpleasantness and sexism to which they had been subjected. Whilst largely unsubstantiated by independent evidence, visits to their premises by uniformed officers ceased, notice was given in future, and specially suitable officers were to be selected for such duties, avoiding entry into the club's premises or disturbing its members. My sergeants considered it the worst of the complaints we dealt with, not just for the bruising and insulting treatment which they received whilst trying their best, but because of the frustration of the exercise at a time when sexism was rife, and even evident within the force, towards its women officers. It was common for an officer whose advances were rejected by a woman officer to

190

immediately spread a rumour that she was clearly a lesbian, something experienced by many female officers.

After a few months at divisional headquarters, I was transferred to Hampstead sub-division, with its sectional station at West Hampstead. This was to be my last posting, as it turned out, and it was fitting to end up at what was one of the most interesting and popular stations, judging from the contentment of the officers working there.

Being a resident there came with high status and pride - the combination of living in an atmosphere which was rather like that of a village or a county town, like Cheltenham, but not too far from London - but at huge expense. On one side the Heath rolled down to Kentish Town, and, on the other, Heath Street and Rosslyn Hill ran through the centre, past the Royal Free Hospital, down to Camden Town. With its bistros, numerous very smart and expensive restaurants, high couture fashionable dress shops, beauticians, pubs with character and menus to match, plus the little arty, antique and gift shops, it was a regular pleasure to walk about and be greeted by its occupants, when taking a turn in uniform with the Chief Superintendent.

Parking was a complete nightmare in the whole area, and gave rise to many of the complaints we had to deal with, but which could often be determined by words of advice, as, so often, the complaint was levelled against officers' attitudes towards a typical Hampstead resident. Taking their statements in so many superbly appointed houses and flats added to our particular pleasure, and the occupants made our job easier, unless the matter was a serious one, and there were few of these.

The Heath was a huge draw especially as it contained Kenwood House, the ancient home of Lord Mansfield, famed for anti-slavery law, which commanded a magnificent view of the Heath, and which was famous for its open-aid concerts, sculptures, and magnificent paintings. Hampstead Garden Suburb was slightly to its north, and there was also a fine golf course, setting the tone. The upper parts of the Heath were much to be avoided by the local residents, as they were frequented largely by S & M deviants, who were attracted by its widespread reputation for such public behaviour. The police left the area well alone, but the odd foray into the territory was attempted, in order to bring in some control and limits, to appease the residents.

West Hampstead was a large conurbation, composed almost exclusively of Victorian and Edwardian houses that had at one time housed servants, but were now subdivided into flats for the young, many of whom were students or worked locally in and around the main thoroughfare, the Finchley Road. This very busy dual carriageway, with a few large stores amongst its rows of shops, garages, pubs, restaurants and cafes,led directly into the West End.

At the station, I was the only Chief Inspector, and so combined the administration unit with operational duties, and ran a small plainclothes crime squad of my own. They came up regularly with decent crime arrests, which made good reading for my senior officers, until other local areas started to complain that the enthusiasm of my squad was causing them to pursue calls ignoring their boundaries. We had to throttle back somewhat, but still maintained promising figures per officer, and for proper investigations (rather than arresting for petty outstanding warrants).

As the officer in charge of traffic prosecutions in the unit I had a most serious allegation that a police van driver had collided with a motorcyclist and his pillion passenger in the Finchley Road, and had ended up dragging them both behind him for some forty yards: both sustained disturbing injuries, and a number of witnesses came forward. Their oral statements, recorded in the reporting officers' accident report books,with full descriptions from the witnesses, made the allegation look damning, and I took over the case.

After some discrepancies were revealed between the witnesses, I decided to involve the local Accident Prevention Unit, and sent them the papers. I had used them when I had been an Inspector at Leman Street, where they had sent me a series of diagrams at short intervals, to indicate the position of the two vehicles involved, with sight lines for both the drivers, revealing just what they could see at these different stages. This proved conclusive in that investigation, and I had been totally impressed by their skills, training and expertise as competent witnesses in court, with full analytical mathematical and statistical qualifications to boot.

Once again I found myself in a tiny office, tucked away at the back of the traffic garage, with two mature constables at work over their papers: there was no supervision or procedure for them to follow, just the determination of two dedicated traffic officers to get to the bottom of who was at fault, and how to prove it, with the correct evidential tools. The fact that they were accepted in court as expert witnesses – a high test – indicated the depth and thoroughness of their training on the academic courses which they had been required to attend.

Within weeks I received their findings, which consisted of examining the position of each of the several witnesses whose full statements had been taken. None had been able to see what they had testified to having seen, and the reason was that the side of the dual carriageway where the collision occurred was much lower than the other side, where the witnesses had been driving. Their figures and diagrams were telling proof that they had either exaggerated what they had seen, or were plainly not telling the truth, but were keen to blame police. With such evidence, the allegation was refuted as without foundation.

We at the unit lost our property return officer, and I had the discretion to recruit another. People were shocked and dubious about my choice, as the successful candidate was black and was originally from central Africa: her parents were diplomats, her education immaculate, her nature serene, witty, extremely articulate and sensible, and her manner superb, with everyone from the constables to the most senior officers. The fact that she was extremely attractive, and was almost regal in her stature, was, I reckoned, going to stand her in good stead. No longer was the property officer going to have to leave notes and messages, or chase individuals personally about their particular piece of property. I figured that the traffic was going to pile up at her door, with everyone who had a property query having an excuse to spend time with her, disposing of their property. I especially liked her unconscious contribution to race relations, for she was a natural ambassadress in that area.

Within months of her recruitment the Hampstead property return was a nil return; every piece of property had been properly disposed of. I had no doubt that ours was the only such return in the Metropolitan Police; it was very much a bragging point for our Chief Superintendent, and something which a promotion board would be pleased to hear.

Soon my position was to change, and I was made the Chief Inspector (Operations) whilst another took over the unit. Having been on the special course, he was tipped for future promotion, but needed grass roots experience – hence the administration unit.

My first step was to sort out a licensing problem between two of our busiest pubs. It was developing into an intense rivalry. They were frequented largely by the sort of undesirables who an experienced CID officer would recognise from associations with notorious gangs, both south and north of the river. Any dispute that would break out would be violent, and dangerous, and would involve serious public disorder.

The money behind the pubs had come from the most dubious of sources, and the reputations of those involved, and of the financial trafficking, had awoken the interest of the CID and the financial authorities.

The pubs operated with the impunity which those with this background and reputation expected (and had probably arranged), and paid no attention to licensing regulations. I saw it as my task to bring them within the law, or, preferably, to close them down, and remove the risk and the danger. With a thorough investigation and prosecution, this would allow the authorities to inspect the evidence and regularise the situation, and stop the strongly suspected money laundering, or other possible financial improprieties.

The conduct of the premises was so blatant and reckless as far as regulation was concerned that both were successfully raided and summonses issued. (I believe that their position changed radically with new licensees later.) One was closed down very quickly, for when I checked the offences committed I had noticed a tiny provision in the Act which referred to access between different parts of a public house, affecting the validity of its licence. I ensured that this was one of those to be prosecuted, but included it almost as an aside.

The solicitor acting for them at court pleaded guilty to all the listed offences, and clearly had not noticed this particular provision, which interestingly made the licence forfeit if proved. Accordingly, the licence was lost through the plea, and the situation I feared was not to develop; I was informed that the authorities were able to dig deep into the finances.

Also, even here, I ran a small vice unit, but it soon wound down through lack of business, except for one occasion when, again, I had to play the would-be customer in order to uncover one very clever brothel which advertised itself as providing French lessons. Again I was left with a naked lady whilst dallying in her bathroom, waiting for the much-delayed knock on the door by the squad, and using an inability to raise interest as my excuse. Unlike my squad, the lady was not amused, and it was the first time she had been caught in many years.

I was now into my twenty-fourth year of my service, and this was the time when the Force sent a letter to those who were approaching retirement on pension. It reminded me of this fact;that time flows by before you know it, and that the future ought to be considered.

It was very considerate of the Force, and I suspect that it was instigated by some thoughtful civil servant, possibly at the direction of a senior officer in that position. I was getting to a stage when I was not enjoying my work, and was becoming disenchanted; my promotion prospects were dubious. Even if I succeeded in being promoted to Superintendent, this was not enough of a change - being a deputy - as the better rank was Chief Superintendent, and that seemed very distant.

There was, however, a more important thought that crossed my mind. I was there and then entitled to a pension, close to half of my salary, which meant that I was working for just under half pay. What then to do? I needed a job that was challenging and prestigious, to make up for my lack of progress.

Putting all this together, I was reminded of my Chief Superintendent, when I had been a young Inspector, and had brought a case against him in court. I remembered his enthusiasm, and how articulate he was in his familiarity with the law and his persuasion; whilst he challenged the officers' evidence, he did so fairly and effectively. He lost the case, the evidence being strong against him, but he did so with grace, and achieved a creditable sentence as a result.

I further remembered, in the sixth form, pondering the future, being attracted by the idea of becoming a barrister but by no means ready to do so. Maybe now was a time to really think about this, as much had happened to me to indicate that this might be a possibility.

I concluded that this might be all I was hoping for, and would provide what was lacking. There would be both a higher moral and intellectual element, in an environment whose culture equated with my ideals.

My views were becoming more out of step in the Force, with no prospect of achieving change, or a favourable audience for my ideas, in the light of my prospects. We had been labelled, and had, to my chagrin, as a member, accepted the label, as an organisation that was institutionally racist. We had a canteen culture, strongly macho tendencies, and a tradition of complete loyalty, which blocked objectivity and fresh ideas. My own thoughts on capital punishment, the totally ineffectual 'War on Drugs', and the belief that the end justifies the means, coupled with presumptions of guilt, would never be countenanced.

The Bar afforded the chance of studying whilst in the Force having a degree, even in Sociology, could help; I would continue

196

to receive my salary and allowances, and leave immediately on qualification. This all seemed speculative, and possibly arrogant, but the more I thought and talked it over with Pat, the more it appeared worth pursuing.

The more I turned it over, the more I realised that I did possess some advantages. I had put together cases for the prosecution in Magistrates Court, even as a young and untrained sergeant. Gradually I had learnt to cope against solicitors, and was able to sway the lay bench and some magistrates. I was able to make an opening speech, and I could interrogate a defendant and his witnesses with confidence.

In the Crown Court, I was able to work with a prosecuting barrister, and to assist and strengthen our case, whilst paying close attention to rebutting defences. Crown Court language and procedure was still foreign to me, but could be learnt. I could tell a dishonest witness, police or otherwise, and could so show him my police experience that he would usually resort to the truth, for fear of being exposed by someone who seemed to know procedures and reality.

I was forty-five, and that was not too late to start a new career, agreeably replete with bright and well-spoken young barristers at the same intellectual level. The next question was whether a set of chambers or a defence solicitor would allow me to represent a defendant or whether the defendant himself would want me, an ex-police officer, to defend him. Would I sound too authoritative, or think I knew it all; would I be sufficiently flexible mentally to accommodate new ideas, or true principles, in legal argument? In a nutshell, could I sound like a barrister rather than an ex-copper?

Having had much to do with Gray's Inn over the years, I sounded out one of their top career advisors, and discussed my situation with him. He immediately convinced me that I was what the Bar really needed; that I had the experience and the ability to communicate easily with all walks of life; that I had the courage and persistence to battle on if I thought I was right, and that I would go far as would be possible.

My pension would help with the difficulties of finance, and I would find many at the Bar who had entered it as a second career, from all walks of life and academic disciplines. I came home to Pat excited, and the decision was made. It was going to be a huge undertaking, but an utterly worthwhile target at which to aim. My determination to adopt a different way of life and an exciting future and, to be truthful, to show what I could give, was all the motivation I needed.

A walk round the car parks of the four Inns of Court, and an inspection of the residents' vehicles, indicated that there was money to be made – no 'bangers' in sight in any of them.

A number of steps awaited me, requiring a great deal of luck, assistance all the way, and no doubters or opposition. Whilst it may seem as though a new chapter has arrived, that will not come until I leave the present career and start anew.

The first step was a preliminary test or examination on law, comprising some fifty questions on aspects of criminal and civil law, Institutions, evidence, British Constitution, well-known Latin phrases (?) and other legal concepts. I had thought, with my knowledge, general and specific, including British Constitution, from my LSE degree, and broad experience, this would not present a problem: we were also supplied with a textbook to assist us for the course.

The fact this was the first exam I had ever failed was a real setback. We were allowed one more chance and this time I worked as hard as I ever had, using the textbook, learning much of it word-perfect. I was determined not to fall at the first hurdle, having clearly taken the first attempt far too lightly.

That meant I was able to take the first part of the course, which was to pass the academic subjects which all students had to pass, before setting off on the second part, which was the professional examination, divided into that for barristers and that for solicitors.

My degree allowed me to reduce the eight subjects to six, which meant I could do a part-time course, completed in under a year at the Red Lion Square Polytechnic in Holborn. After starting we were told that the pass-rate was about 17%. The alternative course was that at the City College, which had a better pass rate, but was much more difficult to attend, especially as I was travelling from Holborn police station.

The subjects were Land Law, Contract, Tort, Criminal Law, Trusts and, I think, Evidence.

My Chief Superintendent allowed me to continue, provided that a full time eight hours was worked. I was able to start early when at the Administrative unit, and set the work for the staff for the rest of the day. After 6pm or so, I was able to take up operational duties, or work on my complaints and other tasks.

He fully supported me, as he could see that I was devoting myself to the full eight hours, with no resort to studying or reading for my subjects, even in the meal break. I wanted it to be seen that I was playing fair with the Force, respecting the huge opportunities I was being afforded to complete the course, yet retaining my job and therefore, importantly, my whole salary with its crucial allowances.

Fortunately, many complainants could be seen after work, and often preferred being seen late. I could also use the office to complete the paper work, and that was best done when the staff had gone and I had the run of the office. Of course, as, occasionally, I was the duty Chief Inspector on the Division, I had to be available for call-outs, but these fitted in with my late hours. In fact, it provided extra cover for the Division.

Having always enjoyed studying (and, I'm afraid, even homework) I threw myself into the academic subjects, all of which I thoroughly enjoyed except Land Law. The rules and regulations, exceptions, and wealth of tiny detail in the provisions were a nightmare, and I was not alone in struggling. If one subject were failed, the whole eight, or six in my case, had to be re-taken, and nearly all the failures were in that subject. It took probably our most brilliant student three attempts before passing to become a most able and successful barrister, QC and, eventually, judge.

Trusts had started off similarly, but a new lecturer replaced the senior, to our relief, as, again we had all struggled under her. Breaking down the cases into deserving cases versus greedy and conniving relatives – or good guys versus bad or famous film stars trying to bend the rules, etc. - all made the subject easier to grasp, and included a sense of morality that helped with the technicalities of the various trusts and their purposes. Once he started teaching, his tutorials ran after the proper time for more than an hour every time, as they were so well attended, crystal clear and dynamic.

The examination in Land Law was truly a fearsome experience. I had prepared one answer thoroughly and dashed that off. For the second, I knew about half the answer so did that. I then tried another which was in two halves. I knew a little of the first half and nothing of the second. I ruled that question out completely, after trying to answer the first part. I came to another, and did the same. In complete panic, I sat watching student after student walking out after having given up.

These failed attempts had eaten up much of my time, but I had to re-group, so I went out and smoked a cigarette, and told myself that I had come too far to give in at this stage.

I returned and crossed out any question I knew nothing about. That left two questions about which I had a few ideas, and at least something to write down. With the little time left, these answers were more like notes than an essay. My friends told me I looked like a ghost during the exam, in an obvious panic for most of the time, and, towards the end, as white as a sheet.

When I got home I adopted my usual practice devised by my old Maths master in assessing the unknown: to mark my answers first as if by a kind and generous marker, and then by one who was really tough. Taking an average between the marks would be my result. On this occasion I reckoned I had passed by 2%. I never found out the actual figure, but from conversations afterwards learned that this must have been absolutely right. However, I had got through, and had cause for celebration, after a dreadful experience.

All this time at college, I had been pursuing, in parallel, my police career. This continued by undertaking the Professional Bar Course which was split into that for would-be barristers and that for solicitors. Many subjects were the same, but that for solicitors was more wide-ranging, and extremely practical: since a barrister had to present cases in court, knowledge of the law, and particularly of evidence, court procedure and drafting, featured strongly in his training. We had several choices, and mine was matrimonial law – an easier option which I was never going to practice, since the trauma of my own divorce and the disputes which inevitably arise, especially over money, had ruled this out completely, as I thought. The thought of losing the argument, and thus the case, over the custody of children, was unthinkable.

The killer subject in this course was tax. It included all forms of tax, and many of us decided to opt out of Capital Gains Tax, thus reducing the area of study enormously, and yet at the expense of only a quarter of the questions. This cunning strategy worked well for all of us, as far as I could tell, and certainly minimised my studies.

The students were a very bright bunch, most starting a second career – which is the case with many barristers, even with those who have done well in their first. The personal freedom of being at the Bar, its challenge and status, and the money that can be earned, depending on which branch of the law is practised, made it very attractive.

There seemed to be complete dedication, enthusiasm, and a burning ambition to be on one's feet in court. The success rate was somewhat higher than at the academic stage, and it was a real pleasure, and still is, to see again my fellow students in various areas of practise, even at the highest courts in the land, or in other specialised walks of life, where court appearances would come as a complete shock.

The last part of the course which had to be completed was the eating of twelve dinners at one's Inn: mine was Gray's Inn, reputed for being the most sociable, which had a higher percentage of women: maybe the two go together, but there certainly seemed to be some truth in the description.

This was tightly controlled, and there was no signing in on entry through one door and slipping out the other – even for someone who seemed to be dashing to three different parts of North London most days.

The food was excellent and relatively inexpensive, and the company always entertaining – the point of the practice. There was entertainment, theatrical performances, silly speeches, and very serious and erudite ones, and moots and challenges between tables, either to sing, to argue or to play. I remember an American barrister whom I came to know better having to sing after a challenge. In true US style he ended up dancing along the long tables doing a very acceptable version of Yankee Doodle Dandy in true James Cagney style, to uproarious applause. The development of self-confidence on one's feet did a potential barrister no harm, and, I am sure, some practical good.

My own contribution early on was a point in a debate on the Police force, made to a very full audience. The principal speaker sought me out afterwards, and, for a few months, became my mentor and advisor. He was an expert on fraud, and had been in the Met at a high rank - another piece of luck, or a lucky coincidence again.

The diners were not all students, but included experienced barristers with a top table of the highest in the judiciary, practising lawyers or academics, and many chose to sit with the students, a practice they sometimes found invigorating. Socially, the mix was thoroughly enjoyable and entertaining, the tone was light, the wit memorable; and there was none of the patronising or pomposity that sometimes accompanies barristers, of any age.

It all culminated in Call Night, September 1981, when we dined in full barrister's gowns, wing collars and bands, hired, of course, at a princely hire cost, but feeling very special, hugely privileged, very self-congratulatory - I am afraid - with the flashing of parental cameras everywhere.

Returning to work after receiving the congratulations of everyone at the station, I was especially pleased with that from the Detective Chief Superintendent, who told me that he was really envious of my achievement. My parting gift was the criminal law textbook *Archbold Criminal Law and Practice*, an essential pre-requisite.

It was not long after that that I was called up as a candidate for promotion to Superintendent. I did not mince my words, and was forthright about my achievements, and the lack of recognition since having been promoted to Inspector, some fifteen years before, and getting one promotion during that time.

I stressed my role in prosecuting case after case, with pleas of guilt in every case, due to the evidence I had presented over the fifteen years; my other achievements were before them, but the nil return for the property return was another high (and unprecedented) point; which all added to the various special tasks I had performed.

They were informed that my talents had to a large extent been unrecognised and wasted, and I think I added that candidates with lesser qualifications or abilities had been promoted over my head.

Finishing with my call to the Bar I stated that I could do better in practice, and felt that my talents would be fully recognised, and that that was where my future lay. It was their loss. Whilst I could have declined the Board, to pass and obtain the next rank would have helped my pension, so I went through with it.

I failed, unsurprisingly, being deemed arrogant. I told them the facts, and they couldn't take it. Apologising was an art infrequently, if at all, practised in the police service. (It is not much better now.)

The next step towards my third life was the hurdle that kept hundreds of candidates every year from becoming a working barrister – in house or out. That was the necessity of getting a pupillage with a qualified barrister, usually for a period of twelve months.

When dining, I had met several other pupils, who suggested applying to their chambers, as they thought I would be what they were looking for, with my police experience to strengthen their defence work with defending counsel. Having written to one very swish set of prosecuting chambers in the Temple, I had one interview in the conference room. Before I could get started, this relatively young barrister told me that they were really looking for a person with the potential to become the Lord Chief Justice. He epitomised the sort of pompous and patronising young barrister whom one often met in such chambers, and I could not let this pass.

I asked him how he would recognise such a person at the start of their career, since those whom I had met at the top of their professions had often had no such pretensions, but had got there by a combination of luck, persistence, courage and keeping their nose clean. The quality of their degree and intellectual ability would, of course, help direct their career and everyday success, but no more than that. I then added that if the others in his chambers shared his failure to grasp reality, and his rather stuffy naivety and self-importance, his chambers was not for me, and I got up and left.

My next interview was in a cafe, sharing a coffee with my prospective pupil master, Gino. We hit it off and had a good interview; his chambers were much more informal, but with members who were going places; and it had a top senior clerk, according to my informant. I found out that he was always acting for the defence and was somewhat critical of the police, having always cross-examined them. Nevertheless, he took me on, was always fair, and possibly softened a little, especially since one of my first actions was to take him as my guest to a senior officers' lunch – which he thoroughly enjoyed, as did they.

I resigned from the force shortly afterwards, on a Sunday, and started with Gino at 4 Verulam Buildings, in Gray's Inn, on the Monday. My third life had started.

Chapter 13
Pupillage: a Headstart: Thrown into the Deep End

There is no magic in the word pupillage. The system at the Bar is for the pupil to follow his pupil master everywhere, and in every court. Usually this is for a period of twelve months, but it can be split into two periods of six months with different pupil masters, if so desired. The first six is unpaid, but one can'devil' for another barrister, who may pay you something for paperwork. In the second six, you could attend court and earn a fee, though you would wait some months for receipt. By the end of the second six months, you would generally receive a few hundred pounds for criminal cases.

Barristers occupy a room about the size of a dining room at home, and sit three to four each at their own desk. They are surrounded by bookcases on the shelves, on which are arranged their briefs. This is designed to make the most of the biggest and heaviest briefs, to impress the solicitors who may come in for conferences. Pupils live out of one pigeonhole.

I was different. In our room there was a small desk, reminiscent of school, with a seat. It may not have matched the desks I had in the police stations; nor was I surrounded by maybe fifteen members of my staff; nor was I responsible for over a hundred officers.

In fact, I was tempted to comment, jokingly, on this contrast to Gino, but realised that this would not be appreciated, as he had put himself out for me. I was in a room with the other tenants, had a place to sit and work at, on which any briefs would be laid out for me to read and work on, like a tenant. Other pupils wandered around chambers like nomads, and could not even enter the clerks' room, so as not to interrupt them at work. As in the Navy, I was at the bottom of the pile, and I got used to it.

In the Crown Court, I was encouraged by Gino to wear my wig and gown. It would make me feel like a barrister, and behave like one; my position at court would be recognised, and though my wig was shining white, my age resulted in my being treated as experienced, and I was occasionally asked for advice. Some pupils were loath to wear them, but I felt that it was a badge of honour which had been worked hard for; in any event, I was used to uniform.

Gino would even take me into the judge's private room with him, if the judge wanted to discuss something out of court, or just to have a private or sociable chat. This was invaluable, and I could be trusted to keep my mouth tightly shut, listen and learn. One day it would be my turn to be invited in.

I did some devilling for others in chambers, and remember an eight -page advice on a commercial insurance dispute. The barrister I gave it to returned it with every line highlighted (strange!) so it must have been acceptable; but, as with, perhaps, two other advices, I received nothing for it but thanks.

Gino gave me written work, though, and I prepared some short advices on evidence, and may have practiced a speech or two as an exercise. Only once was he quite stern with me, when I muttered across the bench that an officer had done something which was out of order. He had realised that himself, and was to deal with it in his own time and way in an ambush later on.

We did have one disagreement, over a case in which his client - a world renowned vivisectionist - was accused of burglary, in rescuing some beagles from an establishment which tested them for smoking. He was going to plead guilty, and my argument was that what he did was neither iniquitous nor criminal, considering his motives and conduct.

Gino disagreed and dismissed the argument I put forward. I found a law report the next day in which, in such a case, the jury had acquitted. I put it on his desk without comment.

He spoke then about the case, and involuntarily complimented me, by saying that the trouble with me was that I thought about the law too much. As an ex-policeman, that was truly one of the best compliments which I had received. Thinking about it, he was surely right, as being practical is often the better course than pursuing a long legal battle which may look as if it should succeed but may not; juries and even Court of Appeal judges make surprising decisions. The client, too, may have strongly opted for a plea. The compliment, however, remained.

In one case he had been devastated. The defendant was a young girl, of impeccable character, accused of assaulting another in a night club; the latter's testimony was supported by her equally unworthy friends. The defendant was convicted, and received a medium-term prison sentence. The evidence was strong, however, and Gino could have done no more.

Another was memorable, in that it concerned stolen animal skins, which were alleged to have been from reindeers from Italy. Every time Gino mentioned reindeer from Italy, he got a huge laugh from the jury, and the case was laughed out of court.

With Gino, I was usually in the Crown Court, which provided me with the experience in that forum I needed: I was used to the Magistrates courts.

In the meantime, I needed to know that the family could survive on my pension, and with nothing coming in from the Bar. Financially, the traffic was the other way; wigs and gowns were not cheap, and there were considerable travelling costs and living expenses. Admittedly, I would recoup much of it claiming back VAT, for which I had to register. Though my earnings would be well under the limit for those claiming for cases on which I had worked, who wanted to claim back their VAT, we all had to be registered.

Though I could earn fees in my second six months, it was clear from hearing the others that there were huge delays in receiving the fees, months if not years, although, in those days, we could claim for each hearing. It was much later that those negotiating for us allowed the rules to change, so that we were not paid until a case concluded – which again could be a year or two after we had dealt with preliminary matters and bail. I never could understand how the profession allowed our main problem to be exacerbated, rather than eased, by those who should have known better.

There were chances to teach law available, and I obtained a post at Barnet College, teaching Tort and Negligence at A level.

It was two hours during the evening, and paid fairly well. As it was my first teaching post, I was conscious that it was established that concentration times were under half an hour so I split my lectures accordingly, and interspersed them with quizzes and other devices. At first the students found this strange, but they came to appreciate the breaks.

The money was useful, but it did not fill the gap totally, so I put a card in the window of my local shop, advertising my services as a gardener and garden designer, at a reasonable hourly rate.

Though my second six months was coming up, this was quite manageable, and the gardening, if successful, would be at weekends. By now, Pat and I were married, and our first child, daughter Katherine, had arrived (in April 1981). Survival now seemed a realistic possibility.

My first customer for the weekend work rang, and I called round to see her. She had a large garden which she had cultivated all her life, she said. As she was over ninety, this was going to be a challenge, as it proved immediately. We walked round her garden, and she started quizzing me about her shrubs, their common and Latin names. I failed with a few, managed a couple, but got caught out when she asked about their habits: did they retain their leaves in winter, etc.?

After a very uncomfortable half hour, I held my hand up, and stated that, though I was a keen gardener, I had clearly established that I was poorly qualified to tend her garden, and that I just would not be up to it. She declined my refusal, and said I was just what she wanted: I would do the spade work, and she would teach me as we went along. She then told me she had been the chairwoman for the Barnet Horticultural society for fifty years, that many of her plants and shrubs were Victorian, including a very ugly and slightly frightening contorted hazel ,and that she specialised in flower arranging with them. We agreed hours, and the fee, and off I went on a learning adventure with her. I had to wait a few moments after we visited each plant, for her memory to kick in, but her knowledge was encyclopaedic. I worked for her for nearly two years, and was able to take on more customers until fees began to come in.

I was re-assigned for my second six months to another pupil master, whose practice was almost exclusively in civil law, and I had to sharpen up both knowledge and wit to live with him.

In a second six months, a pupil could attend court on his own, as directed by the clerk, and working for chamber's solicitors. Our chief clerk, John, was very much aware of the limited work we were capable of, and would ensure that his solicitors were never let down by us, since chambers relied upon them.

He was careful if he needed someone for a first appearance, as legal aid had to be formally applied for, and the form completed properly for the solicitor. As this would be the first time the lay client had been to court and set eyes on one, he would need the 'right barrister', and it was important, therefore, to create the best impression, so that the solicitor might retain the case. I am sure that he would get feedback on each of us in his meetings with the solicitors, soliciting more and better work for chambers, and ensuring that the professional clients were happy with chambers' performance for them.

Indeed, sometimes he would attend court with the senior barristers on important cases, or those where his presence would be useful – a rare move for a chief clerk. Without doubt, he was a superb clerk, and even at my level it was obvious that he supervised the clerks' room admirably. Though it may sound strange, he was also remarkably easy to talk to. This was far from being always the case, as will be explained later, when we come to 'clerks I have known'.

My practice commenced on either my first or second day at court. If I had used the term 'started', it would have been a monumental understatement – the only word for it would be 'jump-started.' I went to Willesden Magistrates Court, to do something for John, and, whilst at court, met one of my bright young sergeants from Holloway. Greg asked me what I was doing there, and I told him that I had just started as a barrister. He replied that he was a solicitor, having left the police many years before. Just looking at him, and noting his manner and familiarity at court, and the great respect in which he was regarded by all at court, including the bench, I realised that he was doing very well. He asked me which chambers I was with, and said little more at that stage – as I remember.

The next week, through John I received a brief about two feet thick, in my name, from Greg, in his own firm in Ealing, featuring a large number of defendants, in a case that was to be committed to the Old Bailey – the Central Criminal Court.

After digesting the essentials of the case, I rang him up and asked him if he knew what he was doing to me sending me such a case, and he just said that he had no doubt I could handle it. I cannot remember my reply, for even at that stage one would not look a gift horse in the mouth, and I needed to read the brief through before deciding what to do.

As I carried on with other appearances, always in the Magistrates courts, I found out the magnitude of my first brief. Not only did it allege a conspiracy to rob banks by a gang, a conspiracy in which there were a number of specific bank robberies, but one of the defendants was a super-grass, giving evidence against all the others (giving Queen's evidence being the proper term). My defendant was one of the conspirators, but his name was last on the list. With more experience, this would have provided some relief, and I realised that this case would be heard openly at the Old Bailey. Counsel involved, both prosecuting and defending, were clearly rising stars and the top defending counsel was one Michael Mansfield.

To conclude this stage, I decided to conduct the committal myself, since the part played by my defendant was to tell gang members details about local shopkeepers, traders and businessmen, carrying their takings to the banks: he had nothing more active to do with the conspiracy or robberies. I further decided that, for the trial, I would need a leader and asked Gino to lead me, which he did with alacrity.

I could then carry on with my practice, and on to my first Crown Court trial, in a prefabricated building off Harrow Road. This must have come from Greg, for there was no one else who would have sent a Crown Court trial to a beginner.

The charge concerned a theft, but on reading the statements, I noticed there was no evidence as to a central fact that needed proof. I accepted the statements, without requiring the witness to attend court, and the trial went ahead. Suddenly we got to the stage where I made a submission of no case, due to the lack of the necessary fact (which may have been one of ownership). The prosecutor was shaken, and did all he could to resist it, but then asked for an adjournment, for the loser to be fetched from home if possible. I opposed it very forcibly, as I was close to succeeding due to the prosecutor's error, but the judge was sympathetic to the very reputable and popular prosecutor, and allowed it.

Needless to say he was brought to court by police, and the case proceeded and we lost. The prosecutor then decided to praise me in open court, telling the judge that it was my first Crown Court trial and how creditably I had performed. On the one hand this was flattering to receive, but it showed the defendant that he had been represented by a total beginner. I would rather the prosecutor had said nothing, as it reflected back on my solicitor, though I heard nothing from him about the matter.

The case at Willesden was committed to the Old Bailey, and I did the committal, rubbing shoulders with some of the most up-and-coming criminal barristers around. It was indeed committed to the Old Bailey, and Gino was appointed my leader. Since most defendants were represented by a silk and a junior, I had no difficulties in getting a leader for my case, even though, factually, it did not pose the challenge which the others presented.

I carried on with the second six months, and managed to go to court with my second pupil master, and do the work John assigned for me. I had not long to spend there, but learned in this six months that tactics played an important part in certain cases – a conclusion derived from some of the civil work I saw.

I picked up one significant case which took me to the Court of Appeal for the first time, and into the Law Reports, as an authority on sentencing. It started when I went to see the client in custody on a charge of indecent assault and causing actual bodily harm. The first thing he said to me was; 'Get me locked up, Mr Forward, I'm dangerous.' He then said; 'One day I'm going to kill someone; I need help.'

He pleaded guilty to the two charges, and was remanded for psychiatric reports which confirmed that he should be detained in a mental hospital. I strove to get him a hospital order, but could not get the order, for lack of suitable accommodation. I delayed the sentencing several times so that suitable accommodation with a skilled psychiatrist could supervise him. I failed, and he was sentenced to three and a half years' imprisonment, split into two separate sentences to be served consecutively.

Since, following the authorities, only one sentence should have been imposed for offences arising from the same incident and facts, I decided to appeal. This would give me another chance to avoid imprisonment, and to get the hospital order he clearly needed. The case came to court the following year and that was not without interest.

Carrying on chronologically to some extent (this will not always be possible, and some cases are better dealt with from start to finish, since this is not a historical exercise), I was getting to the end of my pupillage, and so the next and last hurdle arrived, again one at which many hundreds failed, and at which even those who succeeded took, it was said, three years, on average: to become a tenant.

My chance came from a pupil who had herself been squatting at my chambers, but who had a tenancy round the corner, at 10-11 Gray's Inn. The head of chambers was an ex-police officer, and the set was small, consisting mainly of criminal lawyers, but with a very sociable membership, with, as far as I could see no pomposity, no standing on ceremony. I had decided not to go for a prestigious chambers, but for somewhere where I could enjoy my work and the company. I did not stay with my pupillage chambers, as I considered that I would always be thought of as their pupil, and I left another, who was very keen and liked and able, to try there herself.

I got on well with the Head, and they were anxious for me to start. I would have liked more time, as I was being briefed in my own name, receiving decent fees, and paid no rent. As they insisted (and as I would be secure straightaway) I accepted and started with them.

The gardening continued, as did that in my own garden, where I had reserved a plot half the size of a regular allotment for vegetables, and devoted much of the rest to shrubs for low maintenance. I also built my own greenhouse, which I invited Pat to admire. She took one look and told me that I had built it inside out. Brilliant! I may be a tidy gardener, but when it came to DIY that was typical: I could never read a plan to build or put together furniture etc.; but the structure was turned round, and has been hugely successful with its black Hamburg vine inside. I had remembered my childhood experience with such a grapevine in Leigh-on-Sea. I also cultivated a sweet white grape running through my mini-allotment, in the style of the customary use of a pergola in the Madeira gardens which we had seen on holiday.

My stint at Barnet had ended, and I signed up to teach Contract and Business Law at Middlesex University. Again this proved of no practical use, but the pay was better, and it lasted for another year.

I concluded gardening, as I needed the time to prepare my legal work. The most pleasure came when the husband of one customer came home, strutted round the garden, as was his wont, and complained that the patches of weed-killer were uneven, and made the lawn look unattractive. I told him that, if he could guarantee more even patches of weeds, that would solve the problem.

Having always been circumspect in the police to avoid the formality of a complaint, I then said to him, so that his wife could hear, that, frankly, I did not like him, or the way he treated his long-suffering wife and children. Whilst his wife would be the loser, since she loved what I was doing in the garden, I was not going to work for him again, and took my leave. The satisfaction was delicious, and his face a picture.

Money was coming in, but by the end of my first six months it amounted to only a few hundred pounds. That improved quite quickly, with my own work from Greg, and that from my new chambers. Whilst there was a long wait for the Crown Court to pay, when it came, it paid well, depending on the nature of the case and its size by page numbers; so the more the number of statements and exhibits, the better the fee. Greg had indeed got me off to a great start, as he said when we had lunch at Ealing one day.

He only instructed one set of chambers in the Temple, a large and very swish set, apart, he said, from what he sent me. He could not return anything I received, as he did not know those in my

213

chambers, and did not want to carry on much longer splitting his work, now I was up and running.

In fact, he stopped quite shortly afterwards, when my clerk did not return one of his briefs to me, as he should have, but hung on to it, so as to get another hearing. Greg rang him, gave him a piece of his mind for sharp and unethical practice, and pulled his work from him and from the chambers. He was not used to being treated like that, and could not trust my clerk again. I apologised to Greg for him, and agreed that it was unacceptable; I said that I appreciated all he had done for me, and that we would no doubt meet again in court.

This was the old-fashioned breed of clerk, who had been doing the job man and boy, was in complete charge of his barristers, and whose advice to me was: 'let the solicitors come to you, don't contact them, or tell them the result.' With this I never agreed; his implication, that we were too important and busy to speak to them, I always rejected. The brief he had tried to cling on to was probably worth £100, so it was not greed that prompted his action, but his belief that he could dictate to solicitors. Mine had come too far to accept that.

He had his special friends who would brief us, often for peanuts, and those would be allowed to let all the cases build up for months before being paid. We also had to write a whole summary of the case, usually a traffic case, for a meagre fee that barely covered travel.

You could not talk to him, discuss your practice, or suggest improvements; for instance, after a while I stated that if I drew a map of the places to which we were all being sent, and also showing our home addresses, we would all be criss-crossing each other every day, wasting money and time. He looked aghast at this idea that we had any say in where we went.

If we had a difficulty in attending and declined, he would starve us for a few weeks with no work, to show us who was in charge. In the case of his low-paying cronies, I started to charge for a very generous lunch, and very soon found that I was not being briefed by them – so that strategy worked.

The main problem was a very long lunch hour for him in a pleasant pub in Chancery Lane, and then a scramble to fill the diary on his return. Since he spoilt the head of chambers with the best work, whether he was capable of it or not, he was untouchable.

I went with Gino to the Old Bailey for the bank robbery conspiracy. It was a joy to watch the top performers, but especially to listen to Mansfield. His language, complete lack of all the clichés which barristers turn to, and his vocabulary - and yet his simplicity and clarity - have always been a model for me to follow since.

Unfortunately, we lost the case. When our client started to be cross-examined, it was put to him simply that he was part of the conspiracy, and that he had indeed provided information for the others he had met, to enable the gang to rob them. He readily and unequivocally agreed. Gino was stunned, as was I.

Either he had totally misunderstood the question, or he had been talking to someone and got things quite wrong, or worse. His answer left Gino with nowhere to go to remedy the admission, so he had the charge put again, and the client pleaded guilty. Oddly enough I cannot remember any comeback from Greg about the case, but if there had been any doubt about his evidence, he would not have been put in the witness box, as the prosecution evidence against him was very minimal.

Much of our work at that time was for travellers, since they were always granted legal aid, as they could not read or write. Their criminal cases were often very serious, but we also took on their planning cases, involving their unlawful use of land on which to build or site their caravans.

By now, the Court of Appeal had listed my appeal against sentence for the lay client who had asked to be put away for the safety of the public. As I walked to the court that morning I glanced at the law report in The Times. The headline stated that the practice of one sentence for offences committed in the same incident was no longer correct. I was shattered.

Since this was my first appearance in the Court of Appeal, I ensured that I was last on the list; this was fairly easy, as most counsel were in a hurry, and wanted to get on as soon as possible. I wanted to sit, watch and learn. I was surprised to see counsel interrupting the judges, patronising them, and citing facts when expressly told to deal only with law. Others were dreadfully nervous, and barely able to speak.

One, from the North, opened his mouth, and nothing emerged for possibly a whole minute. The judges bore with him patiently, encouraging him to at least introduce himself, and then maybe indicate the charge, and start off with his first ground of appeal, by reading it to them. Bit by bit, they winkled things out from him, and after quite some time he had pulled himself together. I am glad to say that he succeeded, and went back to Lincolnshire in triumph. The judges were magnificent, and the idea of being bullied in court by exasperated judges, or rushed or scolded, was as far from the practice as could be. My respect for them was enormous, and their example has always led me to reject any other treatment from judges towards barristers, however nervous or inexperienced.

It came to my turn. My client had handed me a press photograph of a prison van, with its doors open, parked in a country lane. It was empty, apart from the fact he was sitting on the bench by the open door, waiting to be captured. I thought this might amuse the judges and lighten the tone: it would also show remorse, and help with mitigation.

The bench enjoyed this, and laughed, as they stated that they had been watching me all day, shuffling the pages of *The Times*, reading and re-reading the law report. They told me they would put me out of my misery by distinguishing the report and rejecting its view. The principle remained, certainly in my case. What a relief; though I did not make the papers, I did get reported in the *Criminal Law Review* as a relevant authority.

Most barristers would complain that some of their most difficult cases were those passed on by their colleagues, sometimes by misfortune or accident, sometimes deliberately. Classically, this would be the receiving of a poisoned chalice, though I prefer the modern phrase: getting a hospital pass. I too have been guilty of such a pass, but with mitigating circumstances, many years later.

The case I received in the first two years would be worth a whole chapter, were this book to take the form of a number of short legal stories. The source was a colleague in my chambers, and I suspect he must have known that the trial would be controversial, to say the least.

The defendant had fallen out with a businessman over the man's wife, and the feeling between them was one of hatred and impending violence. In a nutshell, the defendant was charged with assaulting one of the businessman's friends (an actual bodily assault); threatening behaviour to the businessman (affray was charged); dangerous driving, by crashing deliberately into his car; and causing criminal damage to the car. On the first occasion, it came to trial with my colleague, who was defending. He raised a defence that the detective in charge of the case was pursuing it out of spite to assist the businessman, and that there was an allegation that an affair with the wife was at the real root of the case. The defence had contended that the case revolved around both his sexual behaviour with the wife, and the involvement of the detective ,and that the accusation against the defendant had been made deliberately. As I remember, it was also implied that the detective had misbehaved.

The trial judge adjourned the case for an investigation into these allegations. After some months, the case was re-listed, and the judge, addressing the court, held that there had been no truth in any of the allegations made by the defence, making strong comments on how scurrilous such allegations had been.

My first course of action was to try to persuade the judge that he should not conduct the trial himself, as he would not be able to ignore the allegations, and their refutation, so implicitly leading to the lack of an objective hearing of the case. This failed, and it was obvious there and then that we were in for a rocky ride.

In fact, I told the defendant we were going to lose the case; the judge hated him and was beginning thoroughly to dislike me, and we would lose badly. The only strategy I had was to make every valid submission which I could to infuriate him; it was clear that the more decisions he had to make, the more faults I would be able to find and raise on appeal.

It was a desperate tactic, but what else was there? The defendant agreed that he would continue to plead 'not guilty', and we would go ahead. It was somewhat fortunate that, as my practice was providing some good Crown Court cases, I had decided to work hard on the complexities and practice of arguing evidential matters before a judge. In fact, I had carefully read the whole subject again, as it was cropping up in case after case, where the prosecutor, myself and the judge were continually opening our 'Archbold' (the barristers 'Bible on criminal law, practice and pleadings), on issues of admissibility.

I had not realised, when taking the academic and professional courses, how central this subject was to be in any court work. Standing in court, facing the judge, and a spirited and authoritative attack by the prosecutor, soon changed that view.

My prosecutor at Chelmsford was very experienced, fair-minded, and authoritative. There is no doubt that every submission or application he made was acceded to; every one of mine was rejected, as had been my initial objections. The indictment appeared to have been accepted in the first trial, and certainly any other application or objection on my part would have received short shrift. This was a judge-led trial, and he was in a hurry to get to sentence.

The prosecution case proceeded, with the prosecutor given a very smooth and untroubled ride. The defence was to be self-defence, namely, that he was threatened by the complainant, that he was going to be beaten up by him when he stepped from his car with two friends and an iron bar in his possession, and that he, the defendant, had had to crash into his car to delay him while he drove to the police station to seek refuge to report the threats.

The first witness whom I wished to call after the defendant, who was always called first, was to be his stepson, aged thirteen, who had seen the men step out of their car going towards the defendant, the complainant, armed with an iron bar. My solicitor had taken a statement from the school, testifying that on that day he had missed school, to assist in confirming his account. That could have been served and admitted as a business document if correctly taken (as indeed it had been).

When he was called the judge stopped him, and told me that I would not be permitted to call a thirteen-year-old witness in a Crown Court trial. He told me to leave court, think about this, and then come back and proceed with the trial. I did so, and returned, and again called my witness. The judge became incensed, and told me to go out again, since I could not have heard him - the boy was not to be called because of his age. I returned and again called the boy as my witness, despite the judge's becoming almost apoplectic.

He gave his evidence well and clearly, and was not intimidated by his surroundings; he made a good witness, as I had thought he would. The judge took over the prosecution role, and cross-examined him over the day, the date, and his school, and generally causing such complete confusion in his mind that he could not think straight about the incident or when it had happened, though he had stated he had not been at school that day. I introduced the fact that I had a signed statement from his school testifying that he had not attended that day, but the judge ruled that inadmissible. After destroying the boy's evidence, the judge then said to me that that was what happened when you called a thirteen-year-old to give evidence in the Crown Court. I did not reply, though I was very tempted to do so.

I then turned to my next witness, to testify that he knew both the complainant and the defendant extremely well, and that he was well aware of the relationship between the two men. The complainant had denied any ill feeling towards the defendant, or an attack, or possession of an iron bar. The witness could give the lie to that: he was also totally objective, and there was no bias from him towards either of them.

The judge stated that he was not going to allow this witness to give evidence, shouting at me, ' do you not know any law?' This evidence would go to the credit of the complainant, and was therefore inadmissible, he said, after more of a rant at me. I argued that it went to the heart of the case. Again the judge shouted at me for my ignorance, lack of knowledge of the rules of evidence, and asked me whether I had not learnt anything. He repeated that it went to credit only, and was inadmissible by this rule, which, it seemed, I had never heard of. I repeated that it was crucial evidence that the complainant hated the defendant, and that arming himself, and attacking him, was consistent with this testimony. It was ruled inadmissible in an insulting, patronising and self-congratulatory way.

Needless to say eventually the defendant was found guilty of all the offences, and was given a long sentence, comprising consecutive shorter sentences.

Before sentencing he asked the jury to stay and look at the defendant, as they would never see such wickedness again. He then ordered the Social Services to investigate the boy's situation, and to see whether they could take him from his parents, and put him into care.

I started working on an appeal straightaway. I drafted an Advice, which described in detail the whole proceedings, and the complaints I had about the unfairness with which the judge had conducted the trial. I then enumerated each of the Grounds of Appeal: this, in my case, was a succinct statement of the ground of objection. Some barristers amplify the grounds with argument or evidence; my style is to keep them as brief as possible, e.g. 'the learned judge erred in law by ruling inadmissible the evidence of ... on the grounds that it went merely to credit.'

I had discussed the possibility of an appeal with my head of chambers, but he considered that I had no chance. I then saw the top criminal barrister in Verulam Buildings, one well versed in the higher courts and the law. I sent him my papers. After reading the material he replied that I should continue, that he considered the appeal arguable, and that he advised me to go ahead.

The Grounds, Advice and the covering application for leave to appeal against conviction were then sent to the Registrar of the Court of Criminal Appeal for the single judge to grant leave to appeal. It was months before I received a reply, and, in the meantime I received a spate of cases concerning travellers, for whom chambers were constantly briefed.

Where some of the more interesting cases go to a number of hearings, over months, it assists the memory to keep cases chronological, rather than deal with one case completely and intersperse the others between hearings: in the above case, for instance, things did not run smoothly, and much more was to come.

The first case of this spate concerned a violent disorder charge against a number of travellers, following a gypsy wedding. It was a serious matter, as there were allegations of the possession of firearms and the use of clubs and other implements, and the case was to be a committal at Canterbury Magistrates Court, with the evidence to be heard.

Halfway through the hearing, there came the sounds of a huge fight going on in the lobby outside the door of the court. When one went outside, the scene resembled a bar fight in a cowboy film, with, possibly, twenty men and women all fighting, throwing chairs at each other and causing complete mayhem. After an adjournment, on returning to the court the next day, we found two rows of travellers sitting in the lobby facing each other, with a row of policemen sitting between them. The hearing proceeded, but I was not briefed for the Crown Court, being fairly junior at this stage.

After this, off went three of us to Northampton, in a Crown Court case involving a family of travellers who had obtained money from a number of elderly householders for repairing their roofs. Seeing broken tiles, or houses where tiles, or even one tile, had apparently fallen from the roof, the house holders were persuaded to have their roofs re-tiled. The travellers would then accompany them to their banks to withdraw the money in cash to give them. They were charged up to four figure sums for the repairs, and they were intimidated into having work done, and into paying.

There was evidence that local radio had warned aged householders to beware of such approaches, and a number of householders, all of at least pensionable age, attended court. The prosecution and court were geared up for the most sympathetic presentation of the case, the witnesses being assisted up the steps to the witness box, where, in most cases, the need for this was far from evident. Much feeling was aroused by the allegations, and the prosecutor – a most competent and local counsel - was primed and ready for us.

For our part, we were all from the same chambers, which was most unusual but, for us, helpful, both in terms of our travel, and professionally, as we would all be supporting each other in court and would know each other's cases.

I was representing the wife, who was accused in the conspiracy of threatening the householders, and damaging their gardens so as to get her husband and son paid.

Our lead counsel started cross-examining aggressively, as instructed, since many defendants demand fire and brimstone from their counsel. The second went along the same path, but more circumspectly, since the witnesses were retired accountants, doctors and solicitors. My case rested on descriptions of the wife's behaviour. Whilst it had to be tested factually, there was little to be gained by an attack on any of these professional people, especially on the issue of what they had done to get the work, or what work they had in fact done.

The judge's patience snapped because of the aggression shown to the witnesses, and there was a furious argument when he pulled up counsel for their tone and lack of consideration in cross-examination. Since it was not directed at me, I kept my head down, as it became most uncomfortable, and there was nothing I could say to help.

At the end of the day, the others were called into the judge's room, and received a dressing down. There was a threat that their fee would come under scrutiny if they continued to behave in this way.

I played no part in this, but the next day, as I was leaving court for lunch, the judge met me outside and had a pleasant chat with me, finding out a bit about me, and possibly appreciating my approach, which had been to adduce what evidence I could to assist my defence, by encouraging the witnesses to agree with what I put. Because of their status, I could be subtle; and treating each with full respect obtained useful points, without arousing the jury, who were close to livid at some stages.

The thrust from the judge (and it was an approach I always accepted), was that most witnesses are decent people who come to court voluntarily; they expose themselves to attack, but should be treated fairly and courteously. It will be obvious where this is not the case, and, if dishonest or badly biased or unpleasant, they can be tested. With a jury watching courtesy is still invaluable, and such a witness can be led into further untruths or wild exaggeration. A row between witness and counsel is never pleasant. Seeking agreement is far easier and more effective.

Needless to say, our clients were all convicted, and received long prison sentences. It was not many years later that the father and son were convicted of robberies of aged householders in their own homes, and received even longer prison sentences.

The last of the spate of three was in a case in which another traveller had purported to do work for an aged householder, and was said to have stolen a cheque for £12,000. He denied it, but was convicted after a full trial. When I went to see him in the cells, he asked me if I wanted to know whether he was guilty. It is a matter which counsel never raises, as, if he does, and is told by the lay client that he is guilty, he cannot act for him if he pleads not guilty: this is an important ethical stance to which counsel always adheres.

At this stage I could ask him, and said that whilst I thought he was, there was something that troubled me about his total guilt. He said that he did take the cheque, but had asked for £1200. Finding that the cheque had been wrongly made out for ten times that sum, he kept it and cashed it, well knowing his dishonesty. That satisfied my feeling that he had not been quite as wicked as the prosecution had alleged, and that he had not stolen the cheque, but it had been freely given to him.

By this time, I had received the notice of appeal, on which the single judge writes a short paragraph on the reasons for granting or refusing the appeal, and granting bail or legal aid if sought. He had refused my application for the appeal, and stated shortly that the appeal involved no law. Since the appeal is based on an error or misstatement of law, that is normally the end of the matter.

However, there is an appeal against the single judge's decision; but it must be made before the full court of three appeal judges, chaired at this level of criminal cases by a Lord Justice. I sought an appeal before the full court. It was the first challenge I had made in this way, and I never had to do it again.

It lasted some ten minutes, after which the Deputy Lord Chief Justice found that there was plenty of law in the case, and the appeal was set down for two whole days. That is a long time for most appeals, unless they are in very serious or complex cases, which could not be said of mine. Nevertheless, it was to be my first appeal against conviction, and only the second time I would be in the Court of Appeal. It was going to be nerve-wracking, and downright scary.

Since we are in the Court of Appeal, it may well be sensible to finish this episode, before turning to other work, and very different cases, in a fresh chapter. At the court, I was accompanied by a pupil from chambers, who had worked on the hearing with me, and was there with a pile of authorities, open at the right page, to be pressed into my hand when I held it out. The team worked well.

It started with Lord Justice Mustill - one of the most brilliant at the Bar - asking me whether I realised that one of their number had had to read the twenty-nine grounds of my appeal. I replied that I felt they were necessary, to paint a full picture of the fairness of the trial, but that if I failed on the first three, I would not seek to rely on the others. With that, he appeared satisfied that that would be a reasonable approach, and would, more importantly, save time for the court, which would not have to deal, however peremptorily, with the other twenty-six. The rebuke was gentle, courteous, but pointed.

My opponent was the prosecutor at Chelmsford, and he appeared confident, prepared and seemed at home: I was not. We set off, and the first ground was that the charges should not have been on the same indictment, being neither part of a series of similar cases, in law, or in fact; nor were they part of the same transaction – to put it simply.

The second was that my witness's evidence not being allowed was wrong, since it went to the central issue of the case, namely the need for self-defence towards an impending attack by the complainant, who hated the appellant. The complainant had denied any ill feelings towards the appellant, so the judge had contended that any challenges to that would only go to his credit as a witness. The third ground was not in the same category as these, and it was on them that the appeal rested.

Counsel for the Crown replied confidently and impressively, but the points were well made, and he failed to persuade the court otherwise. My pupil handed me a note saying that it was going well!

The court then addressed my opponent, telling him that they had found for me, but asking whether he wished to address them on the Proviso. This allowed the court to find in law that the appeal was made out, but, putting it shortly, that they could disallow it, because the court was of the view that that was the right course of action in order to dispose correctly and judiciously of the matter.

The tables were now turned (and another note from my pupil said, 'You've got him.') I wished that I had her confidence, but this time he was nervous, having been caught by surprise on a quite unusual and difficult point of law. My role was simpler, and

I could argue my case with confidence, because of their finding, and because of the conduct of the trial and its unfairness. I was required either not to respond, or to say very little.

We had succeeded, and the case was reported in the Criminal Appeal Reports. It became an authority on the joinder of indictments, and the rule about evidence going to credit (and provided a ready example for practitioners). It is one of the leading cases on the former, and, over the last few years has started a line of argument, with other cases following it on the same subject – what may be the crucial issue in a case.

The essence of the judgment on joinder had been that the four cases were not a series where similarity in fact or law existed. The worst part of the case was when Lord Mustill LJ addressed me, asking, 'Putting aside all the legal authorities, Mr Forward, what is your opinion - must there be a similarity in either law or fact or should it be both?' I was terrified at being asked to throw out all the authorities and to speak freely off the cuff on such a subject. Of course, I played it safe, echoing the authorities. He smiled, and seemed to have enjoyed putting me on the spot.

Chapter 14
Vindicated in my most Difficult Case

Luckily, I was receiving some good cases in my own name, and in the Crown Court. The normal work for chambers' newest tenant was in the Magistrates Court, and consisted largely of overseeing bail applications for the other tenants, whilst they dealt with their Crown Court criminal cases. The other work we did were the planning cases for travellers: eviction notices for unlawfully trespassing on land, etc. After the Magistrates Court hearings of these matters, appeals were usually lodged ending in the highest tribunals: instructions were always issued to obtain as much time as possible, and to persist until the bitter end. The further encouragement for such work was the size of the fees paid.

This work required specialism, and I only had to step in for two cases which others had to return. In one, the authorities cited the wrong section of the relevant Act, and the case was thrown out. The second involved a traveller, who had been tending a small strawberry field just off a major road in Hampshire for decades, and was summoned for residing thereon in a small hut.

This contained all his gardening and other tools, and somewhere where he could rest and sleep, as he was an early riser, and transport was a problem. The case was contested, and he was an excellent, truthful and credible witness who was well known to everyone who used the route, and who had been buying his wares for over thirty years or so. I was pleased that he was found not guilty, to quiet applause, and allowed to continue.

Despite my protestations that I would never touch matrimonial cases, or any that involved the custody or care of children, I took on three in all.

The first was at my local court, where the parties were disputing the ownership of their settee. The district judge announced that if they did not agree in five minutes, he would order it to be sawn in half and distributed.

The next took not much more time, again thanks to the sound common sense of the judge. Whilst I had declined this type of work, I readily admitted that those adjudicating such cases had more than a good measure of common sense, which made the work almost worth doing. This case involved a mother of four children, one of whom had the most serious case of psoriasis imaginable. He had to be bodily washed at least every day, and then treated: he had been to school twice in a year, and was homebound virtually all the time. His mother had to cope with this, the other three children and maintain the family home, apparently with no help from her husband. In fact, it was the opposite for all he was concerned with was to alter their surname by changing a z to a k (as I remember), since the word then translated as 'magistrate' or 'leader'. He produced dictionaries to support his case but my solicitor had found entries in others to the contrary.

The judge was appalled by his treatment of his wife, and by his persistence in such a minor and contested matter, bearing in mind what his wife was going through, without the need for frequent attendances in court.

The case was thrown out in seconds, and the claimant was lucky not to get bundled out physically.

The third was at the request of my best criminal solicitor at that time. Since Gerard had briefed me on a number of occasions, and came on a case to North Wales with me three times, it is right to name him, as he became important and a friend. He asked me to deal with ancillary matters in his own divorce. I told him I knew nothing of the subject matter, or the law, and would not even know where to sit in the court. He persisted, and I refused again, saying that the idea that I should represent him was ridiculous, and he would be at a complete disadvantage.

He refused to accept my refusal, and insisted, saying that he would take all the consequences, but he wanted me. He was objecting to his wife's seeking a nominal maintenance order, was prepared to allow her possibly to transfer or to cash their son's insurance into her name, and was refusing to pay their son any maintenance.

In conference, at the door of the court, I informed him that since he was, to my knowledge, still in love with his wife, if she wanted a blank cheque for money he would unhesitatingly give it to her. I then asked why his son should lose his insurance money. And, lastly, since he had the boy every weekend, and spent freely on anything he wanted, paying maintenance in a small fixed sum would be cheaper, and he could control the spending on him. I may have mentioned a tax benefit, too.

This was promptly agreed, and the order drafted and signed. I had gone against every one of his instructions. Afterwards he explained that the result was precisely why he had wanted me: 'It was to talk sense into me!'

As it was a favour he sent me a few Personal Injury claims to advise on, in accident cases, which I polished off sitting in comfort at home at weekends, which helped my finances.

It was not the only case I dealt with in complete ignorance. A colleague of his sent me a case in the industrial tribunal, involving a foreman in a garden centre who had taken home a Christmas tree, allegedly without permission. He had been an impeccable workman, had been promoted to a foreman some eight years previously, and had never been the subject of any disciplinary procedure, but was sacked forthwith. He also alleged he had been given permission, but he could not adduce any evidence of that.

Attending court with my solicitor, and not many papers, I wore my very best suit and tie, and adopted a supercilious and very confident manner towards my young but more experienced opponent. I hardly spoke, but opined that their treatment of him was absurd and totally unreasonable; but that my solicitor, on my say-so, was prepared to agree a very reasonable offer of compensation without fuss. My bluff worked and the offer - actually a rather good one for us - was accepted readily.

The last non-criminal case I remember from these early days was an appeal against a Criminal Injuries Compensation Board, which refused the claimant's compensation for being injured in a street robbery, on the grounds that he had claimed for another the previous year; that it occurred in the same street as that in which he lived; and that an exception meant that he was disqualified for an award because his way of life, living in a poor district where crimes were committed, was such that he was more prone to injury. That remarkable decision was overturned, and he received the compensation which he richly deserved.

Having dealt with a case of repatriation of a client to the West Indies before a Social Security tribunal, and having retained no memory of the facts or result, I was sent to an interesting case in North Wales. It could just about be described as a criminal case, and Gerard came with me on each of the three days for which it went to court.

The case was brought under the Unsolicited Goods and Services Act 1971, the allegation being that a National Holiday magazine had sent an invoice to a landlady in North Wales, asking her for the fees for two adverts she had placed in their magazine. This was a criminal allegation, prosecuted by the local Trading Standards office, and, as it could be dealt with in the Crown Court as well as by the magistrates, we elected a committal hearing in the lower court, calling live evidence to argue that there would be insufficient evidence for the case to go forward.

The court was in a village called Llantrisant, I believe. Certainly, when I looked it up, I found that it was south of Llandudno and near Llanfair. We had found a small eight-bedroom hotel nearby, with a fabulous view of Mount Snowdon directly opposite. Gerard and I travelled with our lay client and her best friend and manager, and were booked in at the same hotel. As proprietors and manager of such a national magazine, they were worldly, well educated and well-to-do, very expensively turned out, and great company; they would make excellent witnesses. That they were also extremely attractive had no bearing on our enjoyment.

The court opened its doors as we arrived: they had no other work that Friday, and this pattern continued the next two Fridays. All the staff spoke nothing but Welsh even in court, except for the actual hearings, when they unhappily used English. Being English, and, worse, coming from London, we were their implacable enemies, especially given that we were making accusations against a Welsh landlady. All the hearings were conducted in a hostile atmosphere by the leader of the Trading Standards, the chief witness and prosecutor, following the landlady.

We went into full attack, and it was not long before we discovered that the documentation completed by the landlady had been overwritten, a crucial date having been altered – the correct word was forged. The prosecution were devastated, and this was not the only suspect evidence she produced: it was obvious, to anyone not Welsh, that she was lying about most of her evidence, and had to accept forgery in her documents, though the bench tried desperately not to hear it.

When we came to the evidence of the chief Trading Standards officer things got more lively as he: a) knew little law, especially on the subject of evidence; b) was a very important local person used to getting his own way, especially before his own people; and c) was one who would not tolerate any objection or challenge.

I stopped him with virtually every sentence he tried to utter, as it was all hearsay, giving evidence of what he had been told by all sorts of people, but none witnesses. He became infuriated, and complained he was not being allowed to give one word of evidence. I replied that there were rules of evidence, and that his was almost completely inadmissible every time he started. As the bench were lay persons, it was for the clerk to advise on the law and to ensure that the bench made the proper decisions: business had to be conducted properly, whatever her sympathies or 'Welshness'. She well knew that we would fly to the High Court in the Strand if she erred and that that would bring down enormous criticism.

Our objections to the evidence of the Trading Standards had to be upheld, and he was right - he was hardly allowed to give any evidence, because of its inadmissibility.

On the third day, the case was dismissed by the bench – through gritted teeth - but in refusing our costs, they clearly felt better. Our clients were fully satisfied, and did not wish to pursue the costs, as they were well off enough, and happy to have paid my solicitor and myself privately.

Having dealt with the business, may I digress about the fun we had with the case? Our hotel was run by a London accountant who had got fed up with accountancy, and London, and had decided to open a small hotel in a beautiful area, and to do all the cooking himself. He proved a wonderful cook. Breakfast, for instance, was laid out on a fifteen foot table, and would display five different freshly caught fish every morning, together with all the conventional breakfast fare: devilled kidneys, etc.

The evening meals were all magnificent, and he would wander round the tables chatting to us all, whilst popping off to finish his chess games with some of his regulars in the restaurant.

The presence of four smartly, elegantly dressed and personable foreigners there encouraged much gossip, and I inadvertently let slip to our taxi driver the words 'Hollywood film producers', to spark off further gossip and speculation.

Our windows opened to unparalleled scenery for the UK, with that snow-capped mountain, and we left by hailing the train to Llandudno – a lovely Victorian seaside town – by standing on the line with our thumbs up like hitch hikers. And we called that work.

What was indeed work was the next case, which became the most difficult I have had. In 1984-85 the biggest change to affect a criminal lawyer was the Police and Criminal Evidence Act

1984. It was to make further provision in relation to the powers and duties of the police, and to regulate their powers and protect the public. It made provision concerning stopping and searching; arrests and detention; investigation; identification; and interviewing detainees. It added, crucially, questioning, rules for determining, and placing a duty on the prosecution to exclude evidence obtained by unfair treatment and confessions. Reliability was to be the test.

It added more and more pages entitled Codes of Practice, specifying in complete detail, and in the custody record, conditions that had to be adhered to, and relevant entries countersigned, to indicate compliance. In that way, rights were fully protected and discretion largely removed. The areas covered were specified as: the right to legal advice; conditions of detention and care and treatment (down to enough sleep and food prior to interview); cautions; and interviews. But, moreover, Notes of Guidance encompassing the spirit of the changes were added to each part of the Code. These also had to be complied with in any test on admissibility.

My case plunged me into the thick of these changes, and it took me weeks to become well-versed in this new law, ready for the hearing.

The case against my client was that he, with others, conspired to bring a large quantity of drugs into the country; it was suggested that their value was about half a million pounds. My client drove a van, containing furniture for his father's business, to Holland; and returned with no furniture, but with a large number of boxes containing drugs. Another employee took over the van in this country, and was stopped in possession of the van and boxes containing the drugs.

The man who employed him to drive, the man stopped with the van and drugs, his employee (or minder), and my defendant's wife were also charged, and committed to the Crown Court for trial: a drugs squad was involved in the case and its prosecution.

At the Magistrates Court I took issue with the solicitor acting for my defendant's wife, suggesting that, as there was no evidence against her other than that she had sat in the van with the husband and their baby in a car park that night, there should be a hearing on a submission that there was no case for her to answer. My concern was that for her to be unnecessarily put on trial with her husband would put him under huge pressure. That course of action was not adopted, and she joined her husband in the dock at Kingston Crown Court.

The evidence against us was contained in admissions in his five interviews, and one written confession under caution. We got to court, and I had the problem that his co-defendants were telling him to plead guilty, and save his wife. They tackled him all the time on this topic, and he kept asking me whether they were not right, as their barristers were saying the same thing (and one of them was leading counsel with a junior). I had decided to challenge the admissibility of all the interviews, relying on the Police and Criminal Evidence Act.

Again, the others put more pressure on him to plead, implying that I did not know what I was doing, and doubtless contrasting my length of call and experience with theirs. I took unusual steps to acquaint those acting for leading counsel with what I was doing, and why, and that my client fully appreciated our defence, and agreed with my handling of the case. I added that since there was no evidence against the wife, she would succeed in establishing that she had no case to answer, so my client's sacrifice would be for nothing. (To my mind, she had only been added by the police to put pressure on her husband, so as to make him plead guilty).

I informed the judge that we wanted a *voir dire*, and wanted all the officers called to give evidence. This included all the squad members and their Detective Chief Superintendent, and many from the police station and custody staff. Also, I required, and had instructed, a psychologist, who specialised in dealing with vulnerable and suggestible defendants in interviews, as my client had a low IQ, and was in that range. After much thought, I decided to call the defendant in the *voir dire*, as well, since that type of hearing was before the judge only, and the jury were excluded – the procedure was known as a trial within a trial.

What he said could not be repeated before the jury, and he made a good witness, and was the only one who could tell the court what the police did: for instance, they produced his fingerprint on one of the boxes. His evidence was that they had taken him to another police station where the boxes were stored in the middle of the night and asked him to pick one up. On the *voir dire* I was able to call the custody officer of that station, where his record disclosed a five minute visit in the middle of the night by the prisoner to that other police station, with a drug squad detective.

The *voir dire* must have been one of the longest ever for one defendant, as it lasted ten days: the others did not participate, but occasionally wandered in to listen to what became a complete rehearsal of the Sections of the Act, the Codes of Practice and the Notes for Guidance.

To go through all that was alleged in our defence would be tedious, even for a lawyer, but there was 'oppression' (a specific provision in the Act), to do with a detective's expressed interest in his wife, strengthened by a note of her phone number on her statement to him. Another section stated that unfair treatment could consist of anything said or done in an interview which could affect the conduct of the trial unless disproved by the prosecution. This could therefore include anything that had this effect.

Many procedures required the authority of a senior officer, but it was alleged his whereabouts were unknown, and that he could not be contacted and countersign. On cross-examining the officers at the police station, it transpired that he was available and on duty that night at a police function close by, and had left his details in case he needed to be contacted as duty senior officer.

Together with many similar minor issues, the principal difficulty for the Crown surrounded the request and provision of a solicitor for the defendant; he was semi-illiterate, but was asked to read and agree to dispense with his rights. The record on the solicitor (and other rights) was completely unsatisfactory, in a nutshell. His vulnerability and suggestibility came into the issue to strengthen all the failures.

At the end of the *voir dire* the judge ruled that all his interviews were admissible and, since it was Christmas, he adjourned the trial.

During the break, I had another stroke of luck. A *Times* law report reported an almost identical case, involving the same breaches of the Police and Criminal Evidence Act, in which the appellant had succeeded. The central issue was that of the failures involved in abusing the right to a solicitor.

When we returned to court the judge called me into his room, told me that he had also read the report, admitted that he had made the wrong decision, and apologised. He ordered a re-trial with a different judge.

This judge was from Liverpool; he accepted without demur the mandatory nature of much of the Act, and that the Crown had a heavy duty to establish the reliability of the interviews. His experience and knowledge reduced the *voir dire* to five days, and he appeared ready to believe the defence case as we proceeded and put the Crown firmly to proof.

It did not help that, in a question from the Judge to the Detective Chief Superintendent in charge, the latter lied in his answer during cross-examination by leading and junior counsel. Whilst they did not pick it up, when I started to cross-examine this officer it was the first thing I put, and he accepted shame-facedly that he had lied in answer to the judge's direct question to him. (That counsel still owes me a crate, so he promised, for that!)

The judge ruled that all the confessions were inadmissible, for the reason that the Detective Chief Superintendent in charge had been responsible for thirteen breaches of the Police and Criminal Evidence Act. That should, we thought, be the end; however, the Crown Prosecution Service and counsel decided to carry on with the trial, on the basis that my clients did take the lorry, and had parked at night in a dark corner of a car park.

Since my clients had the young baby, and had stayed in the vehicle in the car park during the night, it was contended that this was to get the baby to sleep as well as my clients, until the morning, before driving back. The jury acquitted us, the case was dropped against the other defendants on somewhat similar grounds (illiteracy and breaches in their cases, though health also featured in the case of one). The defendant's wife had been found earlier to have had no case to answer, and her case had been dismissed.

The walk into the sunshine after the verdict with my client and his wife and daughter is the moment that has kept me in the profession for all these years. As those in a similar position will know, it is a truly magical moment. It was enhanced, personally, as he had been looking at ten years or so, and I felt that I had played some part in his acquittal.

It even cancelled out the disappointment from putting in the fee note, appealing to the Senior Costs judge at the High Court on the refusal of the Crown court to pay for some hundred hours of preparation, only to be told that one was supposed to know the law, and being cut financially by him to the bone. As I came to realise, I had the best job in the world, and the worst system of payment.

I could write a whole chapter on not getting paid. I was told, a few years in as a tenant, that, on average, barristers will lose about ten per cent of their fees for one reason or another. What I was not told was that in another number of cases you argue, remind, chase up interminably, appeal to High Court judges and the Legal aid authorities for up to two years, before you recover these fees, or not. They amount to some thousands of pounds in many cases.

The other nugget of information, again confirmed, was that most barristers have a perpetual overdraft equalling a year's fees. So, deduct ten per cent of your fees, about twelve per cent for your clerks' commission, fifteen per cent for rent, and more for necessary overheads - it can be a somewhat precarious existence at the Bar.

You are encouraged to write off smaller fees that are proving difficult to chase, or to take a smaller sum to get at least some of your fee. Barristers cannot sue for their fees, and, in many cases, are at the mercy, financially, of solicitors, whose delays, in many cases, are legendary, as are the legal aid, Crown Court and High Court paymasters. Yes, fees are at times very acceptable, even generous; but there are serious drawbacks, money-wise, from being at the Bar and being, not a 'fat cat', but the average practitioner. I shall touch occasionally on such problems, since they have been my main concern for over thirty years. For many of those my wife has accepted that we live in an Alice in Wonderland state where the Bar and money is concerned.

It was over Christmas that I received my instructions to attend Inner London Crown Court, to apply for bail where a bench warrant had been issued and the defendant had just been arrested and taken to court. It was not uncommon. However, when I saw my client, he said they had the wrong man. His details matched completely, and there was nothing he could put forward to confirm this protest. I saw the judge and acquainted him with my concern, I half-believed him, though such facts as existed were all against him. To his credit, the judge allowed me another visit with him, and more details were checked.

The culprit had been involved in a social security fraud, but had absconded before the conclusion of the trial. More details were checked: he had a previous conviction for a similar offence, had been the subject of a psychiatric report with those details, and had the same National Insurance number. I asked him how these details could be the same, and he remembered that at the time of his report there had been someone else there for a report with the same name.

More convinced, I returned to court and the judge was more inclined to agree with me. Judges were encouraged to be more sceptical when faced with mitigating factors and unusual defences, so he told me to try once more to get a fingerprint confirmation for this offence. That failed as at that time it was not the practice to fingerprint for social security matters, and this was the last step. Nevertheless, the judge granted him bail, instead of keeping him in custody for the three-week Christmas break, and he returned to court.

This time the prosecution had obtained the officer in the case, who knew him, to state whether my client was the man involved in the trial. He took one look, and agreed that he was not the accused. The mistake was put right, and the judge wrote a letter for him stating that, if stopped under his name, his details had been copied respecting someone else, and he was to produce it if ever challenged. Whilst logic was staring him in the face, the judge acted humanely, where many would have rejected the explanation out of hand.

What brings this case to mind was that my fee for the two days was rejected: we were told after months of pushing that 'the case was not in the list.' Of course it wasn't - he was arrested after the list was published.

The clerks at the court refused to pay, despite the assertion by my clerks, myself, our diaries and our word that the fee was earned and a proper one. This has been the case a number of times with warrants, and one concentrates on the better cases, rather than fighting every battle for years.

This time I told the clerk's office at court that I would contact the judge and obtain his confirmation of my attendance since, in writing a letter to the defendant, he would undoubtedly remember such an exceptional matter. For once, we were successful, and the fee was paid promptly to avoid my contacting the judge.

Nearly all counsel in my chambers defended, although there is nothing to prevent one prosecuting as well. In fact, the cab-rank rule instructs counsel to take whatever comes. Prosecuting would open me to at least as much work as defending, and, with my clerk's encouragement, we notified the solicitors' branch at the Yard to allow me to prosecute.

I was instructed to attend the Magistrates Court (Uxbridge, I remember) and sent the brief. When I arrived, a solicitor from the

Yard was there to meet me early, and I was already at court. My training in the police had always emphasised punctuality. He then tested me on the facts contained in the brief, which I answered satisfactorily.

It was an actual case, and I presented it to the justices whilst, behind me, he would tug my jacket, and whisper in my ear points which I should be asking. The ordeal was soon over, we got our conviction, and I was notified that I had passed the test. I was on the list for the Magistrates Courts. Cases came in thick and fast, and were, at first, traffic matters. Sometimes there would be two or three to prosecute, though, after the first, the rate of pay was discounted for each, slightly disappointingly. Nevertheless, it was all experience, and many beginners would have presented the case for nothing - just in order to learn.

There was slightly less stress, as the witnesses were mostly police officers, with their notes, and the resulting conviction did not affect one as personally as defending and having your client sent to prison. Mitigation on a finding of guilt was also less stressful, but this time the court would rely on their prosecutor's knowing the law and guiding them, along with their clerk. Higher courts would be very displeased if something went wrong and prosecuting counsel had not put it right.

My next case is a good indication of that. My client was alleged to have caused actual bodily harm to a high-ranking civil servant at the doorway of a public toilet. My client was a Royal Marine, and the matter occurred in the middle of the night. He denied the matter, but the circumstances led one to wonder. I was not instructed to put forward a defence justifying the assault because of something that had occurred between them in the toilet. My solicitor was of the same mind. I did ask the Crown if the civil servant had any previous convictions.

I repeated formally a request again for this information and received nothing. This material should always be provided even if there were none, or at least one would be told before trial. At trial, I asked prosecuting counsel the question again, and nothing was disclosed.

Whilst we were waiting for the jury to return with its verdict, the officer who was sitting next to me told me that the complainant had a conviction and asked whether I knew that it was for importuning a male person. After his conviction, I immediately appealed to the Court of Appeal.

At the Court I stood up and got as far as saying that I represented the appellant when the presiding judge told me to sit down. 'We want to hear from him,' he interjected, angrily indicating prosecuting counsel. He received a complete berating from the judges for his lack of the disclosure, requested three times, and the hearing lasted some twenty minutes. The appeal was allowed instantly.

Chapter 15
Learning my Trade and Polishing up Technique

There is not an even escalation of work at the Bar. One day you are prosecuting a careless driving allegation, where there has been a minor accident, with one driver accused, and another making the allegation, and the next, you get to the door of the court and your client comes staggering out, bleeding badly from a stomach wound. Rushing him into court before it opened, the clerk gave him bail, and sent him off to hospital - such was a case from Bexleyheath, tried at the Old Bailey.

The defendant was committed for an assault in a car park, in which he had struck a man with a weapon, but had himself been stabbed by the man's father. The other two gave their evidence in the trial.

In the trial, the defendant's interview was contested, on the grounds of his unfitness due to the stab wound. The police doctor looked at him through the hatch in the cell door, and could tell that he was perfectly fit for interview(?). That was accepted by the judge, though the jury were clearly unhappy. Important evidence was given of his health and serious loss of weight, which I pointed out to the jury as he stood there in his jacket, which appeared to be several sizes too big, and was hanging off him. The judge stated that he looked alright to him, and there was open laughter from the jury.

A witness called by the Crown told the court how many floors up he was when looking through his window, and all he could see, which was powerful evidence. The incident had happened on the far side of a large vehicle, as they were standing beside it. Calculating the angle which obtained from that height to the roof of the vehicle, and beyond, to where the men were, provided exact evidence that they could not have seen the incident at all. The distances were known, and trigonometry allowed calculation of the angle from the window down to the ground, a certain number of yards out from the nearby wall of the block of flats.

I was quite pleased by this (and the jury was impressed), and the judge asked me if I was proving this mathematically. As the jury and I were getting a little sceptical of the judge's bias, I was a bit flash, and retorted; 'Trigonometrically, My Lord.'(Old Bailey judges, though the same rank as other Crown Court judges, were always addressed as My Lord or Your Lordship – my first experience of this.) We got a 'Harrumph' in reply.

My client was found not guilty, but before he could be discharged, the judge announced he was going to be bound over to keep the peace, on a sum to be forfeited if he failed to do so. He asked if I wished to address him on the amount. This was in the presence of the jury, and was a most unusual step.

I stated that since he had no previous convictions, had been acquitted, and, because of his impeccable character, was most unlikely ever to commit any offence in the future, there would be no objection, and the sum or length of time for the order to continue would be of no consequence. The jury enjoyed that answer to what seemed an exercise in spite.

I am not sure whether biased judges realise that too strong a direction, or an unfair view of, or admission of, evidence, can rebound on them. It is almost a national characteristic that we support the underdog. (Similarly, prosecutors hectoring a witness, or being too long-winded or unfair in their assumptions, can have the same effect.) I was sure that a two-hour speech by the Crown at the end of a short trial in one case would bore the jury, and that was visibly apparent; a most unusual defence succeeded. A concise speech, not repeating all, or even many, facts helps if combined with humour, and if not refuted by insuperable evidence.

The same was true in the case of a football riot between QPR and Portsmouth, when my client from Portsmouth (where I was now being instructed on occasions), with many other fans, caused a riot in which the crowd spilled on to the pitch, and women and children had to be lifted into the higher stands to avoid serious injury. The riot made the television, and we had full coverage to show in the trial.

It is right to say that my client had been in the back row of the stand, and was walking towards, and grinning at, the fight that was taking place among the supporters, and enjoying the spectacle. Nevertheless, he was arrested for participation in the riot by encouraging it, and faced a possible conspiracy charge to go with it.

At a pre-trial review, where arrangements were made for the trial, there were some ten counsel appearing for the defendants. I made a submission to the trial judge that the date set for the trial should be vacated, to avoid its taking place during the World Cup. My argument was that the coverage, on television and in the papers, would inevitably feature hooliganism.

Jurors would see this night after night when they returned home from the trial, would see the hooligans in action, and hear discussions on the subject, and the calls for conviction of those involved and tougher deterrent sentences. Such prejudice would be unavoidable. The judge failed to grasp this, and the trial went ahead in the middle of the World Cup and the well-foreseen coverage of hooliganism. None of the other counsel supported me.

There were about a dozen of the away fans, and one from the home side: the judge was addressed straight away, very ably and persuasively, to dismiss the charge against the local supporter, which he did, although there was plenty of evidence against him.

Our trial carried on, and it became clear from the footage - which showed a truly alarming series of events on the pitch and in the stands - that my client had done nothing to encourage a riot (the Crown's case),but had enjoyed the spectacle from a safe distance.

The judge considered that it had clearly been a conspiracy to cause the riot, because the rioters had gathered at the top of the stairway and down as far as the toilets and bar, and could be seen sitting together, obviously planning their next moves. Some of the jury got the point without the need for the explanation which followed in my speech, and started to grin at the judge's lack of knowledge of football matches.

He then seized on the fact that some of the spectators started to leave the ground early, and that this included our clients. This showed, he said, that they had no interest in the game, and that it was clearly a conspiracy. Again, the jury were there before me, and I not only explained just why this was, but added that, in their present form, if they hadn't scored by then, no-one would expect Portsmouth to score in the last ten minutes. The judge looked perplexed as the jury started to laugh out loud.

His summing up was as biased as we expected, but the damage was done: my client, for one, was acquitted. The others were largely convicted. I received more briefs at Portsmouth, and occasionally at Winchester and Southampton, and welcomed the trips to Portsmouth. My naval service had been there, and it was enjoyable to revisit the town and its neighbour, Southsea. Winchester seemed to have almost the same status as the Old Bailey, and its judges were also highly experienced and testing, so there was some apprehension in going there for a trial.

I also met some of defending counsel from the football riot case there, and several came up and apologised for not supporting me in my application to avoid the World Cup coverage, acknowledging its sense and the likely prejudice.

It was at Portsmouth that, in order to obtain a relatively large number of defendants, the police ran an operation in which they captured many folios of footage of an area of streets where thefts from vehicles were regularly occurring. That lasted for many weeks, and involved a great deal of detailed work. There was little we could do with the wealth and detail of evidence produced, but we had a run; and the weather there was always better, and the court staff so much nicer, even to London counsel.

The local counsel in that circuit seemed much more experienced and capable, and could make decisions without having to be closely advised all the time by the Crown Prosecution Service. Hence they would take a view as prosecutors that would accord with common sense, costs and a sensible result. The judges would welcome such reasonableness and economy.

One typical case was that of an indecent assault on a patient by a male nurse at a local hospital. The Crown produced at least ten other nurses to testify against him, plus the patient; we produced the same number willing to testify for us. Most of the witnesses were to give character evidence as well.

We eventually forced the disclosure of the patient's psychiatric reports, contained in several large boxes, which Gerard and I spent hours combing through. The prosecution gave up on the case when confronted by her reports, and false accusations against other nurses, and, to their credit, did so readily.

Meeting my client at Bexleyheath had been really dramatic, but my worst moment was when I was dealing with a rape matter in another court nearby, and was standing addressing the bench when those on the bench went white, and ran out of the court. On turning round, I saw my client sawing at his throat with a razor blade; there was blood everywhere. The gaoler and I leapt on him and restrained him, and he was dragged off to the cells. He was livid with me, as I had prevented him from cutting his throat in a suicide bid.

It might seem as if court proceedings would be conducted in a calm, orderly and civilised manner, as befits a court. Occasionally those alleged to have committed crimes, or who had admitted doing so, behave dramatically and unpredictably, as was the case above.

Again, routinely entering a cell, to show a man his psychiatric report, I got slapped in the face with it. It may seem ironic that that was how I was assaulted by my own client, but I still reported it to the gaoler, and refused to act for him. Though rare, it is not unknown for the prisoner to leap out of the dock and tear out of the court, making good his escape.

My run of luck continued with interesting cases, in which some of our top barristers were involved. The lovely old well-appointed court at Knightsbridge behind Harrods was the scene. Prosecuting counsel was at the height of his career, and his junior was starting on his way to the top. I was being led by my head of chambers, and other very experienced counsel defended.

The case involved an agency which provided cars and driving licences to their customers; some were serious criminals, who used the cars, with false driving licences, to assist them in their many criminal ventures. My clients, the providers, were charged with perverting the course of justice.

There was little for me to do for my leader, and he would not give me any court work, doing it all himself. In such company I decided that I would watch and learn, for I had been admitted to the ranks of prosecutors by now.

Every morning the leader and his junior met in the Mess, and discussed what was to happen that day. What fascinated me was the grasp of detail which the leader possessed: he certainly needed no help from his junior, but knew his case backwards.

In court he was equally fascinating, as whenever an objection came from the defence, he would tell the judge and that counsel that he could assist with his difficulty, and would make apparent concessions which satisfied them both. When examined closely, these assurances amounted to nothing. It worked every time.

He then produced some schedules, which he proceeded to serve on counsel and the judge. These contained a full list of all the crimes the criminals borrowing the cars had committed; each crime was described in detail, e.g. tying up householders whilst they robbed their premises, etc. The number of crimes amounted to around a hundred.

We were asked to accept the schedules, and this was the one day when my leader was elsewhere and I had conduct of the case. Everyone accepted the schedules, but I thought them dangerous, totally prejudicial, and typical of this most astute prosecutor. Yet the others freely accepted them. I was unwilling to do so, but they went through, with the majority assenting. As the jury saw and heard them being described in full detail, their effect was devastating.

I learned from other counsel that our prosecutor was well known for producing schedules which 'in the small print' or in the end column, e.g. comments, did wholesale damage. If I came before him again in my own trial, there was no way he was going to 'assist' me.

Finally, I was on my own in the Bar mess when he and his junior came over to me, and told me that they were unable to understand what our defence was going to be. I told them that I was certainly looking at the judgment in the Great Train Robbery, where it had been contended that the acts which perverted the course of justice, and foil the police, should follow the crime, and not be planned beforehand.

To my astonishment, the prosecutor launched into a long legal argument, showing how he would distinguish - destroy - such a defence. I walked off smiling, feeling that now I was on to something, if he was already preparing for it. Relaying this to my leader, he was totally unimpressed by the incident and by my law. I got no further when I mentioned that it could be a possible ground if we needed to appeal. I learned much from that trial at Knightsbridge, where I was to put some of the knowledge gained into practice.

The particular case in which I did so was a prosecution of a gambling scam in a well-known gaming club in the West End. The game being played was roulette, and the allegation was that chips collected from losing bets were surreptitiously passed by the croupier to his accomplice playing the roulette table.

The evidence consisted of a huge number of video tapes of the action on the table, where the most that could be seen were the hands, cuffs and wrists of the players and croupier; the next set of tapes were of all the entrants to the club, to establish the identities of the owners of the hands, cuffs and lower forearms seen playing.

To prove the case, we produced, to assist, a full roulette table in the well of the court, and gave frequent demonstrations, with the manager and security officer giving live evidence and using volunteers to play. The jury would gather round to get a better view, and the judge would be peering over his bench to see. (At lunchtime some of the ushers and other staff would have a game themselves, for fun.)

I also produced schedules of each of the incidents that could be seen on the footage, cross-referencing where they could be found in the evidence, and describing each incident in the body of the schedule. Both I and the two defence counsel had visited the club, on the authority of the trial judge (since it was licensed premises, and we had to comply with the rules). We all needed that visit, to help understand our respective cases.

What had to be seen, and grasped, was the procedure where the used chips were returned down a chute, which was part of the table. The jury, therefore, had to watch what did not go down the chute, where the chips were placed on the edge of the table if not then ready for the chute, as the croupier might be too busy at that moment; and, then, how they came to be distributed to the accomplice as if purchased or returned as winnings.

Defence counsel objected to the content of the column. The judge ruled that column inadmissible. However, when the security manager came to give evidence, I adduced the details of each incident from him one by one, and asked the jury to write them back in that (now blank) column, since these descriptions had now been given on oath. This was allowed by the judge; so what had been excluded was then re-entered by the jury, by hand, in the same words.

The task of the jury, in what would have been a difficult trial to follow, with the sleight of hand utilised, and identification of the perpetrators, became so much easier.

Conviction followed of both defendants, and both appealed; the procedures adopted and other issues were mainly directed at me and were quite personal and aggressive. The court did advise me that, respecting one matter, I had been unwise in saying something that conventionally ought not to be said, but that did not affect the validity of the convictions, which were upheld.

The club contacted me afterwards and were delighted with the result, as the manager said that they had lost their cases so many times that this was going to be their last prosecution. They treated us with another visit to the premises which, this time, included their restaurant, as fine as would be expected, to cater for some of their affluent customers.

I had been prosecuting for some time in the Crown Court, having watched others' styles, and listened to their speeches and clichés. The jury have to be told that the burden of proof is on the prosecution, and the standard is to be sure, or it must be proved beyond reasonable doubt (both meaning the same). Counsel sometimes attempt to improve on these phrases despite their being the perfect standard (as advised by the Court of Appeal).

I heard one equate the jury's task with being the traffic controller at Heathrow Airport, ensuring such absolute certainty that aeroplanes would not crash into each other. Surprisingly, he was not corrected, and was pleased with his analogy, especially as his client was acquitted.

The conventional speech, I found from watching my opponents, then dealt with the law, the charge(s) and the necessary ingredients, and then dealt with the facts and evidence, applying them to that law. This is much simplified, but it was the style which I adopted. That is, until I prosecuted a drugs case at the Guildhall, a Crown Court in the City of London. Having opened my case, I went to lunch with defence counsel, who was most able, vastly experienced, persuasive, amusing and laid back.

He was also very subtle, for, as we talked, he stated that what he rather disliked was the prosecutor who, in his speech, started with the legal requirements, the law relating to the charges and other matters (about which a jury must be told by the prosecutor as well as the judge). These contrasted, unfavourably in his view, with those who got straight into the case with the facts, getting the jurors on the edge of their seats. Then they would be left with the legal concepts, the burden and standard of proof, and instructions and advice.

I got home and realised that he had been talking about my own presentation and style. Occasionally, I may revert to my old style, but nearly all the time since, I have hit the jury with the facts, moving them onto the edges of their seats if I can, and gaining their full interest and attention from the start. My 'legal lecture' follows, but the essential directions must be given their full weight.

As a prosecutor, there is no set style for a closing speech, other than to emphasise who has to prove the case and how. Often, having told the jury in opening, there is no need to repeat it or to make a speech at all; sometimes only a few points need be added.

Defending, one deals with the elements of the charge(s), inconsistencies - things that do not add up in the evidence - possibilities and improbabilities, quibbles over grammar or semantics in the interviews, and what was really meant, and, often, an attack on the police. Very often, it ends by telling the jury that the Crown's contentions may well be possible, probable even, or might well have happened, and that you feel almost sure, but for... The standard is higher than all of these, and this reinforces the defence's task, to be sure. The defence deals in possibilities, the Crown, in certainty.

I did develop one particular style in defending, which I reserved for just a few cases that a) contained many controversial facts; or b) came after many of my co-defending counsel had completed theirs. The QPR trial was an example.

It was to ask the jury to imagine that they had met a friend, a fairly worldly and astute person, who was asking the jurors about the case they were hearing,as if it had ended. There follow the questions and answers between 'friend' and juror (you don't need separate voices to make it real!).

The 'friend' asks you, the juror, about the case generally, and you describe the high point of the Crown's case, with the charges. He will express a view - how serious it must have been: the offenders must have been serious criminals to do that, and your answer may be, e.g., 'well, this was a fifteen-year-old schoolboy, with no previous convictions.' You carry on, with more from him, to which you can give the best answers that came up in evidence, stressing those that were uncertain or favourable to the defence. 'Were there independent witnesses?' 'How did they come across?' And others, including, 'what did the judge say about... ? What were his directions on finding some witnesses' reliability suspect...?isn't that normally the case?' or, pointing out to him that the conspirators were sitting near the gangways planning, he might respond, 'well of course they were there, that's where the bar and toilets are... to be first at the bar or use the toilet...'.Told that they would be leaving early, again would come his common-sense answer, known to any football goer: 'early to beat the rush'...But always, of course, one would stop short of the jury's verdict, reminding them the Crown must make you sure.

Apart from reinforcing the defence on mostly common-sense or normal behaviour, the conversational question and answer approach enlivens the speech; the jury enjoy it, and some of the answers, especially those in the vernacular, or those based on local knowledge or custom. In this case, this was most effective, and eliminated the biased directions from the judge.

This style I have adopted for long cases for many defendants, especially when my speech comes last. Most counsels' speeches are naturally repetitive, as facts and warnings are repeated. It has also been successful in cases full of common-sense and of arguable and well-known facts.

Whilst it is not always easy to read a jury, or to forecast its decision, I was amused after one trial at Inner London, where the complainant, and the defendant who had assaulted her, both told such lies, with some interspersed truths, that I felt neither was believable. The jury acquitted, and as they passed me in the street, leaving the court, they shouted;

'Did we get it right Mr Forward? You told us what to do if we didn't know who to believe.'

There are occasions when you do know. For instance, in a trial of a taxi-driver for stealing his fare's purse - she was a tough old Lancastrian, probably nearly 80 - the jury glared at me when I was trying to cross-examine her and to put my case. They needn't have, I was getting nowhere. They each stared at the floor during my speech, and were back with a verdict in six minutes, the time it took to get to their room and return.

A rape of a seriously, educationally subnormal girl with a mental age of about eight, with his defence being that she encouraged him, had the jury staring at the floor for four days whenever I spoke. I had warned him that we had no chance whatsoever, but he insisted on pleading not guilty.

Finally, at Knightsbridge, on a charge of theft of graduates' funds by a student, who had been collecting for a final Ball, he had arranged a massive acquittal party, but was convicted, to everyone's surprise. His family, his friends and his very experienced counsel were all devastated, having totally misread the jury and the strength of the case against them.

During his father's cross-examination the father asked me whether he could change his evidence. I replied that I was happy for him to change anything he liked, to come up with a totally different story. The jury were unimpressed by this effort to fit his story to that of his son, and the defendant and his father failed to realise how bad this looked.

One is never taught interrogation at the Bar, or even in the police service. It has to be picked up. Since there are patterns in answers or allegations, one develops appropriate responses. In a case which heavily relies on: 'Are you saying that...is a mere coincidence', dripping with sarcasm, this can be extremely damaging, and I have used an occasion when, on travelling with my family for a holiday in Florida with my daughter – who was living in Canada with her family –we were on our way to disembarkation at the airport for our hotels. The moment we were ready to board the shuttle, the door opened for us at one of the busiest airports in the world, and there, on the seat facing us, were my daughter and her family smiling broadly.

Now the point to be made is that if I was relying on that as an alibi for a crime committed somewhere else in the area, it would be treated as preposterous. Coincidences, even incredible ones, abound, and that a jury will grasp; but a true example helps, taking care not to give evidence.

I also have a technique for inconsistencies – a staple diet for lawyers – and others which are direct cribs from Rattigan's *Winslow Boy*. In it a famous QC interrogates a schoolboy accused of stealing a postal order. The schoolboy is then dismissed from naval college, but the QC invokes an ancient procedure of appealing to the House of Commons. It is adapted from a true story. answers to three questions have convinced him.

Moving on to another moment of good fortune, I dealt with an awkward case of indecency, in which three young girls alleged that they had been indecently assaulted by a young woman friend in the kitchen of their house, with their parents in the next room.

The case was strongly denied, and collusion was certainly arguable in their evidence. In addition, on seeing the lengthy videos of their interviews, I was appalled by their treatment at the hands of the officer who interviewed them; he had clearly had little experience. They were riddled with leading and suggestive questions, unrelenting persistence when they declined to agree with the officer until capitulating, then praised for doing so; and they were given summaries of the prosecution case, and pressed into agreement to those. All were suggestible and the language for nine year olds was inappropriate, and words were put in their mouths. Each interview could be properly described as a travesty to support a prosecution.

Having obtained a copy of the Memorandum for Interviews of child witnesses, I notified the court that I wished to argue all three were inadmissible according to the procedures and advice contained in the Memorandum, which had not been published that long.

We had the argument as part of the review; my opponent had apparently not been informed of what was to happen, and was caught by surprise, but tried his best. Unfortunately for him, and fortunately for me, the judge was a joint author of the Memorandum, and I had picked up every piece of advice, procedure to be followed, and protection to be offered, virtually word for word. He ruled each interview inadmissible, saying that each was completely opposed to his report's recommendations and its spirit.

The case was then dropped straightaway, and my client was acquitted. There was a whisper I heard afterwards, that this might have happened before, and that compensation had been claimed by the parents.

In a completely different category, but in the Magistrates Court , came another case involving an ex-husband doing all he could to separate his ex-wife and her boyfriend, by practically stalking them and photographing their every move. The aim was to get custody of his son, resident with his ex-wife. As I remember, there was an order restricting his movements near their address, but he found ways to break it time and time again, but in such a way that he could not be caught.

The incident that sparked proceedings occurred when he ran across the street with his camera as they were driving off, to photograph them. As my client had put his hand up to fend off the camera, and prevent himself from being photographed, its owner alleged that he had been struck in the face by it and had sustained an assault (without injury).

The prosecution was privately brought by the complainant, by summons, and my first application was to adjourn the case so that it could be referred to the Director of Public Prosecutions (the DPP). He was entitled to take over a private prosecution if it was in the public interest, and could then discontinue it if he felt that that was the right course to take, again in the public interest.

The district judge would not allow my application. The trial went ahead, and lasted three days.

The complainant called his own fourteen-year-old son as a witness, with a statement which could only have been dictated by the father. This was so patently obvious to the judge in court, that he required no cross-examination of the boy from myself, especially in view of his youth.

The complainant was vicious, and utterly and unreasonably aggressive, and determined to cause as much difficulty to the boyfriend as he could to stop the relationship. The boyfriend was a high-ranking civil servant and any whiff of complaint or conviction would have been fatal to his position (which the complainant well knew).

Regrettably, he was convicted, and the judge addressed to order an absolute discharge, he being clearly sympathetic with the defendant and his partner's position. An absolute discharge was as good for him as an acquittal, career-wise, but the judge ordered a conditional discharge ,which counted for him as a conviction.

He told me that that would be the end of his career, and that he could not continue the relationship, with what was being constantly thrown at him. I was bitterly disappointed, for we had shown without a shadow of doubt the wicked lengths to which the ex-husband had gone, and would still go.

Some months afterwards I met the district judge socially, and he apologised to me, and said that I had been right about the absolute discharge, but it was too late. The future for them both looked grim, but maybe, hopefully, it proved not to be so.

As has been seen, and will be again, despite the emphasis on Crown Court work, the magistrates could find themselves dealing with complicated and difficult cases. I remember the glazed look in the eyes of three lay justices when an argument was powerfully put before them, with a number of European authorities, that the case they were dealing with ought to be referred for decision by the European Court.

It was also at that court that I received my first certificate for counsel, granted orally by the bench on my application in court. Practically every such grant to me that has followed has involved a struggle for money. Awarded by the court in cases described as grave, a certificate could also be granted where exceptional complexity existed: the extension of legal aid was expressly made so that counsel could conduct the case. The fees were greatly enhanced, to such an extent that, when I obtained my extension, my solicitor told me that he would be taking the case. I advised him that I thought that this might get him into serious trouble, and he desisted.

My fee was lodged, and nothing was heard for months. If there were queries on legally aided cases, the problem was ignored without reference to the clerk in chambers, or the error's being pointed out. I suppose that this is the case in most bureaucracies.

In this case, my clerk did ring, and was told that the legal aid was just for the solicitor in the ordinary way. It had been issued separately for a father and son. The legal clerk insisted that there was no grant of any extension for a certificate for counsel in the case.

In the end I had to attend the court in question to pursue my claim, as my clerk was getting nowhere. There, I inspected the court register, and saw the record of the grant. We notified the legal aid office ,and waited. Since nothing happened, we queried the delay, and were told that there had been no extension in the case of the son. Again I inspected the court register, and saw that an extension had been similarly entered, and duly informed the office.

Months later, I rang the legal aid clerk, and was told that the papers were so thick that he had put them to one side.

Next time I rang, it had been assigned to another clerk, who was dealing with it. That the fee was worth some £4000 justified my persistence, as my clerk had submitted the fee, and had other work to do. Without a certificate, the fee would have been at most a fifth of that.

Weeks later my final enquiry elicited that they had written to my solicitor to see if he had received the fee (and so would not have to pay me). I informed them that he had moved from his office and had set up elsewhere. My cheque was sent by return, having been signed at the end of the call. It took well over two years to get paid: interest is never paid.

The next delayed payment took slightly less time to arrive, but I cannot remember the reason for the delay, other than that it was for a greater sum, which seems, ostensibly, the reason for the delay in every such case, in my experience. Either someone thinks we are not worth it or they think that we are exaggerating the payment.

In that case there were three defendants, all youth offenders, who, in their very lengthy interviews, had blamed each other. In law, admissions are only accepted if made by and against the defendant. The bench may well say, and do say, that they will read the interviews, but, as experienced magistrates, they can ignore what the defendants say about their co-defendants. That was not good enough on this occasion. So we all spent the day editing our interviews, and removing any accusations against other defendants, but keeping in material that was helpful in their case. We were duly paid in full.

I had been asked to sit on the Legal Aid Appeal Committee with senior solicitors, being the only barrister I knew to have been so asked in the Hampshire and Reading area. It made for interesting days out, and enormously enhanced my respect for solicitors, who were able, unlike me, to turn their hand to any sort of appeal.

My input was limited to criminal cases, or actions against the police, but, with commonsense, one could contribute marginally - except once. This was an appeal by criminal solicitors for a huge enhancement of their fee, approaching over £50,000. As the other solicitors interviewed the appellants, I sat almost idly, looking at the great pile of papers submitted for payment. That was until I noticed all the claims were for units of five or ten hours work. Mine were never that neat or uniform.

Looking more closely, some related to reading a one page statement. Worse was to follow, for, after noticing that the claims were not even chronological, but quite haphazard, I pointed out that one was claimed for twice. We were assured that this was a computer error. The next query was that one was claimed for three times; but this time my observation received no explanation – just silence. And so it went on, triple and double claims, all out of sequence, naturally, with no explanation from the appellants.

The committee cancelled the fee and refused the appeal, the matter to be reported to the Director of Public Prosecutions.

The concern was, and is, that a legal aid clerk had inspected this claim, and had allowed through a five-figure calculation to be fraudulently claimed, and then, worse, an appeal had been lodged before the appeal committee.

In such a case, a claim of such magnitude should surely have been checked by a second pair of eyes. I had no doubt that this had followed a claim for certificate for counsel. Our efforts were never alluded to by the Board, to my knowledge, but at least we all earned our modest fee that day. To quote a comedian, 'There's more,' but later.

I had developed some expertise in claims against the police from the cases I had won: sometimes winning was not enough for brutal policing, or other deliberate misconduct, and so winning damages as well was more satisfactory.

In addition, as it is a tort, and part of civil law, I enjoyed drafting the pleadings and responding to those from the respondent. It made me feel like a proper lawyer, rather than a criminal hack. It was also something of a punishment for impropriety by police or the Crown Prosecution Service (CPS), and taught them a lesson.

To be fair, some of my cases have been dropped by the CPS. One, for instance, occurred when the only witness to a robbery said that it might be the defendant ,but he could not be sure. On my application, pre-trial, to dismiss, the judge held that the witness might be sure come the trial. This, it seemed to me, negated the whole process, if a trial were to go ahead just in case something might subsequently be put right. The judge's ruling allowed the trial to go ahead, but the CPS promptly dropped it, to their credit.

Nearly all my cases were settled by the chief of police, usually the Metropolitan Police Commissioner, after an advice to my instructing solicitor. Only once or twice did I even have to draft the claim or additional pleadings, like Further and Better Particulars, or a Defence. Fortunately, I never had a trial to conduct, settlement coming at the door of the court in those few cases.

The most notable took place following a conviction in the Magistrates Court of two decent young men, one a regular soldier, the other a territorial, both of impeccable character and the sons of a police officer. After some minor incident, they were unjustly arrested, and had a very hard time at the hands of the police, partly for speaking up for themselves and each other, and yet still behaving in a disciplined way (even to calling the officers sir).

As often happens when prisoners are arrested, and force used, certain police officers resort to allegations of assault on police, with which prisoners are charged and prosecuted. (I have mentioned one case when a court refused to hear anymore of an officer's all-too familiar cases.) Being drunk and disorderly was also often charged, in an effort to justify the force used in an answer to a complaint.

After conviction, there was an appeal to the Crown Court, in which we succeeded, and both appeals were allowed. All were in favour of a civil action, though they had kept their clean records: the father, being familiar with court proceedings, was also insistent.

I asked my solicitor to instruct Mansfield to lead me, knowing that his reputation could lead to an early success, and it was a case in which right was with us. The father was well pleased, as well, when he took the case. The reaction of my clerk (formerly described) was for me to send Mansfield 'a short note about the case'. I sent him a full advice, comprising about eight pages, including a pen picture of the lads.

Meanwhile, he had drafted an even longer advice to me, making me so pleased that I had treated him with the full respect he deserved (my clerk's suggestion was quite insulting and unprofessional).

We had a consultation with the lads and their father, as superbly conducted as one would expect, and at the end he said; 'Was there anything you wanted to add, Barry?' The compliment was appreciated, for he had, of course, covered everything. At one stage I advised considering misfeasance (an officer acting contrary to his duty) as it fitted the facts, and was a most unusual and interesting cause of action. His advice, entirely practical as an advice should be, was to go for the usual assault, unlawful detention and malicious prosecution initially suggested. His view was that it would be unwise to complicate a very winnable case.

The Commissioner soon settled, to the satisfaction of all involved, and the force received, I was told later, a new recruit, doubtless to the approval of his father.

Figure 14. Me and Bernard sailing his cabin cruiser off Exmouth, Devon.

Figure 15. Gary and Tanya's wedding, 1990.

Figure 17. Double Christening. Pat with Amanda, Tanya with Naomi. What a joyous day! Celebrated by party with homemade pink fizz. (Guests thought Champagne).

Figure 16. Like butter wouldn't melt!

Figure 18. I was presented with this as a total surprise by daughters Katherine and Amanda, from Katherine's compilation of a huge number of photographs of children, grandchildren and a remarkable one of pop in the bottom right hand corner. Moved again to tears -a very special moment.

Figure 19. Gary
Bachelor of Science (Engineering and Electronic
Engineering)

Figure 20.
Katherine
Bachelor of Art

Figure 21.
Amanda-Jayne
Bachelor of Art
(History)

Chapter 16
Underway: a following wind in and out of Court

Of all the courts at which I have practised, my favourite has been the Court of Appeal (Criminal Division, of course). The hearings are always courteous, erudite, considerate and fair, but can be testing and challenging. In an appeal against conviction, as appellant, your task is to test the weakness of your case, leaving as little standing as possible with which your opponent has to deal. That the words 'we need not trouble you' are uttered, whichever side you are on, is a real high.

Alternatively, the words 'what would your answer be if...' or,' surely this is similar to . . .' warn you that an analogy is coming which you have to answer on your feet. Of course, it may not be a true analogy, but only an experienced advocate would be able to point that out without rushing to some sort of answer. I have seen my leader blanch at such a question, become practically speechless, and our case crumble.

Nevertheless, the elation if the appeal is allowed (usually less if dismissed when the respondent) is truly joyous, and it is even improved if the case is reported, and becomes a precedent.

The next case was such an instance, especially because of the treatment of my client by the judge (remarked on by the court in its judgment).

My client was accused of the theft of some items from the beauty counter of a large West End store. Her defence was total confusion, and she could not say why she had taken the items. She was the head of an administration unit in a large organisation, with a degree, immaculately dressed and made up, articulate and presented well in court. Although the items taken amounted to less than five pounds in value, she had two previous convictions for similar thefts, and was having personal difficulties.

At two pre-trial reviews (PTRs for short), two separate judges had made arrangements for psychiatric evidence to be given. In the trial, our judge refused to allow any. The Crown gave evidence of her previous convictions in complete detail including the items stolen. The grounds for that were that she had put in her good character - her position and education, and her appearance.

In the summing up, the judge again went through her previous convictions to the jury in the same complete detail, not just once, but twice. He then gave a correct direction to the effect that what they made of their significance was for them.

The two grounds of appeal were the inclusion of the convictions, and the manner in which they were introduced, and the exclusion of psychiatric evidence. The opening words of the appeal court's judgment were that this lady had been very badly treated by our system of justice. The court specifically noted that three times the convictions were described in full detail (that was unusual), and that, after the judge had read the full list twice, he added one line that how they dealt with them was a matter for them. The court considered that that had been woefully inadequate and unfair. That she was given custody immediately, whereupon she fainted in the dock, may have not impressed.

I had argued that she had not put in her good character, but her good taste and education, which were not' character'. The court stated that they did not need to consider this, though they did not dismiss the ground.

Though it was reported, the commentary on it felt that it was not a precedent on the use of convictions, but more on excluding psychiatric evidence and unfairness. The Court of Appeal will always punish unfairness.

Often, in court, some counsel become combative, and seem to enjoy duelling with the judge. I would rather not do so, since he has the ultimate power in his court. One example that springs to mind was when prosecuting a careless driving case in the Magistrates Court, the case obviously having been returned late on a Friday to a counsel who sat at times as a recorder in the Crown Court. This he told me, as he tried to persuade me to drop the case. He failed and his client was duly convicted. Much later, he was my judge in the Crown Court, and, after all that time remembered me; his expression told me that I was now on his territory.

In another case in North London, when I was conducting an appeal for a seventeen-year-old, the judge gave him an awful time as he gave evidence, shaking his head, constantly muttering and tutting and even banging his desk, frequently interrupting, and refuting his evidence audibly. When we came to arguing the law, he told me that as he had been doing his job for thirty-five years, I should take the law from him. I replied I had been doing the job for thirty-seven years, so, if time was the criterion, perhaps...

He was livid but I thought he well deserved it, and was convinced my argument was sound. I realised that war had been declared, and so it proved. He had the last word, as, when he awarded costs against the client, he told him that he had added £200 because of the way his counsel had behaved.

To balance out this rare behaviour by a judge: in the same court building, one court was always crowded, for a judge who would usually deal with pre-trial matters. In doing so, he employed such knowledge, experience and care (having read every inch of the papers), combined with Chablis-dry wit and subtlety, that it was a pleasure to appear before him: the proviso was that you too needed to be equally knowledgcable about your case, and the law, or you would rightly receive your come-uppance.

Sometimes judges have to put up with a task that affects them, and stretches their patience. Such an instance arose at Southwark, when one judge started pounding his desk with exasperation. I was defending a pickpocket on the underground, whose instructions on what was to be put to the detective squad, and particularly to its sergeant, were outrageous. Some were of a sexual nature, about his wife, who was called as a character witness (and an extremely good one).

I put what was required, as dispassionately as possible, and the defendant gave evidence. Half way through, the judge started to lose his temper at the accusations, and then came the desk-thumping. The judge was furious with the defendant, so I rose and addressed him respectfully (and almost sympathetically) that he could be said to have gone over the top, and that perhaps a re-trial was required. He readily agreed.

Two months later, the case returned, with another judge from the Midlands. We got to the examination of the defendant again, when this judge also started, as they say, to lose it. He was almost as close to desk-thumping, too, but was just able to contain himself, and we got to the end of the trial; and I had my conviction.

I have heard screaming on two pitiful occasions on Holborn tube station, where a mother and a group of her children on their way to a holiday flight have had their bags stolen; doubtless my first judge had heard pick-pocketing cases which were extremely affecting, in his long career, for I heard afterwards that these were not the sort of cases he enjoyed.

There have been occasions, to the contrary, when judicial wit could be enjoyed, with a subtle dryness to double the amusement. In a very early case at Knightsbridge, I came before a notorious judge, who would invite counsel, of any call, into his room for a break, and ask him for the latest gossip. I disappointed him, as I was too junior to know any.

Later, appearing before him with my case, I had a witness who had acted courageously in the face of the defendant. The judge stated that he felt that he should be rewarded for his actions. I agreed, respectfully. He continued that he believed that there was a procedure; being sure that there probably was, I agreed. He thought that there was a statute in the books somewhere; I nodded; he thought in the nineteenth century? Again, I concurred – this seemed quite likely. Perhaps it might be found in an Act in around 18. . . I realised that he was playing a game with me, with the court, and his audience. He then remembered the year.

Now, if that was the case, delving into his memory, would not the procedure, he wondered, have been to issue a summons from an important official, to give him the authority? Playing the game with more confidence, my answer was that I was absolutely sure that such a procedure must exist. Again, apparently racking his brain, he said that he felt that it could only be by the High Sherriff in the jurisdiction; might I prefer that he should draft the order for me? 'Such fun,' to quote another comedienne. I gained the clear impression that he winked at me as I left the court.

I give one more instance in the same vein. Having sentenced a defendant at Woolwich, the judge was reminded that he had not the power to order imprisonment. After lunch, he sent for counsel again, and the defendant was brought up. He then said he thought he should re-appear, as he had no doubt that counsel would wish to address him again. The young counsel looked baffled, and very concerned, having been on his way home when called back.

The judge continued to address the counsel: perhaps, he suggested, he was going to make an application to him? Before he could answer in the negative, the judge said that it might be to do with mitigating the sentence further. He continued, 'you might, for instance, raise... as further mitigation, or that...showed some remorse, and that something less might seem appropriate, such as . . .Yes, I can see you do . . . and so, because of your advocacy, and I hope (this to the defendant) you realise how ably you have been represented, I am going to accede to his convincing arguments, and order a community penalty. Counsel was especially pleased with his recognition by a most experienced judge. The clerk and I fought to keep a straight face, and the judge had not lost his.

Rarely nowadays are court witticisms, or short stories of amusing incidents in court, reported: they used to appear in one national paper, written under the pseudonym of 'Beachcomber',

271

and were a daily delight. Only two of mine were reported in the national press. One was in a prosecution for an indecent assault in the driver's compartment of a tube train, where the regular driver invited a teenager into his cabin, and touched him indecently.

I rose to prosecute, with my witness eager to air his complaint and see the driver convicted. The judge declined to hear the case. I sought some explanation, as there was nothing I was aware of to permit him to stop it. We had a further discussion in court, and I assured him that I had a complainant ready and willing, and could see no reason for discontinuing. He said that it was a minor incident, and that the court should not be troubled by such a petty matter – this being the gist of his argument.

The more serious aspect of this, though, was that it occurred as the driver had allowed the teenager to drive the train through much of London. This was not part of the charge (it being a matter that could only be dealt with in the Magistrates Court), but it made the alleged offence more serious. That counted for nothing, and the judge ended by saying he would not hear it in his court and that was the end of it.

The case was headlined in the press the next day with a verbatim account of our argument. Normally, seeing one's words in print can be uncomfortable, but not here. The reporter also discovered that the judge had taken a similar course with another petty sex case, to which the reporter added no comment, but mild innuendo.

The next one was headlined in a long front page article about my prosecution of a gay brothel next to Buckingham Palace. The headline referred to its display of tastefully arranged flower baskets. In answer to the question as to whether those catering for the customers were forced or under pressure to cater for them, it detailed the evidence of the officers. In their observation they testified (in mitigation) that the proprietor would arrange taxis home or to hotels to meet clients, and would ensure that they all were regularly medically examined, not just for obvious reasons, but for dental treatment and other such appointments. They were paid handsomely, and, rather than being forced to work, many enjoyed it, and returned time after time after absences.

Customers were said to have arrived, at intervals of two minutes, all day long, and I sought a compensation order for the vast amount of money that must have been collected. The officers could find no trace of this, though I noted that a parent was living in palatial circumstances. Nevertheless, I obtained my order – one ground being that if a book or film was made about this remarkable and very happy brothel, we could get our hands on some of the proceeds.

Despite this, I did not specialise in sex cases and made sure that I was not on the prosecution rape list. One case involved allegedly obscene videos which I had to view, which, embarrassingly, was in the company of a young woman vice officer. They were less to do with sex than with extreme torture, and I asked her to speed them up, as they were quite revolting.

I resisted the temptation to ask her how she coped with this, knowing that it was, firstly, her job; and, secondly, in watching such tapes at West End Central in the force, I discovered exactly how they coped: they counted the spots on the participants' bottoms, in a form of competition between them.

My opponent in the case had been in the same class as me at Bar school, and he had the case thrown out, on the argument that they were so horrific that no watcher would be persuaded to behave in this way, and so they were not obscene. I did not envy this part of his practice, as he was very experienced and persuasive in this field of law, and had to watch such material at length.

Oddly I never specialised in any particular field, either prosecuting or defending, although I did a spate of licensing cases later on. It so happened that I might have to do a great deal of work and research in an area new to me, might get a decent result, and never touch that sort of work again. Whilst I had the variety, it would have been rewarding to develop expertise in cases that paid well.

One instance, again in the West End area, where I was getting some work: police, with experts, seized a huge quantity of pirate tapes from a stall in Covent Garden,in an anti-piracy campaign. I prosecuted them for offences under the Trade Marks legislation at Southwark, where the case was defended by a QC and his junior, both of whom were specialists in this work.

The case was listed for legal argument, and lasted three days. Two of their arguments were despatched unceremoniously, but the main grounds for objection were that, firstly, the expert on whom the Crown was relying was the leading expert in the country, and was known widely in many other countries as an expert and a sought-after lecturer.

He was a member of the British Phonographic Industry (the organisation concerned with music, tapes, protecting the artistes' rights and reward, piracy, and trade marks). He had examined all the exhibits, and was to give evidence of their contents, markings, labelling and production methods. The argument raised was that, as an expert and a central part of the organisation and prosecution, he could not be objective – a necessary requirement for a prosecution witness.

The second ground was the demand for the matter to be referred to the European Court. It was accompanied in the defence's application by a host of cases from the European Court, with which I was totally unfamiliar.

Suffice it to say, I spent over fifty hours working on these grounds, and obtained some judgments on both issues and speeches from other advocates on the subjects. The judge dismissed the applications, objecting, and the defence pleaded guilty. The concern was that the case might create precedents in this field, so opening the door to defences, whether in the UK or Europe, and the use of the expert in all such cases. I was never instructed in this area again, despite building up unusual expertise on the subject, and the topicality of anti-piracy prosecution.

Around the same time, after prosecuting a defective vehicle selling hot dogs in Trafalgar Square, I ended up in the Divisional

Court, resisting an appeal which could have created an unfortunate precedent. The issue was whether the incident had taken place on a public road.

Certainly it was a public place, one of the elements; but was it a road? Much argument flowed, and many authorities were cited. As things were getting difficult, I remembered that there was an exit from the Trafalgar Square tube station, leading to the centre of the square. From there, it was a common journey by tourists to all parts of the square, and the National Gallery. It was agreed by the judges that this constituted a thoroughfare, and therefore a road.

I was home and dry, and the police would be able to continue policing the Square and its traders, and other possible offenders, in the centre of London. This case was also reported in The *Times*'s law reports, and is an authority. Though I have since won the odd case surrounding the issue of a public road, it was hardly a subject for special expertise.

Whilst there have been a few cases involving indecency, or worse, they have nearly all been for the defendant, especially as I hate to see a successful defendant smirking or triumphant when the jury, sometimes unaccountably, acquits in the face of apparently compelling evidence. It would be troubling, afterwards, to think that one might have been at fault or ill-advised in its prosecution, to the distress of the complainant.

Whilst the consequences of losing such cases when defending are more serious, the odds seem better. The only time I led, with a junior, in a trial, was with allegations of indecent assault – touching – in a park, and in the defendant's house. Digressing slightly (on the touchy subject of money) he paid privately, though he had to be pushed hard to pay our fee for the committal. Come the trial, we got to the stage when he was told that, unless he paid up front, we would not be at court for him since, if we lost, we would not see anything of the fee for the trial, which was quite substantial for both of us.

Two high moments arose in the trial. Firstly, there had been mention of a diary kept by one of the girls by her boyfriend in his statement which, surprisingly, mentioned that she did fantasize occasionally. Calling for that to be produced we found that it contained remarkably frank and damaging material. We called a psychiatrist whom I had used effectively before, and my junior very ably examined him: having been led myself, and having had to watch frustrated, I had always said that, if I ever led, my junior would get some work to do.

That evidence proved most useful and added to the evidence for collusion between the girls: the case was going well.

The next high point was to come, as they both alleged that one of the assaults occurred in the bathroom, and in identical terms, whilst they were sitting on the edge of the bath. The trouble was there was no bath - it was a shower room only.

That could have been put to them to answer, but the possibility always exists that, in such a challenge, a witness may say that they have made a mistake, and change their evidence by agreeing. The point, which looks so good, would be virtually lost.

In this case, I had the girls each supplied with pen and paper, and they were asked to draw the bathroom. As they did so the jury were straining forward to see, as the point had been made before they gave evidence. This happened with both of the girls, and when the drawings were passed round, the jury's faces, and their nods, indicated a clear belief that both girls had lied in their concocted account. It was at that moment that we all knew we had won.

Not long afterwards, another trial at the same court provided moments often repeated, though for different reasons. The first provided a textbook example of the worst thing a defence advocate can do – ask one too many question. The charge had been one of theft of a passenger's suitcase by staff at Heathrow. The loser gave evidence that, having disembarked, he could see his suitcase coming down the ramp, and an employee taking it off. Defence counsel started to ask him about the suitcase.

He answered that it was indeed an ordinary suitcase, quite nondescript. Yes, it was brown and of normal size...the sort you get in many shops in the High street... what you take on a short trip abroad. Then came the fatal question: 'Nothing special about it then?' The answer was devastating, and sealed the defendant's fate: 'Well, we had just bought it in Japan and it had a massive poster of a geisha girl on the side, which I could see as the man took it off the ramp.' I distinctly heard a groan, maybe two.

When I walked past the defendant in the dock, there came another magic moment. After being sentenced to over three years' imprisonment, he held out his hand to me to shake, which I did, and he thanked me for the fairness with which I had conducted his prosecution. That, I have quoted before now, to show how I prosecute. It is something of which I was extremely proud.

These were really good years: plenty of good work, some very decent fees (but still with the inevitable problems), with regular hearings of the Legal aid appeals, on some of which I would take the family, and we would spend the morning on the beach, lunch and then I would go off to the committee meeting to earn the fee and fare, and then enjoy the rest of the evening at the seaside.

For many years, I would take swimming gear, and, instead of a heavy lunch, have a swim at the nearest pool, noting how remarkable it was that so many were close to Magistrates courts. Given time, I would walk out of the Crown Court and be transformed into a child, sliding down the water chutes, at Winchester, or Guildford, for instance, hoping that none of the judges also indulged.

Any visit to a seaside town, and there were many, would find me sitting on the beach for a while, and then, as advised, finding the best fish and chip shop the town had to offer. Otherwise it could have been all work and no play. Similarly, on a case that was to be well paid I would go shopping and bring home a special gift, or something for the house. Often it would be dolls' house furniture, if I found myself near Oxford Street or Covent Garden.

Domestically, all was fine, and we now had the second of our delightful daughters. Golf had to give way, because of the time matches took, with a busy career, but weekends would find me on the water, rather than in it, as I had taken up sailing. This followed a visit to the Welsh Harp, a local lake, providing transport for the eldest, only for the friend I was helping out to ask if I wanted a go. Normally, I refused, either out of politeness, or being busy, or not wishing to try something new. For once I volunteered, saying that, despite being in the navy, I had never sailed and hardly even rowed.

After a few sessions, my daughter dropped out, and I was to continue for many years to conquer the challenge and become able at something which I had found most difficult at first. It provided a complete break from gardening, court work and life at the Bar.

It was also heart-warming in later years to watch our younger daughter and grand-daughter rigging up a dinghy, both about ten years of age, pushing off alone together, taking turns on the tiller and sails, solving all the problems that arose, working together, and enjoying competing with the other boats.

The club was a youth sailing club, and, disastrously, the Local Authority withdrew funding in order to support some comparatively unworthy project, when this provided all the life skills a young person would need. Further, it was coupled with the fun, in central London, of a weekend of such a sport, which included wind-surfing and canoeing. All was conducted in a shrieking enthusiastic clubhouse, with tales of adventures and excitement, and leg-pulling at beating the two old parents, trying desperately to keep up in their impromptu races, or efforts eventually to get my own sailing qualifications.

I could not but write to deprecate the Authority's lack of vision in closing the club down, especially with the criticism of youth which one would often encounter; and that would ignore the club's social nights, with their music, led by the instructor with his guitar, and the rest of the group all rocking along, plus spectacular fireworks, their reflections over the lake alongside a towering bonfire on firework night.

My next volunteering occurred when chambers asked me whether I could take on a licensing case. Having been involved in licensing matters in the force, I knew enough to try – there was no one else to do it – and thereafter took on a number of cases. They mainly involved applying for special licenses, extending hours, or obtaining licenses for off-licences or for off-sales in shops or supermarkets. Since these applications involved the applicant's work and business, the pay was reasonable and paid by the applicant, usually promptly, and occasionally in advance.

One licensee did have the cheek to send post-dated cheques for his two matters which my clerk had accepted, even though they were post-dated for six months. They were returned immediately, and he paid up. One, for the extension of hours for a lap-dancing club in Twickenham, proved, justifiably, quite substantial.

We were offered a view of the club in action to assist us, and my clerks insisted on an inspection in working hours. Their sudden and unprecedented enthusiasm for partaking in a legal inspection was for reasons not too hard to work out! I inspected out of hours, to concentrate on evidential matters. The application was opposed, and lost, so the applicant wanted to appeal to the Crown Court.

The objections were that there were insufficient areas for parking, and that the dancers assembled outside the clubs smoking, and wearing skimpy outfits, causing trouble both inside and outside. The premises themselves were said to attract and cause disorder amongst the customers and passers-by. The hearing lasted three days.

I called some local residents and one pensioner who lived in the street opposite. Another witness was the 'madam' for the dancers ,who is designated as their official chaperone – I was told that all such clubs had to have one. Finally, my enquiries to other licensing officers revealed, to my gratification, that lap-dancing clubs were the easiest to supervise, from a police point of view, as there was never any trouble, due to the pre-occupation of drinkers with the dancers. This I introduced in evidence.

My old lady was brilliant as a witness, and the judge loved her. Not, however, as much as he loved my chaperone, as she had spent much of her working life at the Follies' Bergères, and was their dance leader. She was an amazing-looking woman, in all respects impressive, but all the better for her maturity, wit, aplomb, and utter honesty. The judge fell completely in love with her and her evidence, while answers to his many charmingly put questions took far longer than it should have. She was horrified at the suggestion her young ladies smoked in the street, and disgusted at the allegation that they were less than fully dressed.

It all went so well, until the judge, who had been with us all the way, announced this was all very well, but Twickenham was not the sort of place to have a late night lap-dancing establishment. I think he ignored the likely reaction of a number of typical sporting visitors to the town, but may have been persuaded by the disorder which such visitors might cause in the town in the middle of the night. Had the story ended with an announcement of the engagement of the judge to my witness, it would have been perfect.

My next, and last, licensing matter again took three days to be dealt with, but ended disastrously for me. It involved the refusal of an entertainment licence for an ethnic music and dancing club; its music and culture were very West Indian, and its owner was a charming and enthusiastic music promoter, whose club was his life.

The objections were: disorder on the wide concourse outside; the difficulty of parking; the noise; and the fact that it was a 'hotspot of crime', according to the pages of printouts of crimes. Local residents, councillors, the Mayor and the Licensing Sergeant were the objectors.

There were hearings and representations made to the Licensing Sergeant, in particular disputing his hotspot evidence – the high point of the case against us. Again I indulged my enthusiasm for close examination of detail. I found one allegation amongst well over a hundred crimes referring to a robbery in the club. Close examination of that showed that a robber had sought refuge from where the robbery occurred to hide in the premises. He had been discovered by the staff after a search, the police were notified of his presence, and the staff held him until the police arrived!

Within fifty yards of the club were three foreign all-night cafes, where a multiplicity of crimes occurred throughout the day and night; a park which recorded much drug taking and many arrests at times when the club was not open; other crimes unconnected with the club (and at times it was shut) such as domestic matters and harassment; and, unbelievably, nothing whatsoever which involved the club, not even drunkenness in any chargeable form. If the club were removed, the figures would have stayed the same. The Sergeant could not believe it,or that, in other respects, the case was going so badly, to his considerable dismay.

Eventually the day came for the trial, and I spent much of the time with the prosecutor and the sergeant, coming up with conditions to improve the alleged problems, suggesting improvements to the parking (with leaflets indicating a car park amenable to the club's clients), barriers on the concourse, more supervision, and advice on available street parking. Since the club attracted some five hundred customers a night, the profits raised were considerable, and the conditions agreed and imposed by the court had to be effective and reasonable. The licence was extended for an experimental period, to test the efficacy of the conditions, and I heard that it continued.

The disaster arose when we sought my fee, to be told that my solicitor had told the owner to bring the fee - £6000 - in cash to court, 'since that was the way I liked it.' His courier had then absconded with the money, fleeing to his home country (Bangladesh, I believe), and neither he nor my money was ever seen again. I had to conclude the last two days of the hearing *pro bono* (for free), having worked too hard for its owner to let him down.

I had checked with the clerk to ensure that my fee for the heavy licensing case would be paid. As I remember, he indicated that it would be raised, as he had spoken to the client and solicitor.

By this time, I had moved chambers, with a colleague, as briefing and communication with the clerks was far from ideal, and other chambers were interested in us. It was still in Gray's Inn, but the Head of the chambers was very competent, there were many good solicitors briefing, and the clerk was most personable, capable and easy to talk to.

Unfortunately, it was not long before the Head left, taking her clerk with her. The quality of the work deteriorated, as far as I was concerned, and I ended up doing lists of prosecution work in the Magistrates Courts. This was quite stressful as, on arrival at court, one was presented with a pile of files to read and had to prepare remands or conduct trials with insufficient time to prepare fully. My very first was an old style committal to the Crown Court of a drugs supply case, with a file of papers maybe ten inches deep. Of the four or five defendants, one was a member of the aristocracy represented by a QC with his junior (almost certainly privately paid).

Seeing the evidential difficulty presented by one of the charges, I informed the QC that I was going to join the drugs into one case. He retorted,' do you realise who you are talking to?' and said that what I was doing would be completely wrong and unethical. Proceeding, the charge was thus consolidated, as was advisable, in my view, but I did insist on a CPS clerk to be with me, as I was anticipating difficulties conducting the case (getting advice if I needed it, dealing with paperwork and actually amending the charge) and managing the voluminous papers. The QC opted for the paper committal which I now had in mind, one with no live evidence, and in which the papers and charge were agreed. He left somewhat disgruntled. I did not require assistance any further, and took on some further work.

Again, communication was poor in these chambers, and the clerk started to run the chambers himself, taking over most of the duties and functions of clerk and Head.

After a chambers meeting where I raised unsatisfactory features of the regime, there was a split; as a result, it was time to leave and search for another. This lasted a few months, during which the CPS kept briefing me, and I then moved ultimately to Kings Bench Walk, on my own, after a brief stay in the Temple. Some of the others went as a group to another set, but that folded after a short while, because of the loss of the premises. I preferred 10 KBW (as it was called), and went on my own, knowing a few tenants there with whom I would get on well.

One of the longest trials (and certainly the biggest fee I had received) around that time, involved a Sri Lankan sub-postmaster and his wife who were alleged to have stolen several hundred thousand pounds from the Post Office. This was the amount that had been overpaid to its customers for their giro cheques, which had either been forged, or the amounts enhanced. It was at Snaresbrook, my favourite Crown Court, the nearest to home, in beautiful grounds, with a lake and swans and Canadian geese, excellent food, and a good team of pleasant judges to appear before.

I have mentioned the building's history above, and that it had recently been a home for youngsters in care, which we policed. However, the court still featured showcases in the lobbies, filled with photographs of Royal visits and of the children at work and play before World War II, when it was charity-maintained.

At least one day a year, its former residents returned, gathering in the still-preserved Chapel. It was always rather moving, on such occasions, to pass by a large group of little old ladies, chattering away on their reunion, as we walked past them to court, in our wigs and gowns.

Our trial lasted five weeks or so. The husband was the main perpetrator, and I was representing his wife, who worked part time, and was accused of a relatively few payments. The evidence consisted of over twenty thick folders crammed with schedules, which had to be compared to each other and cross-referenced. The jurors needed to have three folders in front of them at the same time to compare one with the other. The times of the incidents had to be compared, to see who handled the transaction, which was important for the wife's case.

The case put was that the giros were forged by one person and that the post-master had used an unauthorised system which by-passed security procedures, and so his assistant, not charged, would be acting under his instructions.

The evidence started with a handwriting expert, who stated that there was only one writer of the details on the cheque and the signature. Over three days I cross-examined him thoroughly, pointing out differences between the handwriting, and he eventually admitted that there were at least four writers. I very much enjoyed this part of the trial, as I had a strong interest in the subject of forensic handwriting, and he had to concede errors and misunderstandings over differences that, in some cases, were obvious. That helped our case considerably, in view of the way it was being run.

Our defence was that a team had been used to sign and cash the giros, and that my client was just complying with their presentation, but with ineffective security. At the same time there were several other Sri Lankan postmasters being investigated for similar thefts in the locality, which assisted our case.

The case was overwhelming against the husband, but my client was convicted by a majority, after a long deliberation by the jury: we did have a chance, even the prosecutor conceded. I had given my speech just in time for my holiday, so did not hear the judge's summing up.

The husband received a term of several years' imprisonment, but the wife escaped custody, aided no doubt by the fact that they had two young teenage daughters living with them at home.

There followed a confiscation hearing for the full sum, but by this time, counsel for the husband had taken up another job with solicitors, so I handled the case for both of them. The husband would admit nothing, and intended to fight the claim against him, which would have meant that they would have lost their house.

Despite that, and in line with authority, the Crown threatened to ask for the same sum from my client, even though the Post office would receive double the loss. The judge awarded a much more reasonable (and affordable) sum respecting her, but added several years' custody for any default in payment by the husband. I gained the impression that the family would rally round and the house would be saved, and their daughters' education continued.

Next, they both wanted to appeal against the conviction, and, certainly, one reasonable ground was a misdirection to the jury by the judge in his summing up, which I read in the transcript. I drafted the grounds for them both, and obtained leave, but the appeals were dismissed by the Court of Appeal, where I attended. This, combined with the confiscation hearing, and the trial, resulted in the size of the total fee.

That was not the last time we saw the judge in connection with the case, for, as he had spent some five weeks with the earlier trial, and ours followed immediately (with its many delays), it qualified for a dinner for the judge. It was a convention that after a long trial the judge was taken to dinner. (It had happened in my driving licence trial, of a defendant for perverting the course of justice, at Knightsbridge, when we ate at Rules, off the Strand.)

Part of the reason for the length of our trial was the delay caused by the court's listing preliminary or bail hearings before the judge. He had complained that these were eating away at the time we had for the trial, which, I heard, had affected his holiday, and which nearly stopped mine.

To help we called down an official in the List office, and repeated our concerns that the judge was forced to deal with these matters. They were regularly taking up a great deal of time (because of his patient and courteous manner) before we could start our case. The judge appreciated our efforts, which did help a bit.

I was also sure that he assisted with sentence and with the confiscation hearing for my client, and remember, after a suggestion that money had been sent to Sri Lanka for a house purchase, that he gave us a lecture on Sri Lankan land law and found the allegation unsubstantiated.

Finally, I liaised with counsel in the trial before ours, and picked the Savoy which at that time was one of Gordon Ramsay's restaurants. We had a very fine meal, and I had not realised how good a chef he was. The judge selected the wine, and I sat him between two charming barristers, so he could relax, and not talk shop. We all had a great time, and the judge especially enjoyed it. He strolled out of the restaurant replete, and with a wide smile on his face.

There have been times when I have been totally surprised by a case, often at or in court, despite conferences before trial. Mentioned before was the occasion on which my client told me to get him locked up; or another occasion on which, to a simple question in the Old Bailey, the defendant had made complete admission.

The first of a series of these took place at Bristol Crown Court before the Recorder of Bristol. My solicitor and I were defending, in a case of an assault by a wooden implement.

There had been no proof given of any implement, either possessed or used, and we were heading for victory. After lunch, the defendant told us that he wanted to plead guilty. The reason he gave was that he had seen his daughter at court, whom he had not seen for a long time, and did not want to get away with a true criminal charge made against him after he had become re-acquainted with her. We had worked hard to get to this stage and were so close. Nevertheless, he pleaded guilty, his conscience was clear, and he received a reasonable sentence from the Recorder.

In the same vein, two other cases caught me by surprise, one involving a roof (and from the same solicitor), and the other a prison and two prison officers.

The first also served as an example of the coincidences that appeared out of the blue in my career (and life).

Our client had been charged with removing a considerable amount of very heavy sheets of lead from the roof of a nearby apartment block. He vehemently denied it, despite the fingerprint of his which had been found on a beer bottle on the roof near some scraps of lead.

We started to build up a defence against this devastating evidence, which would normally have produced a plea of guilt. Firstly, he had injured his arm and shoulder to such an extent that he could not carry his baby daughter, and so we obtained medical evidence; he did not drive; he was the carer for his two young children, as his wife suffered badly from anxiety, causing him not to leave the house ; accordingly, in good weather they would entertain friends and relatives at a barbecue at their house, and, commonly they would all drink bottled beer; his wife would constantly tidy up and put the bottles (whether empty or not) in the bins in the alley near the entrance to the apartment block (photos to prove this); as it was summer, he thought that they might have had a barbecue that day – interesting that he said 'might' and was not sure – (a printout of the weather report we obtained showed that it was the hottest day of the year); that he will take the case, at great personal cost and they lived a low-cost life, his children (and wife) meant everything to him, and he would not have placed them all at risk. Compared with the certainty of his fingerprint that all seemed circumstantial, but it gave us a chance.

We were ready for the trial, when his sister-in-law told them that she had visited a distant friend in prison who, on being told that her brother-in-law had been charged, asked with what. The prisoner accepted being the person who had committed the crime, and stolen all those sheets of lead (with some assistance in driving it away). He was prepared to admit it to the police.

We arranged for him to make a full statement, without prompting or leading him (Bob, my favourite solicitor's clerk, was very careful about this) and the maker of the statement included having picked up a half-bottle of beer from outside the entrance to the block, and having taken it with him!

The statement checked so closely that it was completely credible and, of course, his admission could have landed him back in prison. The CPS dropped the case, and the defendant walked free, back to the family he loved so much.

Bob became a good friend, and was invaluable with the clients; furthermore, he told a good story, and had a great joke for every occasion. The best example I remember was when I was sitting outside at South-Western Magistrates Court, with a client whose dog was in danger of being put down as part of the sentence.

We had been chatting, and Bob told me that the client was also being accused of a serious sex offence. Since I was not keen on such cases, Bob had not mentioned it before, though I had represented him on another matter.

I told them that in these cases the RSPCA could agree not to seek destruction, if we complied with a number of conditions to avoid the dog's being put down, such as its being muzzled, being always on a leash, being registered, that the owner must never commit another offence, and that the dog be neutered. Immediately Bob quipped, to the client, maybe they could do that for you. Fortunately, the client roared with laughter, well knowing Bob and that sense of humour, and I felt free to join in: it was a good joke. Incidentally, the dog survived my mitigation.

The last in this mini-series of the unpredictable, and this time uncalled-for, came towards the end of a trial, again one in which, it seemed from the jury's reaction, we were doing quite well. (It can be fatal to rely on their apparent support, for the jury room is home to much argument and heated debate. That I knew for myself, as at Inner London, the jury room was next to the male lavatory, and one could hear almost every word. I did not stay, as they might have started talking about my performance. The judge's summing up can also be a powerful factor in their decision.)

The offences charged were of Grievous Bodily Harm against two prison officers inside the prison in which my client was incarcerated. There was no doubt that he had assaulted them in his cell after they had come in, and had started, as usual, pushing him around, nor that he had used an implement to do so. We argued self-defence, in the face of their constant bullying and physical mistreatment of him.

Officers had, he alleged, maliciously fabricated a charge against him before, and, in a disciplinary hearing, had caused him to lose a number of privileges.

The brief had been allocated to me, as I had dealt with him before, but as we were nearing the trial, it was switched to another counsel in my chamber, who also worked for the same solicitors. I never knew why; again, communication was awkward, and to enquire unusual, and it could have been unpleasant (or unflattering).

As the trial was listed, the counsel then assigned had another trial, so it bounced back to me; but preliminary work and arrangements had been made. One such arrangement was to call the prison governor, to raise the disciplinary matter against the prison staff. Personally, I had my doubts about this tactic, but arrangements had been made in the pre-trial review and, if it did prove useful, I could be criticised for changing tack (and the client might have been unhappy).

The trial commenced, and I ensured that the governor would not be called until the defence case was opened, to ease the pressure on the prison. It may seem a minor matter, but I focussed on the refusal of the staff to release items sent by his relatives for his comfort: one was a radio, and the other, new trainers.

This was typical of every request he made, but the trainers became more than symbolic. He suffered dreadfully from athlete's foot during the day, but particularly at night; his sleep was severely affected, and he needed new footwear to help cure it. I hoped that some members of the jury had suffered likewise, but I elicited prisoner officers' wilful refusal to allow him his rights (accompanied by mocking facetiousness, bordering on triumphalism). They knew that his presents had been sent, and where they were, and could put forward no reason for their refusal.

My father had been a prison officer (though a cook and baker) and we had lived in prison quarters. I knew what could go on, and that such matters, which may seem trivial, became significant to the prisoners, since they do not have much to alleviate their conditions (and this is not a plea for soft treatment).

I went into full attack on both prison officers, and, whilst the judge did not like it, and prosecuting counsel was infuriated by it, I was not stopped: the jury were soon with me, especially on the athlete's foot issue.

I had to call the governor on each of the three days taken by our defence, which greatly displeased the judge, even though I released the governor each morning almost as soon as he arrived, and I did not require him. The defence was going well, and occasionally one's own witness can shoot himself and your case in the foot, especially as here he would have been likely to support his officers and malign the defendant.

The defendant gave his evidence well, but passionately. The counsel prosecuting went at him with more vigour, sarcasm and used every trick in the book to make him lose his temper, so that the jury could see his disposition to violence. She got so close to his face in the witness box that I feared she would leap on him.

Then, in a heated moment, he admitted, out of the blue, that he had deliberately smashed the sauce bottle on his table (I had tiptoed over this, as there was some controversy about the implement). He had then ground the broken half into the faces of the officers who were holding and beating him, and he added, 'so I would recognise them when I next saw them!'

I was horrified, and saw all we had achieved wrecked. I made my speech without repeating or alluding to his admission (heartfelt and obviously genuine). The other speech from the Prosecutor was as dramatic, powerful and conclusive as would be expected, and fatally minimised his complaints (a serious mistake, as the jury accepted that he had been constantly bullied by those taking advantage of their position).

The judge's summing up and directions were fair and proper, and we had no complaints on that score.

The jury returned, after some time, and acquitted on both charges. In court there was total disbelief. If asked whether that included me, I would have had to answer No Comment.

That was not the end of the matter as the judge then said he wanted a written explanation of why a prison governor was called to give evidence, seriously affecting the running and administration of the prison for three days.

That had been arranged in the pre-trial review after discussions with the defence team, I informed him. I was left under the implied threat of disciplinary action, and ordered to address the judge in open court several weeks later. The explanation, fortunately, was accepted but after much anxiety and stress. When that counsel asked me the result, on my return from court, gratifyingly, she could not believe it.

Chapter 17
The most Troubling Case against the Solicitor General, briefed by the Attorney General, before the Lord Chief Justice. Then the Wizard

Many of my cases were routine. However, those which follow in this chapter also include a number arguing unusual facts or law and in judicial hearings in situations before different levels, some far from one's comfort zone, despite years of practice.

A short example, in a case I come to describe more fully later, was a claim made for an extra uplift for unusual law and facts, and refused by the Crown Court costs officer. Following the appeal procedure, I asked for a full report from her, explaining her refusal. The next step was to prepare a full bundle to the Senior Costs Office at the High Court, where I went before the Master.

After three pages justifying her refusal, she added, in the last line, that in all her long experience she had never had a case like this. I started with the remark that she seemed to have shot herself in the foot; the judge smiled and agreed, and awarded me my fee plus costs.

It is often thought that it is only the Crown Court which gives rise to important cases or appeals, or other appearances in the higher courts. The lay bench and district judges in the Magistrates Courts were always under pressure of time to get through their lists. This, together with the bias that seemed to arise occasionally in court against defence counsel, or a defendant, were often to provoke further proceedings in higher courts.

Some were quite belligerent, taking advantage of their position. Their task should not have been a difficult one, their environment not unpleasant, the hours civilised, and ,with the assistance of their clerk, and two advocates to help and guide them, they just needed to act with fairness and courtesy.

Two examples to support what may seem unlikely were: firstly, as I was preparing to prosecute an old-style committal before a district judge (a case in which all the evidence was to be called live), my opponent opened the door of the court, to see who was on the bench. One look was enough for the advocate to agree to a paper committal, with no evidence given: his reaction was no surprise.

Another, from a central London Magistrates court, was when, waiting for my bench to return with a decision, I was commanded by the district judge, in a court on the fourth floor, to start a trial in his court. I moved to his court when my bench concluded my case. On my arrival, the judge asked me whether I was some sort of quadriplegic. At first, I was tempted to snap back; but the remark was so outrageous that I burst out laughing to his face, and continued to laugh at him for some little time.

I then reported him to the Lord Chancellor, adding the occasions (with the case names) on which I had seen him ridicule perfectly decent and truthful witnesses and reduce them to tears. He would regularly insult competent and experienced defence solicitors in a bullying or hectoring way, completely demeaning them (and before their clients).

Sent his reply, which was a complete denial of the incident against me and the others, I was asked for my comments on his response. My answer was to the effect that his economy with the truth was rather disappointing, from someone in his position – and accordingly I indicated that there was little further to be gained in making any response. The staff at court heard of this and the words 'about time' resounded around the building. Not long afterwards, he moved.

Coming before the chairman of the bench in the next case, my heart sank, as the first time I had been before him, he had been quite truculent. The other two justices supported him, and the hearing was going to be difficult. The three defendants, all youths, were charged with robbery – better described as a mugging.

They were alleged, by another similarly aged group of girls, to have snatched property from them, and had been arrested near the scene. The papers were quite voluminous, with long statements from the complainants, long interviews and difficult law – being based on 'joint enterprise'. That is, they were together when one snatched the articles, using force and the other two either assisted, or encouraged the girl, threatening her friends as well, and, further, were ready to assist her in making good her escape: these were all conditions to prove involvement in a joint enterprise.

There were problems over identification, with the witnesses being muddled over who did or said what, and the admissions from each of our girls were only evidence against the speaker herself.

It was not long before there were problems, and it was apparent that the bench had made up its mind. The case was not going to conclude on the first day, and one justice let it be known that she was busy for part of the next day, but the chairman was undeterred by that.

When the father of my girl attended court, both he and his daughter recognised another of the justices, whom they knew from visiting the home of one of her relatives. The court was again undeterred by this, and wanted to get on with it.

I sought an adjournment, for the trial to start again with another bench, and my colleagues supported my application. The bench refused. I then applied for an adjournment judicially to review this decision - a form of appeal to the High Court, based on the unfairness of proceedings. Again, the chairman was adamant the case must proceed and that all the witnesses were at court.

The bench were informed that I was going to ring the duty High Court judge, and ask for permission judicially to review their latest refusal. I proceeded to do so, and his Lordship stated that he would listen to my application in full and deal with it over the phone.

For well over an hour, I explained what had happened, and set out in terms my grounds for him and for the prosecutor in court. The judge then asked the prosecutor for his views, and to dictate his response to him in full. He then sought the views of the other two defence counsel. He held that he was indeed much concerned over the matter, but that since the equally young witnesses were at court, and had started to give their evidence, and since the rest could be read, he would not stop it yet.

The case continued, and two of the defendants were found not guilty, as the bench could not be sure which of the two had stolen the items. That left my girl.

The next hearing was before another bench, and again there was a finding of not guilty for lack of certainty as before; the bench believed that one of the first two girls had stolen but did not know which, and so they excluded my client from the theft.

The bench did, however, grant a certificate for counsel for the three of us – to the pleasure of the other two younger advocates, when I explained that the application meant at least a four-fold increase in their fees.

Finally, the judge had ordered, over the phone, that the bench were to explain to him in writing all the matters that had gone wrong in their conduct of the trial. After the trial, the other two counsel contacted me, and were very satisfied by their brief fee. They had learnt that to obtain such a certificate was not immensely difficult, though I was not sure that they were even aware of getting such an extension, orally in court.

There was a grant of a certificate in the next case as well (and again my application startled the other advocates, who were all solicitors, but whose fees would nevertheless be enhanced). This involved a large group of young teenagers, this time on a bus terminating at a bus garage. On board, they were noisy, rowdy and disorderly and the bus driver was refusing to move off. One of the girls then took some of the fare money in the driver's tray and ran off, chased by the driver. One of the youths prevented him from grabbing her, and they both fell to the floor; a struggle developed between them. The driver then threw the youth through the door of his bus and into the driver's compartment, holding him with a head lock and punching him.

Other bus drivers entered the bus, and kept the other youths away to prevent them from helping their friend while he was being assaulted. He was held by his dreadlocks while being punched, and was in obvious pain. My client had pushed on to the bus through the exit doors, undeterred by shouts to get off. On the bus, she went to stand by her friend, shouting for the driver to stop what he was doing.

Her friend freed himself, and tried to run to the exit door, but was grabbed by another driver, thrown across the bus, and slammed against the side of the bus. During this beating he had done nothing physical himself to resist or attack them: nor had my client.

The friend was assaulted on three separate occasions, as described above, and all was witnessed on the CCTV. Police were called, and all the youths were arrested, and charged with a public order offence, alleging alarming the public and using violent and threatening behaviour.

In court the friend was persuaded to plead guilty, having behaved so badly in public, to their alarm, and threatening violence; and several others in the group also pleaded guilty. The only persons present had been other bus drivers and a helper, said to be an off duty police officer, whose remarks were given in court by a bus driver - clear hearsay as to his office and remarks.

I put forward self-defence: my client had been trying to protect her friend, and had got on the bus, despite efforts to keep her off, so as to stop her friend being further assaulted. All of the above was clearly recorded, and perfectly visible, and the district judge watched the video a number of times.

He found several, including my client, guilty, and gave his judgment, of which I made a note. As I continued, it was clear that the judgment contained serious faults, and so my note would become instrumental. Some evidence should not have been given, and the judge was clearly unhappy at rowdy behaviour by teenagers. He seemed to ignore the assaults by the bus drivers, which had justified the protection of my client's friend, and treated my client's persistence in having entered and stayed on the bus as part of her actual offence.

The rather inexperienced prosecutor chose to adduce evidence that because the defendant's friend had pleaded guilty, that conviction could be used against my client. If he chose to do that, the law stated, he should explain why. However, the authorities held that that was not possible in a case of affray. I argued that it was unfair under the Police and Criminal Evidence Act, and cited the passage to the judge. However, he did not appear to have rejected such evidence, nor to have explained on what grounds he was relying on it as evidence against us.

Finally, accepting that the defence had properly raised the defence of another person, he misdirected himself, by requiring the defence to prove self-defence. This was a serious error, going to the heart of the case. It was a well-known principle in self-defence cases that if any element or vestige of self-defence remained, the defendant must be found not guilty.

An appeal had to be mounted. It is the procedure to be adopted respecting this case which makes it especially noteworthy. The loss of a course, picked out for her career, as a result of the conviction, meant that we had to think carefully as to how best to proceed.

The simplest option for an appeal was go to the Crown Court, where the hearing would be conducted by a Crown Court judge and two youth court justices. Such a hearing would proceed afresh, starting with the witnesses, heard live again in the usual way. Whilst the judge would deal with the law, and generally chair the trial and discussion and control proceedings, at the end there must be agreement, and two justices could outvote the judge. Drawn from the same area, the justices might have supported the local decisions, even though made by their own district judge, and be critical of local youngsters. They might also take the same view of the videos: that this was sheer youthful hooliganism, by a group who should know better, and that this was not to be tolerated in the centre of town. I would suggest that the theft of the driver's petty cash set the tone for refusal.

The legal mistakes made by the judge would not be replicated in a new hearing, but there was certainly material on camera to provoke the above 'gut feelings.' This could prompt him, as it had prompted the judge, to ignore her obvious distress, recorded on camera, at the treatment of her friend. No anger or aggression was displayed by her, and she was visibly in tears throughout.

The alternative way forward was to ask the judge to 'state a case' for the High Court to determine. This was a hearing in the Divisional Court, where all the facts were agreed by prosecution and defence, and the argument would then proceed on the errors of law revealed in the documented facts and the written verbatim judgment of the district judge.

Reversing the burden of proof, and allowing in material against clear written authorities, were serious errors, providing our best chance of success. The judge should have ruled out from his consideration the hearsay evidence from the off-duty police officer, too.

Not to have live prosecution witnesses, who could have added more prejudice to their evidence, would be a significant advantage. So, too, the young defence witnesses would not have to give their evidence, and be intimidated by doing so in a Crown court; after which, they would then be cross-examined by the aggressive and experienced prosecutor and the judge.

(In several cases involving teenagers in the Crown Court, I have known Counsel to reduce two to running out of court in tears; another became so confused and frustrated by questioning that he gave up trying to give evidence. His first question before the jury from the prosecutor had been: 'Are you some sort of a wimp?')

Therefore, we all decided to ask the judge to state a case. This involved both the defence and the prosecution exchanging our views of the facts (to save them being disputed and argued in the High Court).

We then swapped our versions, and corrected them as necessary, together with summaries of the legal argument and judgments. This took weeks, until our versions were mutually satisfactory. I had to attend the court to pursue and confirm the initial grant of the certificate for counsel, and chase up the district judge's rulings, rather than relying on my note at the time. Gradually, a complete bundle was built up to be sent to the district judge, specifying the questions which he was to answer for the administrative court.

The district judge's difficulty throughout the five days of trial continued afterwards, despite reminders by the clerk, who provided some confirmation of his rulings. A full transcript was not provided, and there was quibbling over our version of the facts: he then refused the application. The ground for refusal was that the application must be frivolous. That term was defined as futile, misconceived, hopeless or academic.

Misconceived was the definition on which he seemed to mainly rely. That did not seem appropriate for a decision that reversed the onus of proof and allowed in material which was inadmissible, and against plain and clear authority. We were undeterred, and so took the only possible step left: to pursue an appeal against his refusal to state the case.

This uncommon and complex procedure required legal aid from the Magistrates Court. It demanded a more civil approach, and meticulous and fully prescribed paperwork. It was so strict that an error in the paperwork or time for submission would have been fatal. Accordingly, my solicitors were guided by me, and I had to draft all the forms and prepare the bundles (though aided by specialist books and specimens of forms and applications from Inner Temple's library on the subject).

At the same time, the refusal to state a case could only be challenged by a judicial review at the High Court. For it to succeed, the refusal to state a case had to be unreasonable or perverse. The protocol started with a 'letter before claim' to the respondent, setting out the claim so as to give them a chance to make a decision on whether to pursue it or 'back down': if it was to be pursued, full reasons must be supplied to the applicant.

Once acknowledged, the lengthy application form had to set out all the facts and law. That was as difficult to prepare and draft as the stated case procedure itself; this time, legal aid had to be obtained by a direct application to the High Court. Another time limit was applied. Failure to comply could result in the refusal of permission, but with a more generous time limit given. However, such a refusal would often result from overstepping the time limit.

The grounds needed to be specified, with several copies of complete bundles of the evidence (different from those submitted in the stated case procedure, as there was no agreed version) and attached in due form. An application for legal aid was made to the High Court. The paperwork had to be delivered and formally acknowledged in the High Court, with an estimate of its likely success.

More weeks went by, with recourse to books and articles. This time I had to buy the latest up-to-date book on the subject. This included the only case known in which both applications had been heard together. Again, I prepared all these documents, together with skeleton arguments for both procedures, and submitted everything. Allocated a hearing for the joint applications, and once legal aid had been granted for both, I appeared before the two judges of the Divisional Court.

Only given the district judge's full typed judgment for the first time at court, having chased it for months, I had to deal with it on my feet for the first time. The proceedings were for permission for judicial review of the refusal to be granted, and then the stated case application could be heard. Here, the court dealt with application for permission, to be followed by the stated case application. Unfortunately, after a full hearing of the first, permission was refused, even though the errors of law were not disputed. A robust view of the incident and behaviour of the group could be said to have prevailed.

The client's mother attended court, reassuring me that we had done all we could, but once again she was disappointed that our arguments had been brusquely dismissed. At least, as far as I was concerned, the procedures and rules had been correctly complied with, and proceedings at court had gone through smoothly, despite all the technicalities and testing applications for legal aid. For once no payment problems arose.

This case prompts a full examination of the motivation behind appealing, as far as I (and doubtless others) was concerned. The whole appeal process took weeks of research, intensive study of current procedure and precedents, the collation of bundles of evidence, properly paginated and indexed, with detailed statements of facts with bundles of witness statements, full grounds, skeleton arguments and, of course, difficult legal aid applications. All to pursue a conviction for affray against a teenager after a trial conducted by a district judge (he was a qualified barrister),in which she received a non-custodial sentence.

This case can be used as a prime example to answer questions that may be raised. For instance, why incur the cost and the time and use of what may be called scarce resources, and go to the lengths pursued, especially when the judge had said that the first application to him was misconceived? In a nutshell, what is it that drives us, when defending, to take these steps?

It would be trite to say that it is the pursuit of justice. For a judge it would be the dispensation of justice, for us its pursuit. The closest we would get to its administration was when prosecuting, for that was the view which we were exhorted to take in our code and instructions, e.g. by disclosing facts, etc., which would tell in favour of the defendant, or which are put in front of the court, should defence counsel omit them.

Responding to my application in a most serious case, the judge became so exasperated by my seeking another adjournment for psychiatric evidence which my solicitor was having problems obtaining (dates to attend court were always a problem for experts and their reports), that he ordered the trial to proceed and the defendant to defend himself. The prosecutor joined me in my objection with equal force, because of its unfairness. With both barristers against him – he granted the application.

This is an extreme example, because the case peculiarly indicated the whole process, using every means available to reach its final determination: it showed the persistence required in an advocate, and epitomised our task as defence counsel. In this case, as in others mentioned below, the motivation that drives us is to attack and correct conduct that can be fairly described as outrageous.

The above case provided incontrovertible and visual evidence of the beating of a schoolboy who had been grabbed by his dreadlocks, put in a headlock, thrown around inside a bus, and slammed against the side – all by adults. His friend pushed into the bus, in tears throughout, to stand close to protect him. She tried nothing physical to rescue him, but urged them to stop: she was in great distress, and her face showed it. She was convicted of using or threatening to use violence to an extent which would alarm the public.

In seeking a statement of the case, a district judge refused her application, finding, despite reversing the burden of proof, and twice allowing inadmissible evidence to her prejudice, that her application was misconceived. That I did consider outrageous, and its correction had to be pursued to the absolute limit.

These other summaries - mentioned before - all deserve the term 'outrageous', strong though it is. In the case of the shoplifter of the cosmetics, her appeal was allowed in unusually strong terms. The full Court of Appeal took the same view in their first sentence, finding that she had been badly served by the whole judicial system.

The marine accused of assault outside the public convenience had his conviction dismissed without my saying a word. After the ten day trial within a trial mentioned in detail above, in which the defendant's admissions were said to be admissible, in a fresh trial, and in half the time, the new judge found thirteen breaches of police procedure, leading to the exclusion of all the admissions, leading in turn to his acquittal.

Lastly, a High Court judge, who held that there was no law in my application for leave to appeal, had his decision overturned in five minutes by the second highest judge in the country (the Deputy Lord Chief Justice). Such are the best examples of what has driven me to appeal persistently, and to the highest levels possible. Doubtless this echoes the experiences of all defence advocates.

For completeness, outrageous behaviour has arisen leading to appeals from another source – the behaviour of police officers in a case. In general, these were dealt with by a hearing in the Crown Court, to which an appeal from the Magistrates Court was allowed as of right. A prime example will follow later.

Having dealt with lengthy and complicated matters, it made almost for light relief when Bob told me that a brief had come in for which he had immediately thought of me. It was not long before I received it, somewhat intrigued as to what he thought was right for me.

The client was a local celebrity, colloquially known as the Wizard of Wallington, who was a practising Druid. He had been stopped by a police support officer, who noticed that he had a knife with him in the street, and called police to make an arrest. Despite being in 'full regalia', he was arrested and charged with being in possession of a bladed or sharply pointed article. The charge required no intent, mere possession being sufficient, but there are statutory defences: if there is good reason or lawful authority (the latter did not apply), or if he had it for use at work or for religious reasons.

Solicitors elected, with my agreement, a trial before a jury which we considered advantageous, for at times a lay bench or a

303

district judge could appear cynical or impatient. One could not have accused jurors of cynicism. Also, this is a charge which could invite a custodial sentence, but less than the maximum in the lower court. Restricting sentence to no more than six months is, where custody appears inevitable, a good reason to prefer the Magistrates Court.

We took full instructions from our client, knowing little or nothing about Druids, and Bob was enjoying himself. It turned out that the client was a Druid High Priest and a Wizard, which made his need to pop out for a cigarette quite weird. He wore full robes, and carried a wand (like a very ornate and carved crook), and a special ring; but more relevant was his knife which was properly termed an 'athame'.

He explained that when out in public he would make or sell potions, perform acts or services, and sell other articles; but everything required a blessing before sale.The blessing had to be given in ritual attire. An essential article was his athame. In his case it was emblematic, made of plastic, with a very blunt edge, but it had a point which could just about have caused injury. His possession of it was not, of course, disputed.

We decided to call another High Priest and the chief Druid, who they informed me was known as King Arthur Pendragon. As it can be implied that a weapon is likely to be used even in one's defence, it was deemed necessary to indicate the character of our defendant to the jury, and the unlikelihood of his ever using a weapon.

Therefore, the jury were to be treated to Druid history, for which purpose we obtained the services of the most knowledgeable historian in the UK. He provided an eightpage history highlighting their ethical and moral superiority (having been advisers to royalty in ancient times, and more latterly magistrates), and that they had always proved of a totally peaceable nature.

Thus armed, we set off for the Crown Court, where we met with the prosecutor, who had first taken up the case, and who, because of its nature (since he was something of an academic), had retained the trial for himself. We went before my favourite judge at Croydon, whose eyes twinkled with a slight smile when he saw me and my client, dressed in his long colourful robes, go into the dock.

My first application was for the charge to be dismissed, as I had found three cases involving Druids, in which all were dismissed or an acquittal had followed, two for possession of their athame. The judge was against me, and the trial proceeded.

For the next three days, the court was treated to the sight of three druids in their robes, the third, the chief druid, all in white, with a red cross from top to tail. The court room was quite full of counsel coming in to watch and enjoy the spectacle. Each, before giving evidence, had to take the oath whilst holding his sword or athame. I doubt if anyone had heard the oath or seen this procedure before (unless they had been to a druid wedding). I am sure prior notice of the trial had produced the Druid oath, as I have never known another Crown Court to possess one. The case became a definite talking point.

They all gave their evidence well; the judge was particularly interested in them and their evidence, and they handled his questions and the cross-examination in an exemplary way. (They all still popped out for a cigarette outside the court in their breaks.) The jury seemed to enjoy their history lesson too, and the closing speeches. I ran all three defences: good reason; that this was used as part of the Druid religion (though I was a little dubious that it was a religion but left that to our historian); and that it was used in conjunction with his work – more arguable.

After the jury had retired for a relatively short time, my client was found not guilty, and was discharged. Photographs were taken outside the court of the three of them, and these appeared on the front page of the local newspapers, with a long report of the case. My solicitors also received some publicity, and my client became more of a celebrity; he was asked to open fetes and other events around Wallington.

This was also the case (alluded to before) in which the costs clerk had refused my claim for unusual facts, but ended with remarking, fatally to her case, that it was the most unusual case she had dealt with!

My clerk was asked by the druids whether I would assist the movement with legal advice, but, recognizing that this would necessitate a great deal of work for little reward (and no real boost to my career from one case every ten years or so), he did not seem to have acted upon it.

Back to normality as a criminal hack, I had started receiving work from two additional sources, one in the Magistrates Court and the other in the Crown Court. Benefit frauds were becoming prevalent, and were generally dealt with in the lower court, as, starting there, most fraudsters and cheats pleaded guilty, since the result was predictable. All that had to be proved was failing to declare income of one sort or another on the forms which they had to sign. The paperwork was sizeable, and took time to amass, but was sufficient, when served, to induce a plea of guilt.

Some required actual observation, for example where a claimant maintained sickness or disability, but observations would be carried out to show that he was perfectly fit, and the Crown Court would be chosen for trial – though hardly ever in my cases.

The money was satisfactory; there was no undue delay or travel as the cases were always in London; but because of the word count, working in the Crown Court provided a more substantial fee. Prosecuting my cases was fairly routine, none was in any way exceptional, or of sufficient interest to stick in the memory.

Similarly, the other source of work prosecuted was for the probation service, for breaches of probation orders made when a defendant was sentenced, always in the London Crown Courts. The paperwork provided was excellent, and it came with a final report relaying clear instructions, e.g., whether to extend the period with a minor punishment for the breach, take further action, or press for a custodial sentence.

The service provided sensible advice and considerate judgment, and there was a probation officer present at court who knew the case and was prepared to discuss it: recommendations were nearly always accepted by judges who acknowledged the service's expertise. If there were doubts, they would call in an officer to discuss and review it.

One of my colleagues had started to develop a practice in Lincoln, with cases that got better and better. My clerk asked me to support her to allow her to concentrate on the higher quality work. It was from her that I received my worst 'hospital pass', as she could not take it herself. I attended the first day, but pointed out to the judge that I wanted included psychiatric evidence that provided some support on the issue of consent.

The case involved a rape case (to which I have alluded before), the victim being an eighteen-year-old, severely mentally troubled and educationally subnormal girl – with a mental age of about eight. She also had a speech impediment, which made her difficult, at times, to understand. The psychiatrist had stated that because of the defendant's slight educational sub-normality, it might be that he could have believed that she had given consent.

That provided all I had to run with, and although the defence deals in possibilities, the evidence from friends, her school and social workers, presented a consistent and utterly credible picture of total naivety, an inability to be allowed to even cross a road on her own, for instance, and a complete lack of knowledge or appreciation of sex, or any effective sexual education.

The defendant gave evidence, and it was apparent that any abnormality was minor, and his allegation that she had encouraged the sex acts (including oral sex) fully and 'enthusiastically' was unbelievable. Even a photograph of the two of them in a shopping centre together (he was buying clothes for her), proved a double-edged sword. I had told him there was no possibility of his succeeding (mentioned before, I suspect, at the start of the trial) and, as it proceeded, and stronger and stronger evidence came in , he persisted each day with his claim to innocence, taking the view that he would never plead guilty to such a charge.

Because of the victim's mental state and speech defect, I could barely understand her in the witness box, but as I was limited in the questions allowed by her adviser, the prosecutor and the judge, all I could test her on were facts, and she answered that she didn't know to virtually every question. It was the most uncomfortable task ever, and it was made worse by the jury's total antagonism to me and my client. Certainly it was the most miserable time I had known in court, but it had been his choice to run the most unlikely of defences, and to insist on giving evidence of it to a jury.

It took some time for them to find him guilty, probably due to the intransigence of one juror. He received the proper sentence of imprisonment, and it could well have been more. An appeal was lodged, but got nowhere. Recognising the inevitability of the result of both trial and appeal, I did all that was possible, which included treating the victim with respect, understanding and full courtesy and patience. She deserved as much, and aggression would have not been tolerated, even were I to have attempted it.

Lincoln Crown Court is within Lincoln Castle, surrounded by ramparts with a museum, in which I found, in my lunchtime wanderings, an original of the Magna Charter, a few of which were placed around the country. Fifty yards from the entrance was the Cathedral, and together they overlooked the town, with a cobbled narrow road from the town up the hill.

The only problem was transport. Arriving on the only train I could catch in the morning left me at court with an hour to spare, and returning home involved at least two trains to get to North London, long waits, and about four hours' travel in all. I did, however, enjoy higher fees, and excellent instructions, from a most capable solicitor. I finished my spate of Lincoln cases with a Court of Appeal sentence which my colleague could not attend, but afterwards had to decline practicing in Lincoln, and to do without its usual diet of sex and violence.

My lunchtime wanderings had replaced the swim during the break, and it was important to get out of court and think one's thoughts, or mentally prepare a speech. Sometimes it could be a solitary way of life, if lunch was eschewed. Travelling enabled study of the brief or more thinking time, but it made a nice change to have a companion. This is where having one's own pupil proved entertaining, as well as being useful for them, even if they were not studying law.

I had three six month pupils, the first had been a right-wing trade unionist (giving her unusual work opportunities); the second was extremely self-confident, but had little commonsense (I had to sack him, as he was trying to make contacts for himself when we went to court); and the third was a young man who properly exuded confidence, was extremely bright, and is now in the upper echelons of an unusual commercial practice, for which he has finished a widely-used text book.

I took on many more pupils from my daughter's school who were doing work experience. I would take on four, two each week, so that they could keep each other company when I had to dump them in one court if I was elsewhere, or if a trial in the Magistrates Court proved unsuitable. One into which I had brought them turned out, on its opening by the prosecutor, to have involved sex in a graveyard, and the bench were taken aback when, halfway through the prosecutor's opening speech, a stranger dashed in, grabbed the two watching schoolgirls, and shot out.

I could imagine them going home and telling their parents, when asked what they had been doing, that 'that nice barrister took us to a court where these two people were having sex in this graveyard and we heard everything they were up to!'

I tried to vet everything, as other cases could get switched and called on out of order: otherwise, we kept near the exit for a quick getaway.

Taking my nephew's daughter for two weeks must have helped, as she was doing law at school, and was called to the Bar a few years later, despite my warnings over finances. She chose more of a specialist civil practice, with a regular salary, so maybe my strictures were not in vain.

Another from school spent two weeks with me, started her law degree, and rang and asked for a second pupillage. I have no doubt that she is also excelling at the Bar.

We followed the same practice if possible, starting in the Magistrates Court, then to the Crown Court and finishing on Friday at the Court of Appeal, so that they could follow the sequence. I would throw in an immigration hearing, with one of the others in my chambers who was in that line of work. In the meantime, at breaks, they would put up with and seemed to enjoy our wanderings - often to the renowned organ recitals at Temple Church, or their choir performances (the church having one of the best in the country). Fortunately, they never wanted to eat at lunchtime.

The one court where one would not leave at lunchtime on a first visit was at Lancaster, where the courtroom was part of the cathedral, again overlooking the town from on high. The court room was twice as long as any other, but twice as narrow, and taking up the whole of the wall behind counsels' benches was a range of stained glass windows of all the monarchs in England since Norman times. It was a magnificent sight - completely contrasting with the town below, which was totally grey, apart from the display, in shop after shop, of superb Lancashire cheese - a must for the first time visitor. (Well, one has to obtain some enjoyment from the work.)

I picked Fridays for our visits to the Court of Appeal, as the court never seemed to sit late, and dealt with many appeals against sentence, each of which would average between twenty minutes or half an hour. These were always enjoyable because of their variety and speed of turnover, and the input from the judges throughout indicated counsel's chances of success. The details of the facts were not stressed, but because what was coming up could not be predicted, we again sat next to the exit. The pupils also saw a variety of styles and approaches from counsel.

It was not unknown, as you rose to your feet, for them to interrupt, saying that they were minded to reduce the sentence imposed by... and ask if you thought you could do any better:

very few had the courage (or foolhardiness) to battle on. More often than not, some reduction or improvement in sentence would result. Occasionally, it would be so adjusted that the appellant would be released that day.

My most successful and fulfilling Friday was taking a group of American law students from San Diego, whom our chambers had been entertaining for nearly two weeks. We had made them all conduct a bail application as an exercise, and then a full scale mock trial in one of the more historic courts in the Old Bailey. As is so often the case, after about ten minutes of a mock trial it starts to feel like the real thing, even with Americans adjusting to wearing wigs and gowns.

It was a great moment for the students, but the best was yet to come. That was when I took them before Lord Denning, as he sat in his court dealing with a contentious but relevant civil case centring on environmental issues.

At the end of the day I received a note from his clerk, asking if my students would like to come to his room. Would they! Would I! We sat before the great man listening to that delightful 'burr' in his homely accent for over half an hour, as he chatted quite freely. It must have been the students' finest moment of their trip, and mine too, since he had always been an absolute hero of mine ever since I took up law.

The next significant case I received was another rape case, defending, of course; but it did not involve detailed and personal cross examination of the victim, since the defence was not consent but identification. Had the defendant been proved to have been present with the victim in her flat, he would have had no defence. It was therefore an easier and more straightforward case to defend, relying on evidence more in keeping with routine criminal cases. It had its complexities and forensic difficulties to cope with, each one able to raise some doubt.

Ever since then, I have found it my most troubling case, which is the reason for my full exposition of it. It was also the only case where I was asked by Liberty – which pursued cases from a Human Rights point of view - to provide all the papers for their further investigation

The rapist had entered the flat, where the victim lived alone, after midnight, as a burglar, through a half open window. She had entertained her boyfriend earlier in the evening, and was relaxing in her dressing gown. After some conversation, and a search for property to steal, the rapist turned his attentions towards her, threatened her verbally and then raped her. He did so twice and left, telling her not to notify the police 'or else'.

From her flat, she ran out on to the street shouting for help, and was taken, still in her dressing gown, in the police van to the station. A single hair was found on the gown and DNA analysis identified it as that of the defendant. He had no previous convictions, was Nigerian, and was a divorced security guard.

The complainant gave a long recorded interview, in which there was a short passage in which she said that she thought her attacker was her rent collector (which was later disproved). He had searched her room for valuables, opening drawers and a jewellery box and picking up a number of items, opening doors and windows, and then closing them as he left. She described his hands, and so he clearly had not been wearing gloves. He had talked to her at length, given his name, and offered no violence, but said that he was a member of a gang, and she should not go to the police, or she would suffer.

He had sex with her on the same bed on which she had had sex with her boyfriend, some hours before. This was confirmed by a statement from the boyfriend, who had travelled from South London by public transport to be with her. Her clear evidence was that she was raped (which was never challenged). She did as she was told, no force was used, nor was there any humiliation or other sex acts.

There then followed a four-hour interview, with a police artist drawing an accurate picture of her attacker, focussing on every single detail of his appearance. These were rated in a range of one to five, and finally his colour was described as blue-black to get the right blackness. An E-fit emerged, and every feature had been discussed at length in her interview. Thus his appearance was ascertained with certainty, and her description was audible from her transcript.

After his arrest she picked him out in a video-recorded identification parade, to which he consented: he objected to several of the volunteers, after which he accepted the parade: his solicitor could not attend the parade, so he managed it by himself and raised no further objections. To have had a solicitor present would have proved a definite advantage (especially as his solicitor was Nigerian).

His own mobile phone was interrogated, as he stated that he had been staying at that time with a friend up north, he thought. His own address was quite close to the victim, and he had a brother living not far away in the same area. Cell-phone analysis was conducted by the prosecution, and they established that he had certainly been in the area where the victim lived in the days before the attack, and on the day it happened. The analysis did not reveal where he was at the time of the rape, other than in the locality. No calls were made during the time of the rape, and some of the calls that day were to Nigeria.

We were also provided with a forensic report, confirming that the single hair proved to be identical with his hair and DNA. This she considered conclusive proof of guilt (slightly overstated from an expert). There was no other forensic evidence on the bed, or in the room, nor any evidence of his fingerprints on any item touched or anywhere in the room, which had been subject to a painstaking search by the police scientific officers, four in all. Even footprint analysis outside her window failed to elicit any evidence against him. There was no comment on the absence of such material by the prosecution.

Then it was time to prepare his defence, as most of the material had been disclosed. I found him rather timid, and totally in denial, but noticed particularly that his speech was almost unintelligible: the language was English but he muddled up his words strangely, with half of one word joined to half of another word, so I had to keep asking my solicitor (from the same part of the world) what he said, though it was in English. Interviewing him was almost impossible for me, and it was always the same just talking to him.

Having been provided with the cell phone analysis this helped him to remember in his first interview with us that he had been in the locality at the time, and that he shopped around the corner in the High Street, where the victim lived. That was also where he had his hair cut, and now he was sure that he had been drinking and ate at one of two Nigerian drinking clubs, again around the corner by a bus stop (which is where the victim ended up in her dressing gown, before being collected by the police).

The name given to the victim was nothing like his; he was a solitary man, and had no relationship with a gang. It also came out, tangentially, that he always read a section of the Bible every evening before going to bed, and had no convictions for dishonesty, never mind burglary. He had been married, but was now divorced. Finally, he had no convictions for harassment, violence or indecency or anything of relevance.

We now started work. There were pages and long lists of mobile numbers in the cell phone analysis. Our own expert reviewed all this material which contained the sites from which reception was obtained. A vast amount of technical work was conducted and presented for the Crown and the Court resulting in the conclusion that, whilst he had been in the vicinity before and after the crime, and on the day and evening before, there was nothing to put him in the victim's road or flat at the time when the rape occurred. Most of the calls could have been made during a visit to the High Street or to the drinking clubs which he had visited.

Whilst the Crown assisted, at our request, with the facts that the two establishments were open during the relevant time, our own enquiries of the licensees or drinkers there proved of no assistance, though he was known by them. That he had originally lied about his whereabouts made things look bad at first – the reason for the thorough analysis - but with his own disclosure (in his first defence statement), the point became equivocal, and failed to provide the Crown with strict proof: all that could be said was that he was not elsewhere, so could have been at her flat.

The next area of disclosure revealed the video recording of the identification procedure. This was sent to another expert for the participants to be magnified to show their full faces and any jewellery worn (the rapist having worn none). Four were seen to be wearing necklaces, and so they could possibly have been ruled out by the identifier.

Whilst waiting for this, enquiries were made about the name which the victim had been told, and an almost identical name came up, that of a convicted rapist from the area, and a known member of a local gang. The Detective Inspector who responded helpfully to our requests to pursue this, as with all of our requests, which were obligingly met in full, ascertained that the man had been in custody at the time. Whilst it was possible that he had still been able to commit the crime, his E -fit and full description were chased up, and showed (disappointingly) that he had not been responsible.

Nevertheless, an attack on the identification procedure was mounted. The first objection was procedural for the rules in the Police and Criminal Evidence Act stated that volunteers must be as similar to the suspect as possible. Otherwise the evidence of identification was inadmissible. (The fact that the suspect is picked out does not affect that decision.)

This, it must be said, was nothing like the case. The organiser of the parade had an E-fit and a complete detailed description to work from. Of the ten volunteers, only two looked like Nigerians from their colour. The rest were light skinned, several appeared to be typical East Africans, one Mexican, and two from Somalia – even more distinctive. The other Nigerian had a very prominent roman nose, contrary to the photo-fit, and the wrong shaped head, and several had ears that stuck out and other features expressly described that were completely at variance.

The officer in charge maintained in his live evidence in court that he had done his best. After two objections to the first parade he continued with the next. Whilst one cannot expect to find identical volunteers, he had the material to be precise, and to rule out most of the parade from the specific information of the victim, since she had described precisely feature after feature. In identifying, the victim would have ruled out some eight of the ten and the other (blue-black) Nigerian.

Whilst it was not my task to suggest how he could have held a completely fair parade, with his material what he produced was so unfair that there was only one person who resembled the description and that was the defendant. What he could have done was to postpone it, study the material, and get it right (or at least much better). The adjournment would have also allowed his solicitor to have been present, thus protecting the lay client and safeguarding the police procedure.

However, the evidence was before the jury with all the images on the video, plus the E-fit, and detailed notes of her comments on every facial feature. The jury received no direction on the procedure - though in law that was a matter for the judge - to admit or not allow it.

They did receive the compulsory warnings about the possibility of mistakes, even on identification parades. The directions were not tailored to the factual difficulties, or racial differences. They could see the defendant, the E-fit and the images on the DVD, so they had all that material to compare.

I also called an interpreter, from Nigeria, to assist my client when he gave evidence himself. This made clear what he was saying to the jury (and Judge and prosecutor). This served to cast doubt on the victim's evidence, as she had had absolutely no problem on understanding his every word during the long conversation he had with her (if he was the rapist); and she was certainly not African, but spoke perfect English!

The last element of the case was the single hair. Again we called an expert, an extremely experienced and capable scientist, well versed in giving evidence in murders and in other most serious cases. He identified three types of hair, and outlined each type's transferability from person to person. He was far more competent, precise and experienced than the police witness, and his report was a treatise on the subject in itself. Unfortunately, the police scientist had destroyed the hair during her analysis, so limiting his.

His conclusion was that some accidental transfer could not be ruled out, though he did agree with the Crown that some specific possibilities which they had put could be ruled out. His conclusion was that it was unsafe to rely on a single hair as strict proof; had there been a congregation or group, that would indeed have been probative. I do not believe that this was pointed out to the jury, other than their having heard it in his report. Even if just mentioned, it deserved more emphasis.

I made all my points fully, as did my opponent, and the directions given by the judge were surprisingly brief, but which no legal objection could be made to them. However, I felt that more time could have been spent on important defence points such as, for instance, the speech pattern of the defendant, which went unnoticed by the victim, and which the jury must have heard.

Nor was the curious absence of any other forensic material, especially fingerprints, pointed out and stressed, as the rapist had touched nearly everything in the victim's room with his bare hands, and the four Scene of Crime Officers had conducted meticulous examinations. Even the van in which the victim was transported was subject to thorough examination.

Nevertheless, his conviction by the jury followed, and he was sentenced to seven years imprisonment. I thought this the minimum sentence, and, as such, it was not a bad result for a conviction.

The next development was that I was warned to attend the Court of Appeal, as the Solicitor-General had been briefed by the Attorney-General to present the appeal, with a leading QC as his junior in court, to review the sentence for undue leniency. It was a most unusual application, but when we were getting robed, ready for the hearing, the other two counsel involved in their review of their sentence, as also being unduly lenient, asked me whether I had read articles published the previous day in the press (including *The Times*, of course).

That in *The Times* reported that the Lord Chief Justice was considering our cases, in order to set new guidelines for rapes by strangers where they occurred in the victim's own home. This proposed change in the guidelines had come, as far as we were all concerned, out of the blue, though doubtless in high legal circles it had been discussed, and could have resulted from a Law Commission study of the subject. The Solicitor-General prosecuted, accompanied by a high level QC, and presented the full proposal, drafted and fully prepared by the Lord Chief Justice according to the reports, but with no indication which I had seen of the length of sentence favoured by the new guidelines. I also had no chance to warn my client of what was to come.

I could not but agree that my client probably did deserve a higher sentence, and there was little I could have said to oppose it, except that it could have been worse, and that I never consider useful mitigation. There was no humiliation or force used, and factors present in other cases were not present in mine – for instance, recording the crimes on mobile phones or in the presence of others or having committed them in a filthy alleyway or public place.

I was stunned when the sentence was more than doubled, and he received 15 years. Similarly, the others, after guilty pleas, also received double. The Lord Chief Justice gave his judgment, and the central phrase used that stuck in my mind was that a household rape was a woman's worst nightmare, and that fifteen years was the proper tariff.

Once announced, the thought crossed my mind that it was rape which was a woman's worst nightmare, and other aggravating factors could be added on as appropriate: some could have made it even worse than that it happened in their own home (without minimising the seriousness of that factor). Any appeal could not be taken any further, and even if it had been possible, with such heavy guns against me, and the legal discussions that must have taken place at length between all the experts, it would have been pointless.

My appeal followed some months later, and I advanced all my factual arguments rehearsed above, the fault in the identification procedure being central, as well as the lack of full probative force in the forensic evidence, and the absence of any of the other forensic material that might have been expected.

The respondent to the appeal was the same counsel that had prosecuted my client, accompanied by his Detective Inspector, who had been so involved in the case. I was taken by surprise that he showed the full images on the DVD to the three judges, maximised so as to be completely visible in court. However, the whole issue was dealt with by its being held, by them, that one had only to look at the images, and to compare them with the appellant sitting in the dock, to see that the identification was correct. That was a view with which, it must be said, I could not possibly have agreed.

My point about the wrong procedure leading to the evidence's inadmissibility disappeared, and was not dealt with by such a pragmatic approach.

Another view taken by the court was that guilt was reinforced by the fact that he lived in the same area. That too troubled me, as it seemed more likely that accidental transference could more readily have occurred when the victim did live in an area much frequented by my client than if, for instance, he had lived in Scarborough.

After the failure of the appeal, I asked my solicitor to write to the Criminal Cases Review Committee, who had the power to re-interview and find further witnesses, and re-investigate the whole case if there was apparent injustice. The only response received was from Liberty, which, as I have stated, considers the result from a human rights viewpoint, and which could mount a further appeal. As requested, I sent them all the papers, but heard no more.

Chapter 18
Sweet revenge and thoughts on identification

If each matter, hearing or case were the subject of a chapter with a suitable title, the next one would be entitled just 'Sweet Revenge.' It concerned the Legal Aid authority, and afforded me great satisfaction.

Having attended for a three day case, the claim was submitted to the area legal aid authority, and included a number of categories for payment. One of these was for attendance for three days, a fact which makes me sure that the legal aid for the Magistrates' Court was extended for counsel. This sub-total was worked out at around £2000.

After the usual months of delay - I believe it was actually less than a year in this case - it came back with the cheque. The calculations had been written in red ink, and the sum was correct for the attendance figure. The trouble was that it had not been added into the total, which was therefore some £2000 short.

My clerk, the excellent Bernard - the best clerk I have ever had (I don't count John, during my pupillage; my contact with him was fairly limited, but I feel sure that he would also have been top of my list) - queried the matter with the authority, but was told it had been settled despite him pointing out their mathematical error. My junior clerk tried again, and got nowhere.

One of Bernard's gifts was his letter writing, stemming from experience in the Crown Prosecution Service, in a solicitor's office, and, for many years, as a counsels' clerk. He was the easiest person to talk to - so important - as full and frank communication between counsel and clerk, in my experience, had been a rarity. Whilst I pride myself on my letter-writing, especially in making monetary claims, I could not have done any better. He included the claim form, to show the entries in their original red ink.

After the usual delay, we received a reply from the Head of the legal aid area, stating that the matter had been reviewed, but was correct, and that the claim for an increase was refused. It had been signed by him personally, with his title set out beneath.

That was the final straw with my many tribulations over legal aid fees. I could forgive a simple mistake in adding up, or missing a figure, but this was too much.

I wrote back and made an official complaint, asking for an investigation by the Head of another legal aid area. I sought reimbursement of the fee, an *ex gratia* payment - I may have suggested £750 - and a sum for my clerk, because of the extra work which he had to do to reclaim the fee.

The complaint was registered and substantiated against the Head of the first legal aid authority, and fully paid out, plus £750 *ex gratia* for myself, and £250 awarded to Bernard.

Of all my claims and appeals (and more are to come), apart from the hundred hours thrown away by the costs judge in the case involving the ten and five day *voir dire* hearings at Kingston, I have always been paid. However, the stress involved with preparing huge files of papers, and the hearing itself; and, finally, appearing either before the Master, in his room at Clifford Inn, also off the Strand, or the senior costs judge in the High Court itself, can be something of an ordeal for a criminal hack. I am not sure that the trouble taken is worth the result, and I could say that it is the principle that counted; but money always helped.

Another payment found in my account book, when refreshing my memory, was for the rape case at Lincoln, where the fee was reduced. Another appeal, a year later, yielded the £1859 from the Master, but this one had to be argued.

It is surprising how often the struggle has followed a difficult case, though some delay would always be expected in the

Magistrates Court. Legal aid is extended for Counsel in these cases, because of the difficulty involved in the case.

Wood Green Crown Court was the scene for a three day case which was certainly not easy , and which had been returned from another set of chambers, as their advocate was unavailable.

It involved harassment of a wife by her husband, on two occasions where he had driven past her, looking at her threateningly. The third took place outside the matrimonial court which they had just been to, she with the interpreter whom she had used in court. Her husband was alleged to have moved towards her, and behaved threateningly, but with no contact.

In court, when it came to her evidence, she declined to take the oath with the Koran, though very religious, and affirmed. I cross-examined her as to this (her husband having said that she always affirms in their court proceedings).

He and his friend told me afterwards that she had said that she would take no notice of any oath, and say what she wanted. The interpreter failed to interpret this answer (unsurprisingly) as well as omitting the fact that she cursed him in her evidence and said that she would kill him! The interpreter then gave answers which he thought best, and advised her, at times, not to answer.

The husband was acquitted of all matters bar that outside the court, where the interpreter gave evidence that his presence was threatening (they had waited some half an hour for the husband to come out of the court, to allow for the threatening conduct).

The defendant wanted to appeal, but a prerequisite was the transcript of her evidence on oath, with the translation of her answers. This required a visit to Wood Green, to persuade them to release the court transcript. The clerk's office would not grant it, but I applied in any event. The Registrar had the power to order the court to release it, but declined, and leave was not granted.

I put in the claim for the trial, and waited a number of months, only to be told by the chambers that the claim had been refused, as they had put it in too late. The time limit was three months. We sought all the paperwork between chambers for the claim but they retorted that they had understood that we were going to do it ourselves. Paperwork established that this was not the case, as they had told us they were going to claim.

More paperwork emerged, showing that the High Court had sought an explanation to justify the lateness. Their reply had been a brief apology, remarking that they were very busy. The High Court then asked the original advocate, through her chambers, for the grounds of the appeal to the costs judge. Three letters requesting the grounds were ignored, but they were forwarded to me, with the rest of the papers. In the end, I collated everything into a proper bundle, drafted full grounds myself, and explained that, as I was counsel involved, I would be attending court in any event.

The other counsel did not attend, and I went before the Senior Costs judge in the High Court and argued my case. I was successful, and he asked me what costs I wanted, as he was free to award them (apart from reimbursing me for the fee to appear before him).

He seemed surprised that I did not seek costs from the other chambers but since I knew its Head well I thought it uncharitable for her to pay them, even though many hours work had been spent. It could also have been messy if she had appealed the costs awarded, and I only wanted my fee, and to move on.

I had responded to her appeal against conviction some years before in the Court of Appeal, where she had included every conceivable ground and complaint: I thought at the time the judges would be overwhelmed by so many allegations of error and misconduct, and would lose sight of the few valid grounds advanced, as they did. She would probably have contested my appeal, too, at great length, and I just wanted closure.

The next case again occurred at Wood Green. As "Sod's Law" so often applied to the Bar, this was my nearest and most convenient court, in which, of course, I hardly ever set foot. It involved two youngsters who had set fire to a London bus, and had caused substantial and costly damage. Part of the charge was of endangering a passenger on the vehicle.

The allegation was that the boys had started a fire by burning the back seat on the upper deck. The fire spread rapidly, and a passenger was sitting on the upper deck. The charge indicted was a most serious one, and would result in a heavy sentence, despite their age. There was internal CCTV on the bus, and they (and the passenger) were clearly visible.

Both youths blamed each other, and so we had what was known as a cut-throat defence – which makes life much easier for the prosecution, as each tends to prove the case against the other while maintaining their own innocence. It is the most difficult and uncomfortable type of case to run successfully.

In this case, our client maintained his innocence, his case being that he was present, but had spent much of the time looking out for some youths who were bullying him. The other was on his own, at the rear, with his lighter (several of which he had stolen, it was also alleged). The reason for his actions was that he was burning his initials (or logo) into the back of the seat in front.

Our client assured us that this form of graffiti was a frequent practice for youths on buses but that, on occasions, he did walk back to see what his mate was doing. Our client maintained his lookout from further up the bus and was unaware of a passenger's being still on the upper deck.

The quality of the CCTV was poor, but it did show the start of the fire, its progress, and the passenger, slumped down in a seat towards the front. There had been no mention in their statements of why the fire had been started, but each was adamant that the other had done so, and that they themselves were not responsible.

At least we had, from our client, a motive for the fire that did not involve a deliberate attempt to cause major damage; the other defendant did not offer an explanation. His counsel sought, and obtained, an expert, to clarify the images on the CCTV. He then selected those which showed nothing of his client, and refused to share others. The judge disapproved of this, especially as the costs would be met from the public purse. As a matter of fairness this was all evidence to which all parties were entitled to see – out of fairness all round, including the judge and jury.

Nevertheless, we obtained further authority to use an expert ourselves - the same firm who had conducted the hair and cellphone analysis in my rape case - and who proved to be superb. A sequence of images plotted the very first moment at which a lighter was ignited, through its development into a fire, and the exit of both boys, all reflected on window after window on the bus.

Importantly, it showed that the other youth had the lighter and was using it all the time, but did show our client returning to him once or twice, and sitting near him, momentarily. Co-defending counsel was most displeased by these images, but there was nothing he was able to do to prevent their dissemination or use in court.

Our next step was to take photographs of other local buses, on that and other routes, which would be admitted by bus staff. Each showed burnt graffiti on the back of seats facing the rear bench seat on the upper decks. These were also to be produced for my client's defence, as admissible evidence.

Despite this, the prosecution were in a position to run an argument of joint enterprise, as our client had returned to watch, and must have been aware of the start of the fire, the damage and the danger. It would be unlikely that a jury would have been so sympathetic as to acquit, and the possible plight of the passenger was obvious, and was allegedly and callously disregarded.

It was equally obvious that the co-defendant had nothing credible to put forward on his own account, but could be guaranteed, when he gave evidence, to do all he could to make matters worse for my young client.

Our final conference brought forth the good character of our client. He was interested in following a career in the gas (and oil) industry, like his father. Backed by sound academic achievements, good character, and an excellent CV, he had been one of hundreds of applicants, and had been ultimately successful - the only one selected from that trawl. He was offered a position, and the wage to be paid was an impressive one for his age: future prospects were excellent, and the money would increase substantially.

Now we had to make the judgment call. The co-defendant had no choice but to plead guilty - our CCTV sank him. What we had to offer was helpful in some ways - avoiding deliberate and wicked vandalism, but could we avoid a charge of encouraging the actions, or of having   provided assistance if required, of knowing of the actions, of the spread of the fire, and of the consequences that would inevitably follow.

At this stage in proceedings, there had been two developments in the sentencing process which were of considerable assistance. More and more guidelines were being laid down, to cover virtually every offence. They graded offences as to their seriousness, and listed the range of sentence to be imposed for each grade. The process took the guesswork out of sentencing, and imposed standard figures throughout the country in Crown and Magistrates Courts.

Whilst keeping to the broad bands in the guidelines, some mitigating factors were so strong that they could move an offence into another band, so preserving the system, but adding flexibility.

I had always thought that mitigating after a plea or a finding of guilt after trial was an advocate's weakest area. Getting a result, at such times, required just as much effort and careful preparation as the trial. One had less time to prepare, so the same points were repeated. Many had little relevance, or were highly improbable.

Typical and well-rehearsed examples were regularly put forward. Listening to such efforts,one was minded to have them listed to save time – such as Mitigation No 1 - which could be the sudden discovery of a pregnancy forthcoming (without any physical sign or confirmation); a job interview the following week (with no letter to back it up); or remorse shown, from a defendant who could not be less concerned for the victim, and whose only regret was that he had been apprehended. Many other examples could be linked, and named mitigating guidelines rather like the sentencing guidelines - forgive my cynicism when prosecuting. That such cynicism must be guarded against has been recognised by advice to Judges, to temper their acceptance of counsel's mitigation with a little cynicism.

Every advocate faced with a guilty plea was required to start off with the guidelines - prosecutors as well - and the judge would expect it of them. Agreement was necessary for the judge to apply them correctly. Any departure from the guidelines would have to be justified, to prevent an appeal to lessen the sentence, or to increase it for being unduly lenient. A brilliant result that appeared a triumph could rebound.

The other improvement was that a defence advocate could ask for an indication from the judge as to sentence. The rules were that he had to announce the minimum sentence he might impose, though he had the discretion whether to give an indication or not. Occasionally, some judges would do so without a formal application. Many refused.

Since discretion and flexibility were, and still are, the handmaidens of the best sentencing, the procedure allowed for discussion between judge and counsel. With an amenable judge, it was possible to obtain an accurate estimate of what was most likely, rather than concentrating on the minimum sentence for such an offence.

We had a good judge who was well aware that this was a most serious charge, with a high likelihood of a custodial disposal. There were strong factors mitigating such a serious charge, mentioned above, and we knew from the judge that the youth of the defendants would count heavily in the equation. That a full trial would be avoided was another major factor (for we suspected that contesting the matter would prompt the co-defendant to follow).

Plainly, my client's character, future prospects and moral value provided more mitigation: and, finally, my client's ability realistically to offer substantial compensation, not just out of present funds, but given the prospect of increasing annual rises.

327

It was vital that he had to be free to take up the position in the very near future, and we were able to produce an excellent report from the Youth Offenders Team, making the most appropriate recommendations. They were followed by the judge, and a non-custodial sentence was imposed, with confiscation set well into four figures.

With his future assured, and a superb career in the making, following that of his father, his parents were absolutely delighted, as he had come close to wrecking everything for which he and his family had been working. I had no doubt that he would never forget his lucky escape.

Flexibility, combined with imagination by a judge, can achieve long term results to affect a youth's life, as it did with the arson case, if argued persuasively and realistically.

I had to defend a friend of my son, who had caused thousands of pounds' worth of damage to cars by jumping on their roofs in a car park, accompanied by other mindless acts, prompted by drink. It was his first conviction, and the damage again merited a custodial sentence, such as Borstal. That was often the forerunner of a life-time circle of crime and prison.

My son's friend wanted no more in life than to get behind a wheel, as did so many of his age. If he were not deterred from doing so without a driving licence or insurance, this would lead to a further offence: then would follow a disqualification from driving.

The order of the court would be breached by further driving, and punishment imposed as a deterrent. So the pattern would be set, but, this time, as an adult, and a criminal path through life would almost inevitably beckon.

Having heard of a local initiative at Wood Green, again, I researched it, and came before the judge with a plan in place for him to enter the scheme: it involved a form of probation, for a lengthy period, at a Banger Racing stadium, where his job would be to maintain, repair and drive the vehicles in use.

He would be under constant and unrelenting supervision by the track manager, a practical supervisor who would want results and was in a position to demand them, or else. This proved another bonus for the scheme, and for the lad himself. It seemed ideal, but was a stiff decision for a traditional or conservative judge; but this one used imagination, and, in considering the longer term (and effective rehabilitation) his sentence paid off.

I can happily say that the judge was delighted with his progress, and my son's friend went on to become a lorry driver, fully content in his work. Having proudly passed his heavy goods test licence, he did very well driving such vehicles for many years, and provided his children with a good life.

Whilst I have set out before the satisfaction of getting a reaction and some discourse from the judge, instead of addressing a wall of blankness, my opposing counsel did once surprise me, by criticising a judge who offered an indication as to sentence without being asked.

The case involved the guilty possession of two cars by a motor trader, one being a brand new Mercedes, which police discovered hidden at the back of his garage covered by a sheet. Their search had been prompted by having found the other stolen car on his forecourt. There was strong evidence from a recent loser, following a burglary in which her carkeys had been taken in order to steal the car. Enquiries made of the Mercedes revealed it had been obtained by a hire purchase fraud, with some connection between the defendant and the perpetrator of the fraud, who could not be found.

The case was to be strongly defended, on the issue of knowledge of the dishonesty involved. Our case was strengthened by the fact the defendant had had in his possession a second stolen car. Having further stolen property when charged with handling raised, as a matter of law, the probability of his guilt as to the first car.

Before the start of the trial, the judge gave the defendant and his counsel an indication of the likely sentence if convicted. It seemed to me that this was in order to help him decide his plea, bearing in mind that it was a strong case he had to face and he might wish to plead guilty, knowing the sort of sentence which the judge was envisaging.

Counsel's reaction was extremely critical of the judge, and he raised it as an abuse of process to stop the trial. I had little to say and could not agree with my colleague that the judge had behaved badly, though, as the prosecutor, I was perhaps not looking through his eyes. I could see that the judge also appeared somewhat baffled. The application was refused, it went to trial and the defendant was convicted, with an order for substantial confiscation.

We waited a long time for the confiscation hearing, which seemed to have fallen through the system. Meanwhile, I received a letter from the Registrar at the Court of Appeal, my opponent having sought leave to appeal the conviction, on the main ground of an abuse of process. He asked me to express my opinion on whether the judge had acted wrongly, as he was considering leave.

Obliged to answer a request from the High Court, my view was that I had been surprised and taken aback by counsel's reaction. It appeared to me that the judge had been acting to assist, rather than to press the defendant into pleading guilty. I heard no more of that matter, though we did obtain confiscation, as the defendant had substantial means at his disposal.

The next case to arrive sent me and a number of fellow defence barristers to Leicester. It was always a pleasure to attend court away from London, and, equally, to be one of a large group in the same case. The court and staff were always pleased to see us, from London, and everyone sported a smile and old world courtesy.

Being part of a group involved a mix of good minds, the prospect of strong support, and, nearly always, the hope of a cracked trial (one where a deal was reached).The papers were usually so voluminous that a generous payment was assured: the travel allowed much of the work to be done on the train, in my case, as I never enjoyed really long drives to and from court, since lateness was a constant worry.

I had worked for a particular solicitor in the Midlands before, ever since a friend had recommended me to take on a case in Dubai for him the next day. He could not make it, and had thought of me; and, being a commercial case, it was worth a small fortune. As it was not my field, and I hated flying, I turned it down; but the solicitor started briefing me with some Leicester cases before moving to London.

I remembered defending there, in a drugs case, an exotic dancer who kept being spoken of as an erotic dancer by occupation (and she certainly qualified for that misnomer); but she faced an unwinnable case. Another involved a firearm which, when we called an expert, proved to be a hundred years old and so our client was acquitted, as it was legally an antique and the provisions did not apply; and another concerned a burglar in a series of burglaries, where he tied up and humiliated the victims, with their partners watching. He was convicted of all bar one, and leave to appeal was refused.

However, all this had been some fifteen years before, when he changed his practice to a commercial one involving property, but a Leicester solicitor had asked him to recommend someone for his case, and he had suggested me.

The case provoked much thought and discussion, between us and the prosecutor, and with the judge in court, since one view was that this was a serious crime: kidnapping. The alternative view was that this was a family very much concerned over the welfare of their daughter.

There were more than a dozen of us, and we were to be split into two trials, as that number was unmanageable in that court, with all defendants separately represented. The Crown had a leader and junior. The full charges were Kidnapping and False imprisonment, and both trials would clearly have taken many weeks, with a doubling of the evidence by each of its witnesses for each separate trial. All defence witnesses would be similarly duplicated.

The facts were that the complainant was a young graduate in her twenties, who had become besotted with a man who turned out to be married with a family. She left home to be with him, but he refused to live with her, and so she ended up in a refuge for women. Her family had heard nothing from her for weeks, and even her best friend had no contact or knowledge of her whereabouts for a similar period.

Eventually they found out where she had been living, and visited the address, having been told by the man that he did not want to continue their relationship. The mother and her best friend, with her best friend's mother, were driven by an uncle to the address, where they had begged the complainant to come and speak to her mother. She had started to scream that she did not want to but had then been persuaded to come to the car. Another car, containing her father and her sisters, and driven by a family friend, had been present. All were terribly concerned.

She had reiterated that she did not want to go home, but, after getting somewhat hysterical outside the car, had gone silent. The door was opened, and she was cajoled – the appropriate word – into the car, and sat alongside her mother and best friend. The friend's mother may have held the door open to usher her in.

She was taken home, where her parents, sisters, uncles friends and other relatives started to speak to her, ensuring that she was well, telling her how she was upsetting and worrying her parents, asking what she had been doing for that length of time; all had a meal together, continuing to talk matters over.

Eventually they told her that they were taking her back to the refuge; but instead, all drove her to an uncle's flat, up North. The rest of the day and night was spent in similar discussions and worries about how she was coping financially, and what she was going to do to get her life back on track.

In the meantime, the police had come to believe that she was going to be taken abroad immediately to the family's own country, with no evidence for this conviction but the complainant's unjustified belief and fear. That was essentially the prosecution case. The family heard that the police were worried about her, so they took her to the police station where, after interview, she was released.

She maintained that she had been kidnapped, but asserted that she knew that her family would not hurt her, and had only her own welfare in mind. Nevertheless, the Crown were insistent on prosecuting everyone involved and maintaining both charges - the first relating to her being put in the car, and the second to driving up North and staying the night.

My client was the mother of her best friend; my client naturally knew the complainant's mother, and was trying, as a mother, to assist. It was contended that she had helped to put the complainant in the car to sit with her mother and my client's own daughter. At court, my client's main concern was for her own daughter, also charged, and for whom a conviction on such offences would seriously affect the future which she was carving out for herself.

The prosecutor and the CPS believed this to be a serious criminal matter of attempted international abduction; all the defence saw was a domestic matter featuring a large family's concern for their daughter's welfare. These views were irreconcilable, and several of the pre-trial attendances involved attempting to obtain some measure of agreement and the appropriate reduction of the seriousness of the charges. My own stance had been to offer at the most a breach of the peace, i.e. pushing her into the car to sit with her mother and best friend. The witnesses at the refuge provided nothing more except that the complainant, when she first saw her mother, had screamed that she did not want to go home.

At the last review, the judge took a firm hand, and stated that he was not going to have a trial of so many relatives concerned for the welfare of their vulnerable daughter over one matter alleged by the daughter. She was a little unstable and hysterical at the time, but accepted that no harm would have come to her, either from the trip home in the car, or at the uncle and his wife's house later.

He welcomed a charge, of a conspiracy by all involved to commit a public order offence, suggested by the defence team, and eventually accepted by the Crown. I still thought that we should fight for the friend's mother, with every chance of success, before a jury, most of whom would have had their own children.

I had even started to plan my closing speech, using my special technique of being a juror answering questions from a sensible member of the public. For example, what was the case about? 'The family's concern over their daughter, who was having an affair with a married man.' Their cause for concern?'Not having heard from her for weeks, during which time she had not answered any of them, including her best friend, on her phone, and had left a very good job.' There were many telling answers to more questions which I would have been putting. The speech was ideal, as it would also have provided a contrast with all those before me, thus ensuring the jury's full concentration.

My final instructions were that the mother wanted to ensure that her own daughter was not charged. Being a graduate with a very bright future, this would all be ruined, so her mother wanted to plead guilty with all the others.

The Crown accepted our plea of guilt, and offered no evidence against the daughter, and the result was what they both wanted. A non-custodial sentence – a suspended sentence I believe - was the result all round.

Back to London, to my usual court, which, at that time, was Croydon. It was at some distance, as was my other regular court, Isleworth; but public transport made the journeys reasonably comfortable. Whilst my closest was Wood Green, and my regulars were on the other side of London, as usual in a barrister life, I was sent off to places like Bexley or Bromley, which took hours, even though they were in London. Brighton or Portsmouth would have actually been quicker.

On thinking about it, that law seemed to me to operate regularly for some and not others. In all the jobs I have had, there were always some of my colleagues who regularly went home for lunch as part of a contented and easy life; others, never. Possibly that's what ambition does.

I remember talking to the daughter of one of my relief at Wanstead, who mentioned her Dad as just a PC. I remonstrated with her that he was a bright, intelligent and capable man, with a wonderfully teasing sense of humour, and accepted at the station as the informal relief leader.

There comes a time for every officer, I said, to make the choice of a comfortable, domestic life working where he really enjoys the work and the area. Many forgo the transfers and changes, the extra travel moving to divisions that are full of problems and stress, and working with difficult colleagues or superiors.

All can offer leadership in a given situation – indeed that is the job - and one was the only person there who could, or had to, take the lead. Taking the first steps to saving a life after an accident or crime does not require rank, and it is most likely that every street officer has been in such a situation.

She was suitably chastened, as her father could have climbed easily, but chose not to; he put his family first. This false and uneducated view circulates widely, so often serving to put down the value of a police constable. (I should climb off my hobby horse and continue.)

The Croydon case involved another rape, with unusual evidential difficulty. It was a case where two girls had spent the evening with two young men. One paired off with the one she knew well, the other (the complainant) with the man she knew vaguely, but towards whom she had no feelings. Back at the girl's flat, they separated, and, after some flirtation and intimacy she was raped, she alleged, which was denied on the grounds that sex had been entirely consensual.

The rape was reported to the police, and confirmed by the complainant's girlfriend. The papers revealed some matters that seemed dubious in the circumstances, which provided ammunition to defend the case. In the lead-up to its going to trial, the complainant's friend contacted my solicitor.

She alleged that her friend had told her that she had not been raped, and that her allegation was completely untrue. She had made the story up to get the alleged rapist, who was quite well off, she said, to buy her a sewing machine; a detail which I thought, being so specific, added credence to the allegation.

At court, I sought an adjournment so that the allegation, which was tantamount to perjury, should be investigated before the defendant had to face a trial. The judge disagreed, and was of the opinion that it should be tested in court within the trial.

Unfortunately, as the date of trial started to draw near, my attendance became unlikely; and not wanting to spring it on a colleague at the sort of short notice which I had suffered in the miserable rape case which I had conducted with the young mentally disturbed victim, I told my solicitor that it would be best to return it. So, as mentioned before, it became my hospital pass.

The colleague I picked was very capable, had prosecuted and defended rapes, and was also very capable as a prosecutor. For this case, he would need all his cross-examining skills to deal with the complainant and her friend. I did not doubt that he would succeed, and he did so, though he did mention my hospital pass when discussing the case with me. At least he had very adequate time to prepare, received a very decent fee, and obtained an introduction to my solicitor, who had known little of him at that time.

It was just after this that I was briefed by a new solicitor to go to Croydon for him, for a lady whom he considered an important client and for whom he therefore needed a good result. He attended court with her, and treated her most circumspectly. We got the desired result, and though it seems odd to say so, he surprised me by sending a spate of cases. Logically, that would seem unsurprising; but so often barristers come to believe that when they get a good result they hear no more from the new solicitor. Perhaps that comes from our insecurity (or mild paranoia).

The firm was in the centre of Enfield, the closest of my solicitors, and there were three in the office. The solicitor whose firm it was wanted me on his books, and was building up the practice. It was for him that I had taken on the rape case, at Wood Green, that had so troubled me .

The third member came to a chambers party which we held, and after introducing him to our criminal team, I did the same for our immigration team, who were making a name for themselves. They were soon to give lectures in the subject to solicitors, and occasionally counsel, who needed them as part of their training. To clarify, briefly, all barristers had to attend twelve lectures each year as part of their ongoing training, and to refresh their knowledge and keep up to date. Their experience made no difference, and they could not practice without obtaining their twelve Continuing Professional Development points; it was a pain fitting them in as it was.

The main solicitor, Valentine, also briefed me for the case of criminal damage to the bus, and other cases. The second, Chuck, had worked in Denmark in the law of oil rigs, and wanted to bring his family over to the UK, so he added a few criminal matters. The third was Adel, and he had been at Croydon with the first client.

Chuck started me off in a new direction. He was contacted by several clients who were dissatisfied with the performance of their counsel in losing cases in the Crown Court, and who wanted to appeal against their conviction. They retained him, and he would obtain a fee for the work, pre-arranging with the legal aid authority the number of hours and the rate for the task.

This was much more to my liking – I approved the rate, and was going to be paid, and quite promptly. Several needed investigation, but were unlikely to be granted leave, others had better chances; but leave was sought for every appeal. This was the least that the solicitor could do for his clients.

One involved a matter of arson in which the appellant had burnt down his house (which he shared with his wife: burning down one's own house is not arson!). It required prolonged investigation, as it involved: the couple's separation; a third man in the relationship who was a specialist in fire insurance; and a visit to the hospital in which he was detained for months with severe burns, and where he was persuaded by the wife's solicitor and friend to sign away his share in the property, and plead guilty.

Numerous aspects of the fire, particularly its cause and position, with his being in the house, and the discovery of unexplained fuel cans, were put forward by the prosecution. These aspects, and his admissions, were strongly inconsistent with the forensic evidence from the Fire Brigade; and the appellant alleged that his wife, their daughter, and the insurance man were putting him under constant pressure for the wife to receive the value of the claim.

My own total of hours worked were close to a hundred, and at the pay-rate the claim settled was for some £3000. The files, including medical reports, notes of attendances on the appellant at hospital, the case papers, psychological material, property purchases, and financial material from abroad, were extensive, but the work was fascinating. Suspicion was being constantly aroused, and material found to back it. Leave to appeal was not granted, the single judge being unconvinced of any conspiracy.

Another of their cases involved an allegation of fraud against a young woman who was solidly identified, and her every communication strongly tested; all the evidence obtained pointed incontrovertibly against her.

We spent hours and hours with her, as she adamantly denied that it was her, and must have been her cousin. She provided no evidence of any cousin or family photographs, nor would she agree to contact her father, living locally, to assist in confirming the existence of any cousin. Persisting with that defence, she was eventually convicted, having given her defence team nothing with which to work.

There were some cases which I could describe as minor, as far as the facts were concerned, but which were most satisfying for the client. Such satisfaction came in different ways, and the first case resulted in the client's not losing her career, after a hearing that she initially lost – unfairly, in my view.

She was a bus driver and, driving on a route which took her into Marble Arch, she had turned left into the junction, intending to drive down Park Lane. There was a double carriageway for traffic to do so, and buses occupied the outer lane to complete the turn, and avoid stationary traffic prior to the bus stop, some little distance away.

As she was completing her turn, a car overtook her on the inner lane and collided with the nearside of the bus, having nowhere to go due to the narrowness of his lane and the left-turning bus.

A CCTV on board the bus showed the angles, the gap available (narrowing as the car proceeded), and the sightline of the bus driver through its nearside wing mirror. The case was adjourned for the prosecution to produce a series of still photographs of the action, leading from the manoeuvre of the bus to the attempt to overtake by the car driver: the left turn signals from the bus were clearly visible.

On our return to the City of London Magistrates Court, there were clear photographs for the lay bench to study. I found the City's court a little different from the usual. Its staff wore livery, and the justices had fur-trimmed gowns, and were generally councillors or justices selected from city institutions. Their deliberations in court were drowned by a tape of noise, switched on when the cases ended.

The only other court that could muster such individuals was at Wells Street, where, more often than not, a member of the aristocracy would sit: once I had one Lord and two Ladies forming my bench. They were a charming and courteous bench, not all that familiar with the norms recognised in say, Canning Town, but concerned to do their public duties responsibly.

These, from the City, were a distinct bench of high status individuals, who always struck me as most business-like. The complainant was an eminent doctor with a high-powered practice. I felt that his evidence was too readily accepted, and was preferred wherever there was a contest. Our bus driver appeared at a disadvantage whenever presenting her evidence. This, despite the damage to the vehicles, which indicated that he had driven from behind into the side of the bus as it had started its turn and after duly signalling, as was confirmed by the tape and stills.

Furthermore, that route meant that the bus had to pull into a bus stop just around the corner, and needed to move across the carriageway to do so. The other driver appeared impatient and in a hurry.

An appeal was lodged and heard at the Old Bailey, since the case came from the City of London's court. I appeared, but, by this time, we had obtained a union representative, who had been a driver on that route for many years; accordingly, he could be regarded legally as an expert witness, after establishing his credentials. The significance of that enhancement was that he could give opinion evidence.

An adjournment was sought for him to be called, after a full statement, obtained after examination of the CCTV and the stills. I took his statement myself at court, and it confirmed that the pattern of driving adopted by my client was obligatory at that junction, and that the good doctor was in the wrong.

The prosecutor was annoyed for the matter to be stood out, as all her preparation was in vain, and the case could not go ahead. (She probably had better things to come back for at the Bailey.) I attended the list office to get a new date at which my witnesses would be sure to attend: she failed to do so for her doctor, who, we knew from our earlier encounters, had a long list of dates to avoid, due to his impressive practice.

When the case was next called, the doctor had not been warned, and could not attend at short notice. My objection to this adjournment was acceded to, since there had been several adjournments in the past, and benches were very pro-active in avoiding delays and putting cases off. The court dismissed the case. Our client was delighted: she kept her job, received her costs, and I made a friend of an expert driving witness, whom I used in further cases.

In some ways my next case was similar, involving an unusual cab driver and a rather typical police officer – which almost sounds like a Sherlock Holmes case. The client had hired a cab, and, on its arrival at her address, with her friend, there was some argument over the fare. This persisted, and as both the client and her friend had been drinking, the cabbie locked her in his cab and drove her to the nearest police station. Though they passed two police officers, he kept her in the cab, dismissing the opportunity to stop and have the matter dealt with on the street.

He notified police of his arrival at the station, and several officers dashed out. The woman police officer opened the cab door and threw my client out, arresting her for being drunk and disorderly.

Outside the cab there was a short struggle, in which she was manhandled (?) by the woman officer; during the fracas, the woman officer sustained a kick to her leg. My client was then carried by police into the police station (none too gently, she alleged) and charged with assaulting the woman officer in the execution of her duty. At the local Magistrates Court, after a trial, she was convicted; it was significant that the taxi driver was not called to give evidence.

I met her to consider an appeal to the Crown Court, as she was incensed by her treatment, and her conviction. As I remember she was a perfectly respectable woman, though she admitted she did like a drink with her friends. The kick to the officer - which did not require any medical attention - was caused accidentally during the struggle with the three police officers.

Hence we went to the Crown Court which, as with all appeals, was a totally fresh hearing, with all witnesses called, except the taxi-driver, who, from the start, did not wish to make a statement, nor to attend as a witness. (It is better for the prosecution, sometimes, not to call a civilian witness, as they can unconsciously contradict the police view of the matter, or in other ways assist the defence.)

The first offence charged was being drunk and disorderly in a public place; there was a strong defence to the charge of being drunk, and to that of the incident's having occurred in a public place. The defence to the charge of assault was a denial of a deliberate or reckless assault, and the claim that the officer was not acting in the execution of her duty, as the arrest was unlawful. My client gave her evidence well, and impressed the judge and, as far as I could see, the two justices sitting with him.

It took him no time at all to agree with me, and to allow the appeal, with the agreement of the justices, as a unanimous decision is required. The grounds were that the arrest was indeed unlawful, since a hired taxicab could not be a public place. I did not even have to rely on my Trafalgar Square authority on the nature of 'public'. It followed that, as the arrest was unlawful, the officer could not have been acting in the execution of her duty.

The description 'rather typical police officer' above, derived from the fact that, this officer having received a kick in a struggle, she wanted the matter prosecuted, despite having suffered no after effects. Often, in such situations, where the injury is not deliberate, or is minor, a charge is not preferred but is accepted as part of the risks attendant on the job, or the resulting prosecution may seem heavy-handed and unnecessary. With others, where there is a loss of dignity, or a minor scuffle, some officers always prosecute.

The charge, when allied with the officer's being assaulted on duty, carried a short custodial sentence, which could have had a momentous and truly disproportionate effect on her life. This time, it was not just the avoidance of a criminal conviction that made the appeal and its result worthwhile, but the personal satisfaction from triumphing over the female and other heavy-handed officers.

The latest incident in this chapter - of interest of itself - occurred shortly afterwards, but I end the chapter deliberately, to leave the subject for further thought. Airing my dissatisfaction with the conviction of the Wood Green rapist, a case in which I failed in my appeal, could provoke further consideration to improve methods of identification in very serious and unusual cases.

It started with my collecting my youngest daughter from college, as usual, but, on this occasion, when I arrived, she was deeply distressed and in tears. Two youths her own age had pushed her and snatched her mobile phone from her hand quite violently.

We toured the area where they had run off, but failed to find them, though we did notice a small group of slightly older youths standing around. Once more we drove round the block, but this time I asked the group whether they had seen anyone running past them. They had noticed two youths running, and indicated the direction. Whilst we were talking, one received a message on his mobile, from someone wanting to sell a good quality mobile.

We indicated our willingness to meet the caller close by, to buy the mobile, and, as we did so, saw two youths about to rob another youngster further up the road. The group ran after the two youths, whilst we pursued them in our car, trying not to drive like Starsky and Hutch. The youths ran into a backyard, and tried to block the door, but the group soon broke that down, and then went for both of them. They responded by trying to barricade the door with rocks, as well as throwing them at their pursuers. One tried to deny the robbery and to fight them off, but he was soon on the losing side. The other said he had seen no phone.

I stood by searching for the phone in the garden whilst my daughter told them not to hit the other youth who was just cowering and whimpering on the ground. I then saw her phone beside him in the grass.

Both managed to escape, but the main offender had lost some blood in the struggle, and DNA analysis traced him. He was arrested and we were both called to his identification parade, having made our statements and provided descriptions. (You may well think:'I can see now where we are going with this!')

The larger and more defiant youth had nothing with which to distinguish him, as far as I was concerned; hair colour and style and dress provided little to assist. My overall impression was that his features were all regular, making him quite good-looking, white, of slightly above average height and build, but there was nothing specific in any facial feature to help.

We were both shown video images of the volunteers and were told, as is mandatory, that the suspect might not be there, but to look very carefully at each, at least twice, and to take our time. When it came to selection, my daughter accepted the offer to look at the array again, and picked him out.

I could not do so, but needed to concentrate, and take more time. On being asked whether I wanted to see any image again I indicated that there were several at which I still needed to look again. Ruling out some with noticeable features quite quickly, I was left with several contenders.

The same procedure was adopted and I rejected one more, as he possessed one or more features not presented by the robber. I was now getting close to the two who could not be excluded, but after studying them side by side at length, I was able to identify the robber with certainty. He turned out to be the same one my daughter had picked out, as she told me when we were driving home. For the sake of completeness only: he pleaded guilty at court.

At one time, when volunteers paraded, the victim would walk along the line, see if he or she could recognise the offender, and point him out: if he or she could not, that was the end of the parade, unless each was asked to say a phrase which the offender had said to the victim, or to copy something else done to aid identification.

Our parade allowed much more thought, and an opportunity of proceeding by exclusion in order to identify. This is particularly relevant when an E-fit has been prepared by hours of concentrating on each facial feature in complete detail (and with an accompanying interview with the artist). Excluding every one with a different and significant facial detail now becomes possible. When only two out of ten are 'blue-black Nigerians' one arrives at a parade with only two of the twelve volunteers who 'are as similar as possible' which is what the rules of the Police and Criminal Evidence Act lay down.

I can hear the objection now, as before, in the trial, that the officer arranging for the images did his best. That may be the attitude to deflect criticism of the officer, but that will not do, especially where a sentence of fifteen years' imprisonment may hang on the parade, as in my still-troubling Wood Green rape case. Such a sentence could reasonably be predicted (by the sentencing guidelines, for instance) in certain rape cases (as ultimately here), especially when the other evidence - mobile and scientific - did not produce certainty.

That the officer has a detailed artist's impression of every feature presented by the alleged offender allows him to exclude those who are positively dissimilar.

Of course finding ten other persons who much more closely fitted the bill would have taken time in my case, but there was no need for this to have been rushed, since the offender was in custody, and the charge was of the most serious, and a life sentence possible; his solicitor could have attended on the next occasion to ensure fairness; and the whole investigation would have proved vastly more careful, accurate and compliant with the spirit of the procedure, as well as with the requirements laid down.

Other cases could follow the same pattern. It is my conclusion that with an E-fit, or other close description, the officer that gathers the images, or volunteers, has the best possible image for comparison. The defendant is also in the best position to show why he is objecting to certain images, with the help of his solicitor.

An E-fit can be said in my contention to have changed the principle about such a parade's focussing on assisting a witness, in trying circumstances, to identify a suspect whilst maintaining fairness.

Chapter 19
Joab and Israel save the practice dwindling

Adel had been the last of my three Enfield solicitors to brief me, when I acted for his lady client at Croydon. I met him in court with her, and he stayed throughout. It was most unusual for a solicitor at the Magistrates Court to treat a client with so much circumspection. Partly, I believed that this was because he had just started his own practice, making sure that everything was in order, and perhaps learning more about court work as well. Another reason became evident when I found out that my next client from him, an eighteen-year-old named Joab, proved to be her nephew.

He had been charged with Obstructing and Assault on police, and was due to appear at Stratford Magistrates Court. Adel and I started off with a two hour conference with him, and the more I heard, the angrier I became at his treatment. He told us that three police officers had forced their way into the flat he shared with his young brothers and sisters, in the middle of the night and in the absence of their parents. They all believed that his cousin Israel was hiding there, having gone missing from his care address.

Disbelieving his denials that the boy was in the flat, they demanded to search the younger children's bedrooms, insisting that the boy was there and was being protected by my client. He tried to reason with them, and to stop them bursting into the bedrooms, as they were all pumped up, but he was thrown to the floor and held down by all three officers. He was frightened for himself by their behaviour, but even more so for his siblings, who would have been terrified.

No attempt had been made to contact the parents before the visit. Even when it was realised that only their eldest brother was indoors with the children, no attempt was made to contact the parents. Nor were any enquiries made of the neighbours for their whereabouts. Joab was some six feet tall, and heavily built, and was not easily managed by the use of force, which escalated because of his resistance and his attempts to free himself to reassure the children.

He tried to get out of the flat to contact his neighbours, as the officers were struggling with him and holding him down, trying to handcuff him. The next-door neighbour came out watching and remonstrating.

It was probably to avoid the watchful eye of the neighbour that he was dragged back into the hallway of the flat, still held down, and the efforts to control him intensified, with handcuffs. The youngest officer grabbed his testicles and started to squeeze them to make him comply. Even further pain was caused by the others trying to force his arms up behind his back to attach the cuffs.

His brothers and sisters remained in their bedrooms, petrified by the sound of the screams of pain from their brother and the shouts of the officers and their demands to know the whereabouts of Israel. The same officer squeezed his testicles a second time. Trying an even more drastic tack, he grabbed his throat squeezing his carotid artery.

Throughout all this it must be emphasised that he was a respectful eighteen-year-old student, with no previous convictions, nor anything known against his own character, and three police officers were manhandling him ,

Whilst it was conventionally always the role of female officers, when accompanying their male counterparts in such situations, to busy themselves with female prisoners and their children or other youngsters, in this case she pitched in with the other officers to hold him down. She ignored the youngsters, and made no effort to assist in alleviating Joab's plight – himself a youth - or to reassure the younger children.

Like most defence advocates, I tended usually to believe a defendant's account when I first heard it. Sometimes parts of an account may seem unlikely, or prone to exaggeration, or inconsistent with other parts, but, generally, one broadly accepts the first account.

This was to be my future client; a client's solicitor acts for him, and the client needs the solicitor's support, having being charged and facing a criminal court. Disbelief would be a poor start to the professional relationship which the solicitor needs to be adopted, a relationship which would lead to his continuing to be instructed and his choice of counsel being briefed. For counsel to lose a client would always be a disaster.

Doubts or challenges were better left to the time when the papers were received, or a CCTV viewed. Rarely would guilt be accepted unless a foregone conclusion, or totally admitted: such as, for instance, the remarkable admission made by the client who, when first met, told me that he needed locking up.

Here I was stunned and shocked by what I was being told, by an apparently remarkable and credible young man, and the dispassionate way he recounted it - as if he too could not believe it had happened. He recounted it convincingly without drama or playing for sympathy.

Even more remarkable were the officers' accounts in their four page statements, which corroborated everything my client had said, openly and factually, to justify their physical attempts to restrain him. They freely, and almost proudly, admitted to using holds that they stated were approved by the Home Office for the purpose of making him submit to being handcuffed.

I was dumbstruck by such arrogance and lack of care or of any concern, as well as by their utter naivety in making such admissions. I could understand adrenaline, but this went much further. Never in my experience had I heard of such truly appalling behaviour, so readily admitted.

A date was fixed after a not guilty plea had been entered, and a full day was set for trial at the Magistrates Court before a lay bench. My concern over the potential cynicism which can at times be encountered from a district judge led me not to seek one, especially as there were no legal issues or unusual complications for him to resolve. The familiarity of lay benches, who often specialise in youth trials, with training in their treatment, and the understanding of their behaviour was infinitely preferable in a case like this, with a defendant of such outstanding character and innocence. The presiding chairmen are specially chosen.

It was also obvious that preparation in this case was to be the key to success. The first step was to obtain testimony from the neighbours, a task I delegated to my solicitor; the next, to challenge the validity of the supposedly approved holds applied, and the circumstances in which any extreme hold could be used. I had no doubts myself that these holds were not approved, but extreme force may have been permitted in major life-threatening circumstances.

The best way to obtain such information was by completing a Defence Case Statement, a (DCS) setting out the whole defence to the charge(s). Every detail to be advanced in court, setting up the defence, had to be contained within it, so that neither the judge nor the prosecutor could allege that what was advanced in court was inconsistent, and so that it did not contain new (and therefore untrue) material. Transparency was the criterion.

In the Crown Court such a statement was obligatory, not so in the Magistrates, but, if prepared, compliance with the same strict rules for disclosure of the material requested could not be avoided. My statement was therefore sent off to the CPS, specifically seeking to know more of these powers, of the approved holds, and the circumstances in which they could be used.

Finally, I asked Joab's mother and the solicitor to ensure that a full statement as to his character was obtained from the Headmaster of his school and from any religious or other influential person or scheme (such as the Duke of Edinburgh's award, which always impressed a youth bench).

Meanwhile, my practice continued mostly with cases for the prosecution in the Crown Court and the occasional Department of Work and Pensions prosecution for variety. Only one trial was listed in this period, and that was to be for a Newton hearing, so named after the case involving the defendant Newton, which authorised a special procedure after the hearing for the plea. It arose where the defendant wanted to plead guilty, but not to all that the prosecution alleged. Here, he had assaulted the victim but had not used a weapon to do so, as the prosecution contended. He would be required to put forward the basis of his plea. The prosecution (and/or the judge) would consider the basis, and decide whether it was acceptable for him to be sentenced on what he was prepared to admit, or whether it was simply unbelievable, and the prosecution wanted to prove their full case.

He maintained that he had only punched the victim once. The injuries must have been caused by an unfortunate incident prior to the assault.

The sentencing guidelines recommended that the use of a weapon indicated a higher level of sentence, and the hearing was to determine the correct sentence. So there was to be a trial of that issue, without a jury; witnesses were to be called, and the defendant was to give evidence, before sentencing by the judge.

The judge wanted to discuss the matter, and decide whether he could still impose a satisfactory sentence, looking at the whole case in the round together with the strong mitigation which his counsel put forward. There was little for a prosecutor to say, other than to reiterate the guidelines, of which most judges were fully aware. Some judges may look to the prosecutor, who has a right to address the judge if his sentence is unduly lenient. It proved unnecessary for me to intervene, the judge's decision being completely reasonable.

Since it was classified as a trial, the fee for the hearing was enhanced so it was an easy day, certainly, for me; and the judge eventually decided that he could do justice to the victim and the public without the hearing, sentencing him at the high end of the level. The procedure saved a full trial, without empanelling a jury, and just concentrating on the central issue.

It was during this week that an incident occurred in the first day of a trial which became the talk of counsels' mess and robing room, and caused considerable amusement. Having retired during a mid-afternoon break, the jury returned from their room past the doors to several courts, filed into court, and sat in their prescribed order in the jury box.

Counsel started reading from his notebook, continuing his speech, whilst the jury paid close attention as usual. As he did so, several jurors consulted their notes, but with apparent difficulty. Others looked hard at counsel, and then turned to whisper to their neighbours. Finding that they were in the wrong court, after a few minutes they swiftly retired to their room, to find their way to the right court. It caused something of a stir.

The time had come for me to return to Stratford Magistrates Court for the trial. The prosecution had their three officers present, whose conciliatory tone outside court, and efforts to be friendly with us, and particularly with their victim, I found most offensive. I also took some pleasure in their very apparent nervousness and ensured that I kept my distance from them except to ask if they had brought their notebooks to court, to add to their unease.

We had our witnesses present, and were ready to proceed, but had not been served with the disclosure I had sought concerning the justification for the officers' admitted treatment of my client. I then visited the prosecutor in the CPS room and sought the disclosure I had requested; it had not arrived and could not be served. I accepted this quietly but indicated this was not to be the end of that issue. Meanwhile, I handed her the testimonial I had been given by Adel, typed and ready for production in court.

It was more than I could have hoped for. My client was the head boy at a prestigious school, with, as I was told, the highest academic qualifications; he was undoubtedly their most promising student in every regard, and the one forecast as likely to be their greatest achiever.

When it came to his personal qualities, such as integrity, honesty, decency, even his high regard in matters where he had assisted the local police and the community generally, everything was outstanding. I watched the prosecutor's face as she read it and noted with approval that it had coloured up. It could have been guilt at what could have happened in court to this young man, or even at his reprehensible treatment at the hands of the policemen she was representing.

A few minutes later she emerged and, because of what she had read and that testimonial, she was pleased to tell me that she was dropping the case, and both charges were subsequently dismissed. It was, once more, a walk into the sunlight moment for him, his parents, Israel's mother and, of course, myself.

Sent later that year to Croydon, for a remand case, I entered the cell of my client to be faced with the young man who had been the subject of 'my most difficult case' (chapter 14), twenty years after my first walk into the sunshine. He had pleaded guilty, but the report on him was routine and superficial in dealing with the difficulties he had experienced, which had been exposed in our previous trial. I fully detailed the evidence of his problems for the judge. It was a most fortunate coincidence as I was the only person able to do so, enabling a sentence to be passed that was tailor-made for him.

With the next case I began to feel like an Adel's family retainer, as all three cases had involved the same family. Israel's mother had been charged with the civil equivalent of abduction in that 'in October 2011 knowingly and without lawful authority or reasonable excuse she kept Israel away from the responsible person', contrary to section 49 of the Children's Act 1989.

As we found out in a four hour conference with Adel, the circumstances were that he had been put into the care of the local authority and then fostered to a number of foster parents over many years. To put it shortly, he had absconded from the latest foster parents, and had returned home to his mother. Within a few days of his being home, his mother heard that her father was terminally ill and likely to die imminently; she took Israel to the Nigerian embassy, obtained flight tickets and documents, and booked them onto the aeroplane for the flight. It was on the plane that they were arrested, and taken to the nearest police station. There she was charged and detained, and Israel was returned into care.

The arrest details followed, and we had our conference. Again the case was set down for her appearance at Stratford Magistrates Court. Israel had been put into care because of allegations made against his mother and of abuse by her partner, she stated, many years ago. He was then rehabilitated and put back into her care, but, some time later, had been caught reading pornographic material at school with older boys.

He was put into the care of his first foster parents, but, over the years the foster parents were changed, again and again: in all he was fostered by about ten different parents. Some treated him badly, necessitating these numerous changes. Recently, his mother saw that he had been badly bruised by the latest, and took him away, though not before taking photographs showing the injuries. She started proceedings, using her own solicitor, which were due to come into fruition within months, with a final decision on his being returned to her care. The result of this criminal case is to feature heavily in Israel's mother's efforts for custody. These efforts would have to succeed.

The mother had been refused contact with her son unless through a solicitor or pursuant to a court order of 2011. The hearing which had laid down that ruling followed a dispute with the court's supervising care officer in a session with Israel and his mother on 1st October, in which Israel indicated that he wanted to return to her so strongly he could not live without her. (Any dispute between them had long been resolved.)

That day he went missing from the foster parents, returned home, and may then have gone to his aunt in South London. On the 4th they attended the Embassy, obtained their documents, and, on the 5th, travelled to Heathrow and boarded the plane.

353

They were arrested for trafficking, on the grounds that the mother and son had different surnames and an all ports warning had been issued because of his absconding.

After his release back into care he immediately went on the run, and spent many days living rough on the streets.

It was on the 7th that the three officers had arrived to search for him at his cousin's house, and Joab was arrested. On the 10th Israel had given himself up to police, as he could not cope without his mother. After she was granted bail, contact was permitted and the care proceedings were pursued.

We started work on the criminal case using the conference notes and information from Joab's mother - her sister - and considered the legal position and possible defences outlined in the legislation. Though the charge was under the Children's Act, its provisions, as set out in the long title (which explains the purpose of the Act), were made 'with respect to fostering, child minding and day care and adoption.' This focussed on parental responsibility, largely embracing recovery orders and those family law rulings made in matrimonial cases. It also covered parental abduction.

Non-parental abduction, or kidnapping by strangers for criminal purposes, was governed by the Child Abduction Act 1984, and proceedings under it required the consent of the Director of Public Prosecutions (DPP). This prosecution was brought under the lesser Act, probably to avoid the need for the DPP's consent, since that was for child trafficking, a more serious allegation with heavier sentences.

Both Acts dealt with the issue of consent by using the more modern formulation of acting (knowingly) without lawful authority or reasonable excuse. This being part of the charge, it was clear that the prosecution had to prove that these general elements did not apply. Again, crucially, in both, the main criterion of the child's welfare, that it was paramount in any proceedings, was repeated. (In fact, the district judge accepted both of these propositions, despite their being set out in different Acts.)

One provision in the Children's Act held that a parent does not cease to have parental responsibility for a child, even if they do not have care of him. That was part of the general defence of lawful authority, since it was a specific provision in the Act.

Seeing his grandfather for the last time (as well as his natural father in Nigeria, of whom he had seen very little, but to see whom, in the circumstances of his grandfather's imminent death, would provide considerable solace) was proof of reasonable excuse, on at least the grounds of psychological welfare and well-being.

The Child Abduction Act provided a specific defence, if the defendant believed that, in the absence of consent, consent would have been given, had that person known all the circumstances. This was strongly arguable, as we had a document in which the objecting carer had said that mother and son were reconciled, and that contact was to be allowed.

A further specific defence available was in a case where she had taken all reasonable steps to obtain the consent, but was unable to communicate with those objecting. We had evidence maintaining that she had attempted to make contact, but had been unable to reach that person.

These specific defences contained in the legislation could also be presented as factual examples of the 'reasonable excuse' provision in the Children's Act charge. It too was arguable, and the district judge accepted my 'rolled up' defence as valid.

I set out a complete defence case statement setting out the full defences; a chronology to assist the court; and a document which set out all the relevant provisions of the law and legislation, and its purposes, expressed in the long titles of the Acts, and in the relevant Home Office Circular on Abduction.

The judge had everything to hand, and the prosecutor had a copy. There was a statement from the social worker in the case, which actually assisted us, since it described the huge improvement in the mother and son's relationship. It repeated his passionate desire to be with her. There was a copy of the

Recovery Order, and photographs of his injuries at the hands of the latest of his foster parents.

The Recovery Order contained several defects, with Israel's surname wrongly entered, with a different family name; and the order asked for recovery of Israel and his sister. That she was named on the order was also an error. The date on the order signed by the judge was incorrect, as he was not in court on that day (it transpired from enquiries made), and there was no expiry set for the order – either a specific date or 'until further order.'

I asked my solicitor to enquire of the counsel in the matrimonial case for an opinion on whether this affected the validity of the order, and waited for a reply. Even more essential was a document testifying to the death of Israel's grandfather, which my solicitor was strongly urged to obtain. We kept being told that this would be extremely difficult to obtain from Nigeria without testimony from a wide range of relatives, no documents being available, according to their system (or lack of it).

In the meantime, as enquiries were being made ,and evidence gathered, my clerks had been asked by the CPS to use our chambers to book some days for Magistrates Court trials, around the London area in the first instance. We all took our turn, as they were unpopular: though they were fairly well paid, at a daily rate, they were very stressful. Career-wise, they were also a step backward, as I, for one of many, had stopped taking on such lists many years before.

The papers for the trials, which still could vary between four and ten each day, were received at court in the morning. They had to be read, the law consulted, copies of statements, etc. run off and then the witnesses seen, put at ease, and important points of evidence confirmed with them (without leading, of course).

All this had to be done by 10am, when the court called the first case on. Depending on the whereabouts of the court, and the vagaries of travel, it proved a real problem to arrive punctually without fail. Actually to find the papers on arrival caused further aggravation, depending on how familiar one was with each court. Finally, defence advocates would arrive, often at the last minute, and would seek further disclosure, want to edit and dispute contents of interviews, argue the law, and discuss possible pleas. Summarising accurately, lists of criminal trials in Magistrates Courts were mostly something of a nightmare, day after day, in court after court. The words: 'We know it's not your fault Mr..., but this is not good enough, and something must be done about it' resonated in court after court.

The contract with our chambers had to be fulfilled, as other work was dwindling for criminal work. There was competition between many chambers, and advocates in other branches of law (e.g. immigration) were taking on court lists. Accordingly, our clerks had to accept whatever was sent to us, including those returned at the last minute from other chambers, who could not cope. Though we were at first briefed in the London area, returns from other areas had to be covered, despite very difficult travelling arrangements, as parking was normally impossible.

Even then, motoring problems would generally favour public transport. Finally, the unfamiliarity of attending some courts, with their arrangements, and lack of guidance or instruction, made it impossible to be ready at court, so incurring the wrath of those on the bench, who mostly lived in the area.

Refusal to accept a brief placed the clerks in a very difficult position. However sympathetic my junior clerk Kerrie was in taking notice of personal difficulties, and in at least asking whether I could manage such and such a court, we could not afford to let down the CPS. It is fair to say crack-of-dawn journeys were not my favourite, but court opening times limited the time available to be briefed.

I cite, as an example, one actual attendance before the Maidstone magistrates. Many aspects of such problems were present at other courts, but this turned out to be an amalgam of many, and is totally accurate (in case it is feared that I am exaggerating).

Parking in Maidstone was impossible – my parents used to live there (it was not their fault). The one time I tried, and found a tiny car park off the beaten track, it took me an hour to find the car park again when I returned from court. I had a similar experience in Oxford.

So I set off from Barnet through London by tube, and then by train to Maidstone, using the fastest route but the furthest from court. On my arrival at court I was told that the CPS room where the papers were to be found was upstairs. I returned to the security at the door admitting I could not find it. I was taken upstairs and shown the door, but the CPS sign had fallen off. I was then told the papers were always at the police station, down the road some distance.

After waiting at the police station to be attended to, the satchel was handed to me. On my return, the CPS room was unlocked for me. I then struggled to open the new-fangled security lock on the satchel: the security officer was again required to undo the lock and release the papers. Several of the files were quite thick so I only managed to skim the first two and was then called into court.

I had not met any of my several witnesses, nor spoken to the defence advocates. Whilst the bench were courteous for the delay, as it happened so frequently, they gave me five minutes, and I had to start with something. For someone who liked to prepare a case thoroughly, and in detail, the tension can be imagined. It was no wonder that prosecuting these lists away from one's regular courts had little attraction, as normally help could be summoned, or an officer chased up (or the case would be lost), and phones were actually answered by CPS personnel.

This time, sent to Wimbledon as I remember, I arrived to seek the papers for court five. I was told that there was no court five. I showed my note and a CPS in-house lawyer stated 'No. That sits at Richmond.' I was perplexed; it was explained that that was an overflow court. The same thing happened the next week, when it transpired that court six at Wimbledon was an overflow court, to which I irritated answered, having spent an hour and a half to get there, 'And where the hell does that sit?'

Similarly briefed for Tottenham Magistrates, I was sent to Wood Green Crown Court – another overflow court, and several

358

times more to Kingston Crown Court which sat occasionally at Wimbledon Magistrates. Don't even mention what would happen involving Highgate and Highbury Magistrates Courts. My disbelief was total when, after that mistake, and my complaint to my chief clerk, of being sent to the wrong court, he answered that he was sorry, but 'getting to the right court is completely your responsibility, Mr Forward, and the rules are that you will be liable'. I stifled the query what was I paying my clerks for - this being territory where in any dispute counsel was always in the wrong. It followed that your clerk (or the CPS) needed to give notice of the court location, with the courtroom number - assuming they knew, or took the time to find out.

Back on more familiar territory, my last case in the Court of Appeal concerned an appeal against sentence. As we were about to start, each of the judge's attendants entered, with their judge's papers, books, notebooks and other personal items. Yet another coincidence was to occur, providing a most pleasurable moment.

The presiding judge was always a Lord Justice, the others Mr Justice... or the Recorder of... Crown court, where he sat regularly. I was amazed to see the Lord Justice's attendant, clad, I am sure, in his gown, staring hard at me: his face lit up. I recognised a fellow National service seaman from HMS Redpole. (The appeal was allowed and the sentence reduced.)

Our paths had crossed in the police force, as he had also risen to Chief Inspector, and we had been able to share a few words on some ceremonial duty or other.

It would have been an enormous pleasure to have got together and indulged in nostalgia, but the circumstances failed to allow it, and we were unable or unwilling to make contact to do so. He certainly knew how to find me; finding him might well have been quite awkward.

The time had come for the trial at Stratford, for which we were allocated half a day in the afternoon, before a district judge. A case as difficult as this was always reserved to a district judge, who, having been a qualified barrister for many years, could deal correctly and expeditiously with both the facts and the law.

On occasions, one would seek such a judge for both reasons; unfortunately, it did not work the other way round, and with this case, had I had the choice, I would have plumped for a lay bench. I needed a sympathetic bench, especially trained to deal with juveniles. Whilst my client was an adult, the considerations to be borne in mind very much affected the welfare of the child in the exercise of the bench's discretion against the Recovery Order imposed by a court.

My fears were fulfilled, as little I said had much effect, the judge appearing concerned only with a deliberate breach of a court order, albeit one designed to protect the child in normal circumstances. These circumstances were most unusual: the alleged abductor was his mother; the situation was not one where there was a battle for custody between parents; and there was no intention to permanently remove the boy, but to allow him to visit his grandfather (to see him for the last time) and at the same time to visit his natural father (whom he had hardly ever seen). Whilst the judge did not demand the death certificate, for which I had pressed several times with some force, I felt this would have confirmed the authenticity of the reason for the flight without a shadow of doubt.

Verbal evidence of the cultural difficulties of obtaining such proof was given, but the judge was unconvinced, and was generally unimpressed by the defendant and her account. Nor did I have any authority to challenge the validity of the order, though counsel in the civil case did attend court for the trial.

The trial went as I suspected it would, and she was found guilty and given an appropriate community sentence. However, as far as I could tell, the damage had been done to her custody battle in the High Court.

We decided to appeal to the Crown Court and for this I ensured that our top criminal barrister took the case, as all the work had been done via my written arguments. He had only to use his superior persuasive abilities, but was also unsuccessful. The court, we believe, may well have been troubled by the appellant's testimony, and the lack of important corroboration.

I remained unaware of the result of the final custody proceedings, as my solicitor had moved from his office, and proved most difficult to find. We did eventually make contact in our struggle to pursue the fees for both the latest cases in the family saga.

It took over a year, using the auspices of chambers' legal aid liaison officer, to contact the appropriate legal aid officer for cases at Stratford. Kerrie's and my persistence in pressing month after month, and making a full written claim to the legal aid department responsible, paid off when they told us the solicitor had been paid by them. With that, our next effort saw the fee for Joab's case secured - the sum a little short of £800.

The fee for the abduction trial took longer to arrive, but I was grateful that the district judge had certified in court that legal aid was to be extended for counsel.

Dire threats were made, I was told, as to the legal aid franchise if not paid, and, after many more months, that too was received. In order actually to receive it, I had to take a lower offer from the solicitor, otherwise I would have seen nothing of it. Some £2000 in the hand made the offer acceptable, and very welcome.

So far, I had defended all manner of clients through nearly all the procedures that obtained in the courts. Now, towards the end of my career a most demanding client and a new procedure awaited me, after a call to the Redbridge Magistrates Court. The very transparency of the law, and knowing where to look, at least enabled an advocate to start to cope.

Indeed, the applicable procedure was so unusual, as were the facts, that I came to feel I was becoming the expert in court, and directing proceedings. This was added to by the fact that the solicitor assigned to the case was a trainee, and it was necessary to instruct her as well on every step. For her it was a strict learning curve.

I met my client and his family in the waiting area. Only the father spoke a few words of English, and the family were clearly Eastern European travellers. The client, their twenty-year-old son did not speak. His appearance suggested that he had real issues.

It transpired when the interpreter arrived that the family were Polish; her son could only communicate with his mother by reading her lips as she spoke to him in Polish. The interpreter translated for me what she was saying, and the answers she was getting. The summary from the CPS set out an arrest for shoplifting and urinating in Boots, assaulting police officers who came to arrest him, and criminal damage which arose from freely and uninhibitedly urinating all over his cell. His behaviour was described in the case summary as 'feral.'

Legal aid was applied for, and we entered court, where I explained to the judge that the proceedings would be translated into Polish by the interpreter and passed on to the mother; she would lip-read what was said to her son in the dock, after a struggle to understand. His answers, such as they were, were relayed back to the judge in the same way. Typically of a district judge he took all this completely in his stride, needing no more than just to look at the defendant to realise that there were going to be very real problems in the case.

He was informed that we would need a medical report from his GP, as some papers in Polish, which the mother handed to me, told of liver disease, brain damage and deafness in both ears. He was seeing a hospital consultant psychiatrist, and a further report would be required from him, too, as to his general fitness and especially his fitness to plead. Obviously these would be served on the prosecution, and a review sought, ultimately, as to further court proceedings.

A condition of bail was imposed for him to be supervised in any shop he entered, and the case was remanded for a month. My instructing solicitor was told that she must arrange a report from the GP about his general health, and a psychiatric report.

Numerous attempts were made, but for a variety of reasons –the mother and her son's illnesses, and lateness, or failing to attend appointments - the only report received was one that referred to the mother's carer allowance. The previous bail condition was said to be unworkable, and was varied to a condition of ensuring that he attended appointments. This proved of no effect.

To facilitate the psychiatric examination for his fitness to stand trial and plead, I instructed my solicitor to inform the experts of the criteria to determine fitness. They had been laid down in an authority called Pritchard, decided in 1836, which I cited. They amounted to: can he put forward any defence? Can he challenge any juror to which he may be able to object? Can he give instructions to his lawyers, or tell them what his case is, and whether he agreed with the witnesses or not? And, finally, can he follow the evidence?

If he were fit to plead and give instructions, he could have the trial in the Magistrates Court or go to the Crown Court. He thus keeps the chance to be found not guilty. This was proving impossible to determine without the medical evidence.

The importance of ascertaining his unfitness was that the only sentence to be imposed was a hospital order. That was our aim. First, however, the facts of the allegation were on the CCTV. They still had to be accepted by the jury to find the case proved: his mental state or intentions formed no part of the hearing, only whether or not he had done the acts alleged. If so, then the sentence would be a hospital order.

As one of the charges was theft, he could have elected to be dealt with by the Crown Court. Since it could not be decided by the judge where he wanted to be tried on the last of the remands in his court, because of his possible unfitness, he ordered the defendant to be committed to the Crown Court. He added that, if he had reports before him, this could be reviewed. No reports were forthcoming, and he appeared at the Crown Court.

Matters were fully explained to the Crown Court judge in the pre-trial review, whose inclination, as I was hoping, was to deal with the whole matter robustly and swiftly, in such a way that avoided any form of trial. There seemed no realistic likelihood of any proper reports being completed, without which progress was not possible. I had put before him and the prosecutor a chronology, listing in detail the nine previous hearings, hoping that they would be persuaded that we were all coming to the end of the road. He adjourned the case for one more effort.

The next judge was of the same opinion, but was more conciliatory and optimistic - being of the view that further efforts would be successful since they were ordered by a Crown Court judge. He added that the Pritchard guidelines (those which determined fitness to plead) were well known to any decent psychiatrist, and a report would come easily to hand.

Prosecuting counsel commanded much respect and authority with the CPS and, being as sanguine as I, was sure that reports would never be forthcoming. He would be taking the decisions from now on himself. Ironically, in view of the judge's comments that this was a case he was pleased that I was handling, the next hearing was in the hands of another counsel from my chambers, as I was unavailable.

I suspected that the experienced prosecutor ensured the most suitable judge was available for what was to be the last hearing, when he offered no evidence, and the case against the defendant was dismissed. All this had taken over a year and we had achieved nothing conclusive. The public interest test for a prosecution clearly indicated that this was the proper result.

Whilst it was thoroughly unsatisfactory for the defendant not to receive treatment in a hospital, medically (for severe hepatitis, we were told, and for further psychiatric treatment), the unfitness to plead route was too problematic: for him the solution was through his GP and psychiatrist, without dragging him through the court.

Eventually, I am sure that he received the treatment he needed without any involvement in such complicated and protracted criminal proceedings over such relatively inconsequential matters.

The day after my first meeting with my young Polish client and his mother, I was sent to Camberwell Magistrates, when, in the morning, I dealt with two cases, one a plea of guilt and a first appearance for a trial the following week. The defendant's case was so hopeless and utterly unlikely that I never believed a word of it myself, and he was well and properly convicted the following week.

In the afternoon, I had to defend a youth in the adjoining youth court; he was one of five defendants to have been charged. I was looking forward to this as the facts were contentious, the hearing would last several days, and we would all get a certificate for counsel, as far as I could see.

Furthermore, with younger counsel or solicitors, they would leave me to start off the legal arguments and objections, sweep up after they had completed their interrogations with the witnesses, and make the last defence speech. Unfortunately, this time I was not instructed by the solicitor handling the case, who was new to me, and so I also lost the opportunity of widening my briefing contacts.

But as one door closes, so they say, another opens. Kerrie had developed a new CPS contact who wanted someone to prosecute traffic lists in the Magistrates Court. These contracts lasted for three months, and paid the same as the criminal lists - both very reasonably and promptly - but traffic cases were very different from criminal ones.

Since they were largely prosecutions for mobile phone use, for not having insurance, for defective vehicles or overloading, and, especially, for failures to return notification of a driver in response to a speed camera offence, the facts could be digested easily in the time allotted before appearing in court. One source of stress was instantly removed.

Furthermore, as I was conducting the cases I could make decisions on prosecution without further reference, unless in an exceptional case. For instance, if a witness was being called to prove that he was the defendant's employer, and that the driver, in a nutshell, was driving in the course of his employment, and believed that the vehicle was insured, this was a proper defence. All I needed to be sure of was that the witness came up to proof. No more formalities were required, no more time expended, and the bench were invited to dismiss, to which they would agree on my say-so.

The discretion I was able to exercise greatly assisted the business of the court in cases where there was a high degree of hardship, or where there was no merit in a technical prosecution. With my agreement, such were dismissed by the bench on the facts, without embarking on a trial.

A relaxed approach found favour and brought equitable results, an instance being the attendance on a speed camera case, in which the defendant and his wife appeared, having travelled down from Cambridge. He, a celebrated mathematics don, reminding me of Professor Stephen Hawking, had asked for disclosure of all the documents for him to test. Ordinarily, allegations from the defendant that the equipment could not have been Home Office approved, or must have had defects or not been tested or properly calibrated, were not admissible, unless there was evidence of a defect in the equipment, or lack of due process. The presumption was that the equipment was correct, and the results admissible.

However, as a mathematical expert he wanted to test the whole process, and so was to be afforded full disclosure. A very able traffic officer attended, with a whole series of photographs, charting the speed between each given marking and piece of 'road equipment' at specified distances. Combined with the timings of each, this allowed the speeds to be accurately assessed, and a proper average obtained.

The professor was fascinated, and thoroughly enjoyed following and approving the methodology. Both the bench and I were seeing this for the first time, and it proved most interesting and proved its reliability. Of course, he then pleaded guilty and was lightly sentenced, taking account of his trip to view the evidence. Both he and his wife had thoroughly enjoyed the experience, and the slight latitude afforded was of interest to all of us, as well as saving a long trial challenging evidence to no avail.

The bench liked this sort of sensible approach, increasing their knowledge of a process. They always allowed time to talk to witnesses, or with defendants, for them to understand aspects of the law which, because they could not dispute, the offence had to be admitted.

The one that nearly always arose was the belief that if a handheld mobile was not used to make a call, there was no offence, and copious call logs were produced to that effect. Since the term 'used' was interpreted extremely widely, to cover any use there was virtually no defence. Once explained to the offender, the log could be disregarded and a plea of guilt nearly always resulted, thus saving at least half an hour per trial. A short hearing would follow, with an argument against disqualification, or dispensing with penalty points because of some special circumstances.

Whilst these cases became fairly repetitive, there were different characters, facts and officers involved, and the most ingenious or desperate defences, and totally dishonest excuses, were constantly advanced. The defences came as a surprise, since they did not have to be disclosed. That, at least, brought a challenge. Practically no-one pleaded guilty to using a mobile phone - the very allegation, and the penalty points involved, had the same effect as being reported by a traffic warden.

I was now able to pick my court for at least two days a week. Willesden provided a free parking place next door, a choice of satisfactory cafes for lunch, a superb police liaison officer, who readily chased up missing or late officers and papers, and a total travel time, by car, of around half an hour. I also filled in at Waltham Forest Magistrates Court, which would also list one or two careless driving cases a day, such cases being more akin to criminal trials, with more witnesses. Attending at this court, I had the good fortune to park virtually outside Michael's ex-wife's house, and to return after court to drop in to maintain links with his daughter and her own daughter: sadly, we had just lost Michael.

This work removed the three reasons for stress at work. Travel posed no difficulty; the pay was guaranteed; its sufficiency and promptness were entirely satisfactory; and the necessary preparation was brief, and fitted into the time available. If I were to retain or even to increase this work the fees would level out, leaving me a smaller but reasonable profit, and I was sleeping much better.

Routinely, I would go to the CPS room and obtain my few files, read them through, and then sit outside my court, waiting for customers. This very much contrasted with the criminal advocates or in-house CPS prosecutors reading their papers, meeting with the private and police witnesses, ringing the Branch to get further evidence or missing papers, or to get the police liaison officer to chase up necessary officers, prepare their cases and be available for defence advocates.

I suppose I looked too comfortable, for on one occasion it was suggested that, as counsel, I should be doing their criminal cases. My response was that I had done my time and share of all manner of cases, and was happy now to deal with this level of work, in conditions that were, for once, most amenable and convenient; and that many advocates thought the work too repetitive or beneath them. They also knew that my court would finish early, and I would then assist the others. There was no further comeback, and occasionally I could help out in discussions, using my experience.

On the days when the traffic courts did not sit, I had my usual mix of other cases, mainly pleas of guilt, but they were run of the mill, and I had, by now, virtually finished chasing up the bigger fees I was owed.

Chapter 20
The most demanding case ends on a High Note

My career was winding down, and perhaps I was getting too comfortable. A phone call from Bob put an end to that, as he told me that John had a new client, himself a solicitor, who wanted me to represent his son - whom I shall call James, to preserve anonymity.

A massive bundle of papers arrived, the pages of statements alone numbering close to two thousand, and the interviews, from the large number of defendants, nearly the same figure. I waded through these, and the more I read, the more convinced I became that this could be won.

Of even the most difficult of my cases, this may have involved the most work; but it was fully merited by the facts of the case, and by James's impeccable character. It must be recognised from the start that I was vastly assisted by him and by both his parents, and we spent many hours together, often with Bob, on the preparation.

The case was notorious, and involved charges of Manslaughter, two of Grievous Bodily Harm with intent to cause grievous bodily harm - this amounting to really serious bodily harm (with a life sentence, the maximum sentence, because it couples an intention to cause really serious harm, and so is deliberate).

Another was of Actual bodily harm - varying from minor to serious injury, with five years' imprisonment - and the rest charged with Violent Disorder – one step down from Riot.

Reports of the incidents featured on the front page of most local papers, alleging that enquiries were in hand to trace named individuals (including James) wanted for murder. Police were given the task of talking to local residents to calm their fears.

This was the outlook facing James, and his parents. That I believed from my first reading of the papers that the case would be won indicates that it must have been remarkable given the stark facts. I think my clients were bemused by my optimism, but as we discovered more, it became supportable. From the outset my approach was to throw the book at the prosecution.

As so often it began, according to James's account, with a group of friends having a drink to celebrate a birthday. At the pub, another group was doing the same. A remark from one of James's group to one of the other, about the latter's sister, whom the former slightly knew, had started it off. There was not, for once, the question, "Who are you looking at?" which often preceded such situations.

An argument broke out, turned into an altercation, and the one of James's group making the remark was challenged to a fight by the other. Not wishing to lose face, our man allowed himself to be dragged out for a fight. James's group tried to pull him back, while the others egged on their only too willing member to fight in a nearby alley.

Our man began to have second thoughts. His would-be attacker was then pushed into him, to encourage the fight, and he in turn hit the person, pushing his attacker on to him, and then ran off.

The would-be attacker, and the other who had pushed him forward to fight, chased our man and, rounding a car, both punched him simultaneously to the head. He was knocked to the ground, becoming unconscious. James bent over him to help and ensured an ambulance was called. As a result of the attack the injured man was taken to hospital suffering from fractures to skull and jaw.

As he was looking after the injured man on the ground, James noticed a melee nearby, with his best friend in the centre of a group of three or four of the others. He had been knocked to the ground, so he went and stood over him, protecting him so that the attack could not continue. He was assisted by the younger brother of his best friend, and they both tried to keep the others away.

Three times his best friend (with whom he had come to the celebration), tried to get up, but he was knocked to the ground each time, by, it seemed, one of the men who had, earlier, caused a fracture. On the last occasion, as he rose, James swung an arm to prevent his friend from being knocked down once again: he could not be sure whether he had connected. The three of them tried to get away, as the attacker who had initially wanted to fight was approaching them now, armed with a metal crutch to bring down on them.

Another used a glass as a weapon and, from the other side of the group, struck James, causing large lumps to both forehead and neck. The man with the crutch struck the younger brother over his head, as James and the brothers tried to get away. The crutch split open his skull, and he required stitches at the hospital.

Several hours later our client was told that one of the other group had been taken to hospital where he had died. This had arisen from an argument between two from that group, where one had spat blood into the face of the other's girlfriend, and had been knocked down. It transpired that the one punched was one of the two who had caused the fractures to the skull and jaw earlier; they were also best friends.

James went to the police before the story was leaked, and made, at the first opportunity, a full witness statement. All the press reports had published on the front page an erroneous account, muddling up the fight outside the pub with the separate incident which involved the fatal assault.

The first appearance in the Crown Court was for a preliminary hearing, where such papers as were available were to be served formally on the defence, and arrangements made for the rest, so that pleas could be entered on the next occasion.

The defence case statement (DCS) was normally served on that occasion on the judge and prosecution, and on this the judge so ordered. This has to reveal the full defence(s) of each defendant, to enable him and the court to make necessary arrangements; it is given to the prosecutor, so that he is not caught by surprise by any defence advanced. Another important function was to disclose specific material requested by each defendant.

It could not be stressed enough that before this was drafted we needed a long conference, always with James and his parents, as well as Bob. At first we had only the prosecution's DVD which was of poor quality, jerky, and not easy to follow. The first task was to get our expert to enhance and provide stills. He was the same I had used for the Wood Green rape, as he was the best and the quickest.

The more we talked, the more personal material emerged, and it became obvious there were two separate defences to advance - the obvious one - of self defence of his friend but another, equally powerful, but more unusual where there is self-defence - that James was involved in the prevention of crime respecting the whole incident near the pub. I suspect that James were the only defendant also to advance that defence, which I thought the better.

The DCS, in some cases, may just present the defence as 'self-defence', but it can be tailored where necessary. From the enhancement of the DVD, and the extra material I was receiving, there was a very great deal of helpful material to set out. Although James and his parents did not want us to make specific allegations naming individuals, our DCS could indicate James and his friends' maltreatment on the DVD. So if we were not allowed in the trial to raise this, or chose not to antagonise or to provoke the offenders, our DCS would serve to rebut any defence which they might put forward in theirs.

The DCS had to be complete; every point made had to be included. If any element of the defence were not contained in it, the prosecution could draw the jury's attention to its absence, and comment adversely on the fact. Thus it would be asserted that new material introduced in the trial, which had not been disclosed, had been added as an afterthought, or to strengthen the defence after, for instance, conferring with one's legal team. Because of the damage caused by such allegations when challenged, the DCS must always be signed by the client, so that he could not blame his advocate for any omissions or mistakes.

It had to contain every point, legal or factual; any hearsay (things said to witnesses by others not in the trial); counter-allegations against others (mostly other defendants); any alleged impropriety or overbearing conduct or bad practice by officers; and, indeed, all material which may prove helpful even without direct proof.

Our conference yielded much that could not but help. Our expert improved the DVD and stills as well as was possible, and, at the same time, concentrated on highlighting all James's movements and positions throughout the incident. This sharper focus made James' recollections and prospective evidence much clearer and more positive.

A DCS could always be amplified, or otherwise amended, if further material were to arrive. Details of the incident became clearer, and we were able to amplify my client's defence with side issues, which told about his caring nature and character. If evidence is given by the defendant in court when it has not been put in the DCS, it can be attacked as providing, e.g., a false alibi, using dishonest witnesses. Very considerable damage could be caused thereby to the defendant's honesty or integrity. These were the virtues our DCS was designed to present.

At first sight the main defence to be raised in the trial was reasonable self-defence, in the circumstances, though not of the need to defend himself, but another – here, his best friend.

Accordingly, the facts were provided by the DVD: after James's best friend was knocked down several times, he intervened (with his friend's brother), and, to protect him, threw out an arm. This was to save him from further attack, and to get the three of them away.

This incident where they were surrounded was the height of the prosecution case against James. To reinforce their case, the prosecution had alleged that James had punched one of the attackers twice, and that he had done so in revenge for the attack which had, earlier, caused the fractures to his friend's brother. The prosecution got this wrong, muddling up the two assaults; claiming that the reason that James could not remember matters in his witness statement was because he had been drunk; and that he had been aggressive throughout. All this came from the Case Summary, a document prepared by the Crown to tell the jury about the case in their opening.

My first draft put these matters right, though I had to accept that James had thrown out his arm; that was all that could be said with certainty from the DVD. There had been no other moment of aggression, but, on the contrary, assistance was provided by him to the man first knocked down. Firstly, by trying to pull him away from the one-on-one fight into which he was being dragged, and, secondly, when that man had been knocked unconscious by two of the others, in helping him, and calling an ambulance.

In conference to refine the first draft, James explained that he had been struck by a glass to the forehead from one of the others coming in from one side, after the rescue attempt. At the same time, the main protagonist who wanted to fight, having caused a fracture with his first blow, was rushing towards them from his other side. He attacked them with an upraised metal crutch, with which he split open our best friend's brother's head as the three of them tried to get away.

It became obvious that this allowed me to strengthen the self-defence argument, by adding that James's actions had been to prevent his own physical injury, which was evident from the DVD.

In the prosecution's response to my first draft, the interviewing officer had failed to include, in his summary of the evidence about this incident, that the two brothers whom James was defending had stated several times, in both their witness statements for the prosecution, that James had come to their rescue whilst they were surrounded and attacked.

This omission was grossly unfair; furthermore, it was a clear breach of the rules of the Police and Criminal Evidence Act, which decreed that any interview, or summary, must include matters telling in favour of a defendant. In their response, the prosecution failed in their duty to disclose, and put this right.

Finally, on this; talking to James, whose memory was now coming back, he gave us further information: a) that he was a qualified first aider and a swimming coach; b) that he had just been offered a place at University; c) his injuries to his face were visible on the video, and would be enhanced and corroborated by the brothers in their prosecution evidence; and d) he had assisted in a traffic accident later that night, in which a girlfriend had lost a leg, and he had helped her out and called an ambulance.

That had added to his trauma, which was exacerbated by having been told that one of those involved had died in hospital. That I included to explain his state of mind, inability to remember much about that night, and to rebut the charge of drunkenness.

It was now time to prepare a further DCS, including the new material he had remembered, and attaching copies of the press reports, including that of the tragic accident with which he had helped, a still of his injuries, a copy of his acceptance for University and its impending date, and the certificate of his lifesaving qualification and employment as a life saver.

Finally, and most importantly, it also included an insistence that the prosecution confirm to judge and jury that James was of impeccable character. This provided a major advantage, since the jury had to be told, firstly, that he was less likely to commit any crime, and, secondly, if he gave evidence on oath, he was more likely to be believed. The judge had to tell this to the jury in his summing up, as a matter of law, at the end, as they were sent to their room.

I also added a request for information about police instructions, to interview local residents to reassure them about the violence. As they would therefore be talking to potential jurors in the trial, I wanted to know if there had been any prejudice to James. That request for disclosure was also ignored.

With all this material to put before the jury, directly adding to his character and credibility, I realised that I was in an excellent position to advance that he had been acting to prevent crime throughout the whole incident. This was yet another sound defence, and, furthermore he was the only defendant able to raise it.

To summarise briefly: he had tried to prevent the one on one fight; had stayed with, and called an ambulance for, the person involved in that; had stayed to help defend his best friend from further assaults; had tried to get him, his brother and himself into safety, behaving reasonably in what he did, under a most violent attack with a weapon; had assisted a girlfriend in a dreadfully serious traffic accident, staying with her and calling an ambulance; and, finally, he had gone to the police as a witness almost straightaway. His character was unassailable, and all would be confirmed, with documentation to be served and used in court. For these reasons I thought this a better defence, especially as both incidents, including the later fatality, would be drawn up in an indictment (the list of charges that goes before a Crown Court) full of grave and serious charges, all arising from crimes which he had tried to prevent.

I had already decided that these were the seeds of doubt with which I was going to regale the jury in my closing speech, using my question and answer style between juror and informed observer. There was little doubt in my mind of their likely impact.

Of the eight other participants, one was arrested on the same day on which we had made our witness statement. He admitted to having been the main protagonist, and to having used the crutch on someone's head.

The others in his group all made no comment to all questions, although one, on arrest, denied having been there. Once seen on the DVD, he too admitted his presence but said that he had tried to break up the fight, which the DVD failed to support.

The defendant accused of killing his friend had not been charged so far, as medical evidence had suggested that the cause of death might have been the punch received during the egging on.

Once charged with Manslaughter, it was proposed that his count would be joined with the others in the same indictment, for a trial of all charges and all defendants together. This - the ground in my first appeal from Chelmsford Crown Court, won so many years ago - was to be repeated.

I now list the applications to the court:

(a) The objection to the Crown seeking joinder. I drafted a skeleton argument. Firstly, each count had to be founded on the same facts as the other counts. This could be reduced to the question as to whether they had a common factual origin. A test for this was whether the lesser charge which faced our client could not be alleged but for the facts giving rise to the primary charge. It was argued that both were entirely separate.

The only connection between them was that two of the people involved in the manslaughter were from the same group who had been involved in the first incident. The facts were quite different, one being an altercation leading to a fight between two groups, and the other a fight between two friends within the other group, at a different place, and some hours apart.

Even the cause was different, in that one had spat in the girlfriend of the other's face, which is why he had been knocked down. They were utterly distinct, specifically arising from different motivations; there were no common witnesses; and no connection between the facts of the two events. It was held in two cases, one mine, that still applied from twenty-five years ago, that a common feature of violence was not the same as being based on the same facts.

The second justification for a joinder was whether the counts together formed a series of offences of the same or similar character. The legal term was a nexus (a connection) making a series. This was simplified by explaining that if the offences exhibited such similar features as to establish a case that the public would expect to be answered in court, they could properly and conveniently be joined together in the interests of justice.

This test would need to consider the interests of the parties and witnesses. None of these, I claimed, would justify joinder, as there were no joint witnesses in both trials, and other parties to the manslaughter would be much more likely to prefer a separate trial of the most serious, distressing and emotional charge. That the evidence in one trial was inadmissible on the other, raised a further difficulty in establishing a nexus, this authority derived from the Krays' trial.

The next complication was that being of the same or similar character could be determined by either the facts, or the law in the cases, or a combination of each. This was precisely the question of which I had been asked for my opinion by Lord Justice Mustill, in my first appeal. In his judgement, he had advised that if it were to be only the law or facts to allow it, each would have to be very powerful on its own: combining the two would be easier. He had held, in his judgement, that a common element was insufficient on its own. There was also insufficient factual similarity, as there were different elements of violence – one was an assault on an individual, the other damage to property. Another principle invoked was that having different victims in the trials made joining charges against each inadvisable.

A final argument levelled was that the disorder offence could involve just a threat to punch or push away, rather than an actual blow. Being an offence of public disorder, it also needed to be capable of alarming the public.

Two of the charges preferred against the others, other than manslaughter - the two grievous bodily harm counts - alleged an intention to cause grievous bodily harm, and so were deliberate acts. Because of this intent accompanying the grievous bodily harm, that created a considerable dissimilarity in fact and in law.

The manslaughter could be caused by reckless conduct without an intention to cause serious bodily harm - another dissimilarity.

All my points were set out, served and reiterated in court with the authorities. I included the success of my own case - now a leading authority. The judge disapproved of the fact that I was relying on my own case which was, he considered, not a valid argument. My response was that it was to show that I knew the law and principles, and it was right on the point of law.

The Crown opposed my objection, merely asserting the criteria, and maintaining that there was a proper series. Little law was cited or responded to. The judge agreed that it was a series, and was properly joined, and my application failed. The parents watching - one a solicitor - was unimpressed (even dissatisfied) by either the opposing argument, or the perfunctory judgment expressed.

I knew that I could always pursue the matter by an application to sever (severance in legal terms and an alternative if the prosecution succeeded in joining the counts in the indictment) where it was desirable to cut out certain counts. So there could be one trial of the manslaughter on its own; one trying all of the others; or even one just of James on my own. The test was what was desirable and fair.

I was fired up by the treatment of this application, and was going to 'throw the book' (here, our legal textbook, Archbold) at the Crown. I was, frankly, expecting them to stop the case eventually, as it was becoming difficult to see how it could proceed, in the light of the strong defences the prosecution would have to disprove. There was also a CPS instruction on the care to be taken in cases involving self-defence, and the strength of the evidence necessary to back me up.

Before the consideration of a severance application, there was the prospect of having the count against James dismissed by a defence application, prior to any plea from our client. This was a rare application, based on the lack of evidence; I had attempted such an application before, when another similar application of mine at Harrow Crown Court had been rejected (wrongly in my view). Immediately afterwards, the CPS, agreeing with me, had dropped the case, as the evidence was insufficient.

Still convinced that our client would be found not guilty, and possibly in the same way (by the case's being dropped if the application was unsuccessful), this was to be our next course of action. Despite some of the other advocates having said they too would be making such an application, it transpired that I was the only one to do so.

b) The defence application to dismiss the count of violent disorder. Once again, I decided to draft a full skeleton argument, setting out every conceivable point possible. We were not going to fail through lack of effort. I could rely on much of the material quoted in our DCS, in the DVD and the storybook put together by James' parents from the stills, and all fully served.

We had received a summary of the Crown's case, their response to my first draft of the DCS, and had dug up a copy of the CPS's own document which dictated the policy and guidance on our defence.

I also consulted the relevant criminal procedure rules which govern every procedure in the criminal court, and attached that which set out the procedure to dismiss the indictment, or a count therein. The rule for dismissal was found in two different Acts: both were identical in their terms and tests for the application for determining the application.

This wording stated that the judge shall dismiss (thus it was mandatory - meaning, in legal language, compulsory) if it appears to him that the evidence against the applicant would not be sufficient for a jury properly to convict him. Simply put, the judge must dismiss if he considers the evidence insufficient for the jury to convict.

This is his decision, and he arrives at it by assessing the weight of the evidence - at the time of the application, of course. In my case at Harrow, my application to dismiss had been refused, as the judge, having considered the witness who was unsure about identifying my client, had felt that he might, possibly with prosecuting counsel's assistance, change his mind about giving evidence in court in the trial. That should not have been done. To consider further evidence that might arise in the trial is not permissible.

I have found, on occasions, that judges were reluctant to withdraw a case from the jury, even if it was their duty. This particularly has applied in cases where self-defence is raised in evidence by the defendant himself, or is put to the prosecution or to their witness, which is all they have to do for it to be considered.

A specific example was in the Uxbridge bus riot case, where the district judge expressly reversed the burden of proof, requiring the defence to prove self-defence.

This is because, as said before, there must be no vestige of self-defence left at the end of the case. If such evidence remains, the defence is made out and the defendant must be acquitted. It is the same with the defence of the prevention of crime. I hope this has not been over-stressed, but it is vital in being unusual, and a restraint on a judge's leaving matters to the jury.

It was important that the CPS's own policy statement - entitled Policy and Guidance on Self-Defence and the Prevention of Crime - that I had found in my research confirmed this. I was quoting their own guidance in furtherance of my application. It went on to advise in terms - that the prosecution must satisfy the jury beyond reasonable doubt that the defendant was not acting in self-defence or for the prevention of crime. It added that prosecutors should take special care to recognise and ensure that there was a sufficiency of evidence in those cases where self-defence was likely to be an issue.

Under the rules, the application should be accompanied by any document relied on by the applicant. In compliance, I exhibited the still showing the huge lump on James' forehead, and his life-saving qualification and employment document attesting to his occupation for some years as a lifesaver, which supported the likelihood of his attempting to prevent crime. The relevance of the newspaper report of the traffic accident, and the rebuttal of drunkenness, I thought might have been considered relevant, so these were added.

The bottom line argued was that there must be no evidence of self-defence or preventing crime, and, if there is, the judge's decision is for dismissal.

James, his mother and father and Bob all worked for many, many hours, enhancing the DVD, and producing the stills, and a very full storyboard. The extent of such perfection revealed, for instance, which of the group was mainly the one knocking his friend to the ground; our position throughout in relation to the person being knocked down; and his time and time again struggling to his knees to stand. With precision, even the shoes and the direction in which they were pointing showed the main one responsible face to face with, and punching, James' friend, with the others grouped closely around, all visible with complete clarity, and with obvious evil intent.

Our combined efforts at such enhancement went before the judge, with the production of over 100 stills, (41 exhibited in the trial), with the complete story board highlighting in colour every movement and the position of our client throughout, from start to finish, and including every injury sustained by any party. Every image in the story board bore a short commentary for the judge to rule on this application. Another set, with no commentary on each image, was supplied for the trial untouched, in the event that, in the trial, our commentary might be ruled inadmissible. The jury would be told to make up its own mind as to what they saw themselves, as happened in the Croupier fraud at Knightsbridge, where they had had to write in the evidence for themselves on the blank form.

In their summary, the Crown accepted that not a single witness had seen him behave aggressively. Thus the evidence rested on his admissions, and on the contents of the DVD.

What was said in his original statement and the interview was to the effect that he had swung an arm, which might have connected. He might or might not have connected; so what might have been does not amount to proof against him. The interviewing officer agreed that there was an attack by several others, but was unsure of actual contact, though at one stage he had thought that it looked as if there might be. This lack of certainty cannot amount to strict proof: the evidence must satisfy the jury so that they are sure. Back to the DVD!

Unknown to him at the time of making his statement, without sight of the enhanced DVD, running towards him, and clearly visible, was the main protagonist, armed with a crutch raised over his head, in full attack mode, and, then, bringing it down on their heads. From his other side, another, with a raised glass, was also rushing to join the attack. Both weapons were in fact used to inflict injury, and to commit crimes against the three of them; the body language had been explicit.

I submitted that the case stood or fell on the DVD. His admissions added nothing, not being probative. Any physical contact from him could only have arisen during the later incident when he was surrounded, his friend beaten, and all were threatened with weapons. As we knew from their statements, his best friend, on the floor, had stated in interview that the beating had included being hit on the jaw and falling to the floor, with three of them around, and having been punched several times to the back of the head.

Finally, from both brothers' interviews as prosecution witnesses, they themselves stated that our client pulled some of the attackers away from the brother on the floor. His younger brother also helped the elder away, and the three of them started to escape. They were unable to avoid further assaults.

The storyboard, stills and the DVD itself showed the complete picture of the action: nothing was missed or obstructed, and intentions were readily apparent.

No allegations were made against James about the first melee, where the egging-on took place. However, I could bring that in as clear evidence of an intention then to prevent crime. The evidence would indicate from the start that he was trying to prevent crimes that occurred.

During their chase, he can be seen, back to the wall, keeping well away, and moving to help the victim of the double-handed attack. The Crown in its response had inferred that this movement showed his guilty intention to fuel the disorder. Once there, he was seen standing protectively over the victim.

His actions thereafter were to protect, and allow his friends to escape, and they were struck whilst trying to do so. Every action was to prevent the crimes which were obviously intended, and which occurred. It was my contention that this defence – relatively little used compared with self-defence – was the stronger in this case, and that the instances of violence charged reinforced that view.

The last point was that there must be 'sufficient evidence for a jury to properly convict'. If the jury were not given the good character direction, providing him with a distinct extra advantage - a lesser likelihood of him committing an offence - the conviction would not be proper. So I added that to my other submissions.

The skeleton argument was read by the judge and parts of it stressed in my address to him. He was first told in the case of this defendant that all the evidence was visibly before him. Secondly, that it was for the prosecution completely to disprove the elements of self-defence and prevention of crime - reversing the burden of proof, a matter which did not always come across properly.

Thirdly, similarly, judges always emphasise that it is the jury that should make decisions properly left to them. However, this was an exception to that normal practice. This application was for the judge alone.

He refused the application. He then turned to my next application, and the skeleton argument that accompanied it, and gave his rulings after the end of this application. He appeared to me to be suggesting that the severance argument was the more promising.

This was to be the last application at which I could have the case against James dropped. It also provided for a third review by the CPS for them not to proceed.

To summarise and clarify, as there are similar points made in the three applications, the first had been to object to joining the dissimilar counts and defendants in one trial. In the second, the prosecution evidence did not disprove our defences (actually supporting them). The third operated to separate the violent disorder charge against James from the manslaughter charge, which had nothing to do with him. Proceeding in a trial with both counts was unfair and undesirable, for the entirely practical reasons set out in the procedure.

c) The Defence application to sever. Severance should be decided by common sense, and criminality should be the watchword for inclusion or exclusion of one or more counts in trials. As always, the ultimate test is the interests of justice.

The desirability of trying joint offenders together may often be outweighed by the difficulties which could arise for the jury from having to deal in this case with a number of issues, a host of directions from the judge, and a great volume of evidence. This would clearly arise with eight defendants' evidence and interviews; defence case statements; oral evidence from the attacking group against James and his denials; the pictorial evidence and the storyboard, dealt with by all the advocates defending their clients in the violent disorder counts. (With the grievous bodily harm counts it was apparent that those accused would be pleading guilty.)

The finest quotation of the general principle that should be adopted in a jury trial states that 'in a jury trial, brevity and simplicity are the handmaidens of justice, length and complexity its enemies.'

The second deals with the necessity for a trial: that nothing short of absolute necessity could justify the burdens of a very long trial (five to six weeks or so).

Further advice recommends that any unnecessary or makeweight counts should be jettisoned. The lack of aggression from James, agreed by judge and prosecution, would be a powerful reason for his trial to be severed from that of those charged with similar counts, even making the assumption that he needed to be charged at all. There seemed little advantage to the Crown (or in the public interest) for James to be included and, in fact, many disadvantages for the Crown, the judge and the court. Again, it prompted yet another review – this time looking at the practicalities. I was still optimistic.

Severance allowed the prosecution to go ahead, if they wanted to or if it was necessary, but in a way that was fair, desirable and most convenient to James. The best place to start for guidance was, as always, with the criminal procedure rules. They set out in some detail the overriding objective in conducting criminal cases.

All cases were to be conducted efficiently and expeditiously - getting on with it. Whilst this applied to any case, the rule went on to emphasise that decisions for prosecuting cases should specifically take into account the gravity of the offence; the complexity of what was in issue; the severity of the consequences for the defendant and others involved; and the needs of other cases listed in court.

Ample authority existed to strike a balance between desirability for a defendant, and the interests of prosecution and public. My written skeleton relied on many factors found in the cases. But following the overriding objective, the count of manslaughter falls within the factors of the gravity of the offence, the complexity of the issues for this case, and the consequences of sentence imposed.

Of itself it includes complicity, and a long trial of five or six weeks would, realistically, be anticipated. Any other counts added would lengthen this estimate, and delay other cases (affecting their needs - another criterion in the overriding objective above).

Applying the above principles to the practicalities for trial discussions at court had indicated that the grievous bodily harm matters would 'go short' – there would be pleas of guilt acceptable to the Crown and to the judge.

Thus the possibilities were: (i) a trial of all matters together; (ii) a shorter trial of the manslaughter by itself, and the second trial of the other matters; and (iii) a further possibility, then, of James's having a trial on his own.

The first and most important advice to assist on severance generally is that evidentially unconnected count(s) of the most serious weight should not be included with other lesser matters. Here, the evidence on the manslaughter applied only to that count. This was indeed the most serious charge, and James was not even present. The rest of the evidence in the case applied only to the incidents outside the public house, hours before.

Continuing with (i), the manslaughter charge would feature the case of one best friend being killed by his other. Since a death was involved, there would be a great deal of medical evidence traumatic to a jury, with photographs of injury, autopsy evidence, matters of drink and drugs found, with a number of private witnesses seeing the events, and, most traumatically, the girlfriend at the root of the incident. There would also be a legal question and directions on intent, character and an allegation that an earlier punch was material. It could be said that that was enough for any trial, (without the consequences of life imprisonment being at stake as well).

The next piece of advice is that 'in complicated cases the difficulties of disentangling matters can cause confusion to a jury.' That very much applies when some eight or so defendants are added, with each facing an entirely separate allegation, in which seven are bound, through their counsel, to attack James's evidence and to assert their own version, relying on DVD footage.

From my point of view, the predictable discomfort to James over weeks in court under personal attack could be accepted as at least undesirable. The loss of his University place would make his situation no less dire.

Further complications abound: the judge would have to give directions to the jury on whom to believe and why, known as a Randall direction. Added to that, he must properly direct the jury as to their good or limited good character (tailored to the history of each one).

It goes without saying that the most careful consideration must be given to such a serious charge, without any distraction by other and lesser matters. Being as objective as possible, it was almost impossible to see any advantage for anyone in the trials' being merged. Necessity recommends the contrary.

If I persuaded the judge to sever in situation (i), that would lead to a second trial on the other counts of violent disorder: the assaults would be dealt with by pleas of guilt. The next question was whether James should be tried with all the others: (ii).

Being part of such a trial would mean that he would be under constant (and personal) attack. Each counsel for the others would cross examine him, putting their own case. That trial would last some weeks, with many of the above issues explored, as well as their attempted explanations for giving no answers, examination of their DCSs versus that of James, with its demonstration of his good character (and directions thereon by the judge). With the DVD, the others would have little room for manoeuvre – which would not of course deter their counsel from trying.

It follows that, as far as counsel for the other defendants in the second trial would be concerned, they would gladly do without James. They could attack him with impunity, as he would not be there to demonstrate all his virtues, and emphasise the difference between him and them in the DCSs and his voluntary statement. This would be in the public interest in substantially reducing the cost to the public and the advocacy.

Thus everyone's interest in severing the second trial with James to face trial alone would be unopposed and mutually advantageous (I refrain from contemplating any advantage which the Crown might see in such severance). In fact, the other defendants might agree facts amongst themselves whilst presenting a common face on dealing with James in his absence.

As far as James' situation in (iii) would be concerned, his trial might possibly last for two days, with the evidence of the two brothers in his favour and the DVD, it having been agreed that that was all that the Crown required in order to prosecute.

Thus he could attend University, arranging to miss a few days for lectures, and be on his own in the dock. He would also avoid the mental agony of being on trial for five to six weeks at court, in the presence of a group of his attackers and their counsel or solicitors. Finally, the court calendar would very much benefit.

It was submitted that the advantages of severing the manslaughter, and then his own count into, three indictments would be massive. It was difficult to see any advantages in refusing severance.

The judge then ruled, firstly on the dismissal application. He stated that no reliance was being placed on the defendant's interview or admissions, and that he and the Crown were content to rely on the DVD alone. (This was most favourable to our submissions.)

He continued that the Crown's case was perfectly clear and that of the defence totally consistent in their defences of self-defence and the prevention of crime. The evidence would be deployed in front of the jury, and there was an apparent swinging of an arm causing no physical injury, otherwise there would have been a charge of assault against him.

No aggression was seen from the applicant, nor had he moved with others in what, so far as they were concerned, was a violent disorder leading to horrific injuries. This would be before the jury. He had come to the firm conclusion that the application must fail, but 'this must not be taken to be my firm belief of the situation.'

Further, he himself had no belief, and stated that a judge had a very limited effect in analysing the evidence, which did not suffice for a judge to conclude something over which he cannot and should not decide. It might well be that they (the jury) concluded in favour of self-defence, and the law had been set out, and applicd.

In relation to the severance application he said, as if in an aside, that he would have thought that a full trial would have been in my client's interests.

James saw little advantage in pursuing a long trial in such circumstances over what may prove (according to the judge) a minor tactical advantage. Success was inevitable, in any event.

In adding that a leader should be obtained for his trial it must be said that the expense of the trial would be considerably increased. For James, on his own in a trial of the kind envisaged in (iii), thousands of pounds would be saved with leading counsel and a junior over a period of weeks.

So a leading counsel was to be instructed. The lay client's father, a well-renowned solicitor, chose a QC he had known for many years, and I sent all the papers to his chambers.

It was several months later that Bob rang and told me that our client had been acquitted, despite being attacked by all the others in the trial. That, I am afraid, came as no surprise, as did the result. I was naturally delighted for my client and his family who had had to bear so much pain and anxiety.

The end was marked with an e-mail from them, thanking me 'for all the spadework I had put in', and telling me that the defence case statements had been a crucial part of the trial: that too was welcome, as we had all worked so hard on ours.

Chapter 21
Epilogue

It transpired that that was to be my last case at the Crown Court. Within a week I was in hospital, and booked in for what they called 'a procedure.' It came about somewhat fortuitously, following a visit to my chemist to complain that it had been over 2 days since I had urinated. (I am inclined to avoid mentioning more details, as it is the sort of problem which grown men cringe to talk or read about).

I was told that if the situation persisted for over a week, then I should see my doctor. I ruminated about this, and decided that I would see him straight away, not having been convinced by the advice received. Within two minutes of seeing him I was told to get myself to a hospital, and given a letter to show the consultant.

The nurse at the hospital whose task it was to arrange preliminary matters for the procedure was not on duty, so I was advised to come back the next day. I insisted on seeing the consultant, brandishing my letter in support, and he very kindly completed the procedure himself; I was booked in for tests, and then given a date to return for the procedure. For a few days I was detained for observation. There I saw the registrar, and told him that I would be having the treatment with my private health insurance. As he did both NHS patients at this hospital and private patients at the one across the road, he assured me that I would be seeing him again.

The preliminary matters put in motion ensured that I was to be off work until I was finished at the hospital, with a few months of recuperation to follow. The thought of any attendance at court was out of the question, so the career, if any, was put on the back burner.

Attending for my procedure, and ready for action, the most senior consultant sat with me and chatted (I was told, reassuringly, that I had the top man). By now I had ascertained that the bank had, some months before, missed by one day a payment on my direct debit, prior to substantial funds being transferred. Unknown to me, they had cancelled the policy without troubling to inform me. Having worried for some time about whether they would carry on with the procedure, I was told, gratifyingly, that I was now under the NHS, and matters would proceed: another worry resolved.

After tests and form-filling, the 'top man' started to discuss with me what was to happen, but at my request not in too much detail as it was my first time in hospital for surgery. He began by telling me that, whilst he was ready to start, it was not really ideal for him to do so as there was still an infection which the hospital had not rectified.

I asked for his advice, and he responded by saying that he could carry on and treat the infection afterwards, but that was why he did not think it ideal; but he had been told that I was in a hurry, so he could go ahead.

However, I was not in that much of a hurry, and since the surgeon had said that it would not be ideal to proceed, that was enough for me; my decision, I thought, should be to come back after the infection was treated. He agreed that that was sensible, and that that would be his preference, now that I had decided. Whilst I had hoped that he would decide, being the expert, I felt that I had made the right decision. I was reminded of occasions at court when I advised on pleading guilty or not, always adding, after full discussion, that 'It's your life and you have the final word and must live with the consequences.' He helpfully told me that a slot was available in a few weeks.

A month and a half, or so, later, I returned and the procedure was completed. A few more nights in the hospital followed again, with hardly a wink of sleep. On the first occasion, the ward was full of chronically ill patients, and the noise all night was horrendous. My neighbour in the next bed confused me with his son, and all night he was directing me on building a roof, being a builder!

On the second occasion, they took pity on me, and moved me to another ward with just one patient. On the first night, having procured a sleeping tablet, the nurse stood the water jug on it and crushed it. I gave up and settled down, until the other patient, who was both violent and paranoid, and who never stopped talking about his international tennis career - just bearable - went berserk in the night, fought all the staff and had to be dragged off.

Then followed recuperation; and I was, by now, feeling fragile and somewhat lacking in self-confidence. I occupied myself, firstly, by indulging in a long correspondence with my bank and with the private health insurers, especially as they admitted that a substantial payment had come into my account the day after the direct debit payment was due. Concerned as to the awful conditions which patients in NHS wards suffer at night, I hoped to rectify my private health, but it proved too costly, and neither bank nor insurers would take any responsibility. I also made sure that the chemist realised that the error of her ways could have proved disastrous.

Secondly, my last case had required considerable work on the claim. Whilst I had been briefed originally, and had read the huge brief, with thousands of pages of statements, interviews and exhibits, DVDs, stills and storybook I would not be paid for this, as only assigned counsel could claim. My solicitor, at the clients' requests, had opted for a leading counsel well known to the father.

I was paid for my appearances, and, after studying the legal aid provisions for wasted or special preparation, found that payment was permissible where a case was transferred by the solicitor for other counsel to be assigned. Research on these provisions and their conditions, and on the role of solicitors, was required, with a full count of all the pages and full copies of all my skeleton arguments, summaries by the prosecution of their case and responses to my applications, with draft and final defence case statements.

This extremely thick bundle took forty hours to compile, and had to be sent with the brief by the chambers of assigned counsel, for taxing.

We chased those chambers for news, and, after nearly a year received the reply that my claim had been granted, minus a few hours, totalling just over ninety hours' work. The rate was some thirty-five pounds per hour, and, after another six months or so, the cheque was received.

This was the last straw, and things had to change back to the practice which I had been developing with the traffic lists in the Magistrates Court. Crown Court work eventually paid better, but all the stress would resume. Additionally, I could negotiate a new rental agreement, becoming a door tenant, which meant that I could still be briefed by chambers, but only up to a limited amount. The door tenancy charged rent of only £100 per month instead of about £600, a saving of some £5000 per annum. This very much helped reduce the overheads I would have to cover before making any profit, which, in all, approached £10,000!

It was back to Willesden again, but just the one visit per week. I turned down any cases that involved extra travelling, any different court (even as a relief), or other work. There was no fee-chasing, and I was able to keep within my allotted income, and still keep in touch with chambers, as before.

It was not to be the happy ending envisaged, as, on my first day back to Willesden, when I was driving out of the car park, a 'hoodie,' attending court with face covered, stepped out a foot or so in front of me and I felt a tremendous crash in the back of my car. A huge 4 x 4 had smashed into me, as the drunk in the 'hoodie' staggered off oblivious. The damage was extended to the whole car ,and it proved a write-off.

When I had recovered, with the driver's assistance, we went back to court, and watched the CCTV which had recorded the accident. The security there told me that they had ejected him from court because of his condition. That was quite obvious as, when he stepped out in front of my car, he had put his hand on my bonnet, presumably to hold me back. The other driver said that she had seen this, but there was nothing I could have done, other than to slam on the brakes to avoid running him over. She also had no time to stop.

Fortunately, all I sustained after the shock and headache was the whiplash. I was still able to work on the one day I had organised, after a short break, and was able to drive with slowly increasing confidence, unless a 4 x 4 pulled up close behind and seemed in a hurry.

We got a very decent offer for the write-off and ended up with a brand new car for us, picked by my younger daughter Amanda, which stops her and her sister, Katherine, complaining about my old car.

To my surprise, the doctor accurately predicted that the whiplash would slowly improve over a few months, and, after six, would be fine. I carried on with this work for the best part of a year, averaging one case a fortnight, and then decided enough was enough: just routine cases with nothing to report. The barristers' perennial overdrafts were paid off with fees which were at last received, with the compensation for the accident, and with a tax rebate on ceasing to practice. Other small amounts, due for rent and the clerk's percentage were also paid off.

But the problem now was: what to do? A hard winter prevented me from gardening, and I was not really fit for hard work. Even at court, I was beginning to feel that I should not be doing this work anymore, almost expecting a clerk or a member of the bench to ask,' 'Shouldn't you be retiring now?' Or, 'Can you hear us alright?' Our daughters, I am glad to say, were both still living at home, so I still got to hear echoes from the past, as they argued about which of them was to be my No.1 or No 2 in helping out, and were threatening, despite their university degrees, that someone was in need of a well-deserved knuckle sandwich!

Both were well pleased that I was to retire at last, as was our son, Gary. He, however, had taken his family to Turkey for a few years, to set up a new branch for his employers; but it was Amanda who first suggested writing down my experiences. Sue, in Canada, had changed her profession from master gardener to become a carer for the elderly, and happily approved both of my retirement and of my writing a book.

Then it came about again, early this year, that a good friend and a professor, to boot, had just finished and had published his first novel, having written and edited most erudite and highly respected academic books for many years. He also encouraged me to write, 'as I must have a tale or two to tell.'

The more I thought, the more I remembered, considering, at least, that if my families read my history, I should be able to refrain from telling old and dated stories over and over again. That would be a considerable relief all round. He would also look over my stuff (red pen in hand), which gave me the confidence to try (and I had my chambers accounts and diaries to prompt me). So it came about, and all the better for his editing skills, turn of phrase and appreciation.

So, here we go. Every incident recorded accurately and without gloss, poetic licence, or even exaggeration, and with superb technical assistance on my PC from Michael, the professor's son, and Amanda's boyfriend. Without his patient and helpful response to my agonised shouts, upstairs, of 'The computer seems to have messed up,' or 'I seem to have lost ten pages,' or 'How do I complete . . .', this book would never have been written.

Finally, consulting certain members of my family for a chapter title for my last chapter, I was almost overwhelmed by their ingenuity. However, I thought 'Epilogue' was a little more classy than 'The End'.